GENDER POLITICS
IN LATIN AMERICA

GENDER POLITICS
IN LATIN AMERICA

Debates in Theory and Practice

Edited by Elizabeth Dore

Monthly Review Press
New York

For Matthew and Rachel Dore-Weeks

Copyright © 1997 by Monthly Review Press

Library of Congress Cataloging-in-Publication Data

Gender politics in Latin America : debates in theory and practice /
    edited by Elizabeth Dore.
                    p. cm.
Includes bibliographic references.
ISBN 0-85345-975-4 (cloth : alk. paper). — ISBN 0-85345-976-2 (pbk. : alk. paper)
    1. Sex role—Political aspects—Latin America. 2. Feminism—Latin
America. 3. Women in politics—Latin America. I. Dore, Elizabeth.
    HQ1075.5.L29G46 1997   97-9552
    305.3'098—dc21   CIP

Monthly Review Press
122 West 27th Street
New York, NY 10001

Manufactured in the United States of America
10 9 8 7 6 5 4 3 2 1

6/5/06

$18

Amazon

CONTENTS

PREFACE

This book forms part of a bridge between the strong twentieth century tradition of Marxist feminism and constructions of gender politics for the twenty-first century.

Monthly Review Press has published pathbreaking books on socialist feminism. *Toward an Anthropology of Women,* edited by Rayna R. Reiter (1975), presented early research on women and social change. Several years after that, *Capitalist Patriarchy and the Case for Socialist Feminism,* edited by Zillah R. Eisenstein (1979), communicated the passion of theoretical debates. A decade later, *Promissory Notes: Women in the Transition to Socialism,* edited by Sonia Kruks, Rayna Rapp, and Marilyn B. Young (1989), assessed the record of Marxist feminism on theory and practice.

This volume aims to carry on this distinguished tradition. It examines feminist debates, radical political action, and the relationship between them in the crucible of the *final del siglo* in Latin America. Each chapter was born out of controversy about the future of Marxism and feminism. Each maps debates about the politics of gender and class in Latin America, and each proposes new ways of thinking about radical social change.

This book is the product of a collective effort, initiated by the Gender and Development Research Group (GENDLA) at the University of Portsmouth, UK. It began with a conference in July 1994, which brought together twenty-five feminists from Europe, Latin America, and the United States with the purpose of assessing recent advances in gender theory and practice in Latin America. In addition to most of the authors in this volume, Catherine Davis, Susan Frenk, Deniz Kandiyoti, Malena de Montis, Magali Pineda, Sarah Radcliffe, Alison Scott, Jean Stubbs, Verity Smith, and Georgina Waylen participated in the workshop. That conference and this book were made possible thanks to generous support from the School of Languages and Area Studies of the University of Portsmouth.

Many people contributed to the success of this project; I thank them all. Helen Greenslade organized the conference, corresponded with authors, provided research assistance and put together the final manuscript of the book. Susan Lowes, at that time director of Monthly Review Press, provided invaluable editorial guidance. She insisted that the book be written in an accessible style and asked all of the authors to explain how their analysis might affect political practice. In so far as we did what she asked of us, the book is better for it. I regret her departure from Monthly Review Press. Other important contributors to the publication process were Karen Judd and, from Monthly Review Press, Ethan Young, Judy Ruben, Akiko Ichikawa, and Renee Pendergrass. The book has benefited from the experienced hand of John J. Simon, who joined Monthly Review Press just as the book entered production.

Jane Freeland, a member of GENDLA, provided excellent comments on virtually all of the chapters and has been central to the political and intellectual development of our research. Gail Martin and Beatriz Echeverri also advanced the team's collective work in important ways.

David Cubitt, head of the School of Languages and Area Studies at the University of Portsmouth, always was generous with time, critical assessment, and praise, as well as with more material forms of assistance. At the University, Liz Clifford, administrative head, and Tacey Hurd, research secretary, helped the research team in countless ways over the years, and Barton Crouch gave invaluable technical assistance at every step.

Research grants from the University of Portsmouth, British Academy, Fulbright Commission, American Philosophical Society, and the National Endowment for the Humanities all contributed in providing me with time and opportunities for research incorporated into this book.

Finally, I thank John Weeks for his constant support, tangible and intangible.

Elizabeth Dore
London
January 1997

INTRODUCTION: CONTROVERSIES IN GENDER POLITICS

ELIZABETH DORE

Controversy is at the heart of gender politics. The history of women's movements and gender debates centers on serial conflicts over theory and practice
which have advanced the politics of gender. This volume is in that tradition. It
analyzes current controversies and, no doubt, will create new ones. Addressing
central polemics in Latin American gender studies, the authors map where
debates have broken new and fertile ground, where they seem to be caught in
a rut, and where to go from here. The book also analyzes an array of everyday
struggles over gender politics in nine Latin American countries. Together the
chapters examine the interface between political action and conceptual debates,
highlighting innovative and often controversial aspects of the politics of gender
in Latin American societies.

Gender is the social construction of sexual difference. It is the outcome of
struggles over the ways societies define and regulate femininity and masculinity. By its nature gender is multidimensional. It is recreated and transformed

through an inseparable mix of norms and behaviors that are cultural, economic, historical, sociological, linguistic, scientific, and always political. For this reason, the authors adopt a multidisciplinary and explicitly political approach to the analysis of gender. We examine the gendered politics of history, language, power, and culture. And while all of the contributors to this volume are on the left, we do not speak in one voice. This multivocality reflects the heterogeneity of who we are, the diversity of gendered struggles in Latin America, and the fragmentation of left politics. Despite differences, we share a collective purpose: to bridge the separation between academic and political work in our analysis of how the gendering of power has institutionalized exclusion in Latin America. Taken as a whole this book challenges many commonly held notions about gender politics in Latin America.

In "Women, Work, and Empowerment: Romanticizing the Reality," Sharon McClenaghan underlines the romanticism that characterizes much of the literature on women and economic development. Drawing on her study in the Dominican Republic and on analysis of regional trends in women's employment, she questions the view that waged work is empowering the majority of Latin American women. First, there is much less female proletarianization than is sometimes believed. Second, entry into factory work at a time of increasing labor deregulation and harsh economic conditions is not conducive to political or gender militancy. Although the period from 1950 to 1980 saw the female workforce more than triple, McClenaghan concludes that this did not, as many had hoped, bring the degree of empowerment for women that was first imagined.

The next four chapters analyze different aspects of the gendered nature of formal politics. Anna Fernández Poncela, in "Nicaraguan Women: Legal, Political, and Social Spaces," refutes the widely held belief that the Sandinista revolution in Nicaragua greatly expanded women's political participation.She argues that few women exercised political power; with the increasing institutionalization of the revolution women were progressively marginalized from formal politics. However, during the revolutionary years women's decision-making in less formal political spaces—such as the family and the community—increased notably.

Tessa Cubitt and Helen Greenslade, in "The End of the Dichotomy," unravel the ongoing debate about how women's activities in the public and private spheres are interrelated. They conclude that in practice the conceptual dichotomy between public and private spheres does not help us to understand women's political action. In its stead they develop an analysis of gender politics based on the dialectic between structure and agency. This analytical framework is employed to evaluate the activities of an umbrella organization for autonomous social movements in Mexico.

In "Engendering Human Rights," Elizabeth Jelin calls for the gendering of human rights. She sees contradictions as inherent in the nature of rights, and argues that "solutions" are historically constituted, rather than absolute truths. Drawing on the experiences of women's human rights movements in Argentina, Jelin argues that the concept should be expanded to include reproductive rights and freedom from domestic violence.

Ann Matear, in " 'Desde la protesta a la propuesta': The Institutionalization of the Women's Movement in Chile," examines the challenges for the women's movement thrown up by the transition to democracy. Elites successfully subverted the gender barriers to political participation and made the transition from the movement to the state and formal political institutions. This chapter explores the idea that the more lasting obstacles to political participation and representation may be due to social class rather than gender.

The historical construction of gender in Latin America is the subject of four chapters. In "The Holy Family: Imagined Households in Latin American History," Elizabeth Dore shows that the universal patriarchal family is a myth. The male-headed household was universalized in elite discourse and the law, but was less prevalent in everyday practice. Dore argues that the male-headed household was so naturalized in elite discourse that historians were hesitant to conclude that female-headed households were almost as common in Latin America as male-headed ones.

In "The Charm of Family Patterns: Historical and Contemporary Change in Latin America," Ricardo Cicerchia examines the effect that ahistorical notions of the family have had on contemporary social policy. He analyzes the sacralized character of Catholic church family doctrine in Latin America and concludes that its definitions of family are grounded in ideological pretense to reinforce appearances of homogeneity and harmony. Cicerchia maintains that official family discourses in Latin America are an obstacle to the design of family policies that might be relevant to current social problems. Because it is impossible to disassociate the word "family" from the ideological meanings and value judgments that are embedded in it, he proposes that we discard the word and use instead "family patterns," which emphasizes the social, historical, and multicultural nature of kin and residence groups.

Muriel Nazzari purposefully invites controversy in "Sex/Gender Arrangements and the Reproduction of Class in the Latin American Past." First she argues that sexual asymmetry results from the way current modes of human reproduction articulate with the current mode of production. While some feminist scholars agree with Nazzari that women's reproductive role is the main cause of sexual asymmetry, this general perspective often comes under criticism as "biologist" for deducing gendered oppression from biology. Yet Nazzari's formulation is not so simple. She does not propose a fixed relation between reproductive roles and gendered oppression. Rather she posits that changes in the socially constructed nature of reproduction and in the socioeconomic system, and the interrelation between them, have been the main cause of sexual asymmetry. This is hardly an essentialist view rooted in unchanging biological roles. With this theoretical framework Nazzari looks at, among other things, the gendered nature of slavery in Cuba. She argues that there was sexual difference but little sexual inequality because there was no specifically female role among the slaves. Neither slave owners nor slaves wanted female slaves to be mothers. Slave owners found it cheaper to replace slaves by buying new ones than to subsidize the bearing and raising of children, and female slaves usually refused to become mothers, practicing abortion or infanticide. The chapter concludes with a discussion of how sex/gender arrangements reproduce class relations as much as gendered asymmetries.

In "Reading Gender in History," Carmen Ramos Escandón analyzes the ways in which taking gender as a central analytical category alters our vision of the past. First she draws out the important strands in debates over the historical category gender; then she shows how a gendered analysis suggests an alternative periodization of Mexican history.

The politics of culture is the theme of four chapters. In "Problems of Definition in Theorizing Latin American Women's Writing," Deborah Shaw argues that the category "Latin American women's writing" is essentialist in that it disregards variations in class, race, nation, and so on, which characterize women's literary production in Latin America. It is unlikely that anyone would seriously suggest that "Latin American Men's Writing" could be a useful category. Shaw shows that critics who have tried to collapse women's writing into a single genre tend to biologize it—to find in it assorted "feminine" characteristics which give it less literary weight than "male writing." Following her repudiation of a unitary women's writing, Shaw argues that gender is an important aspect of the identity of all writers, male and female, of all national origins.

The politics of language imbues William Rowe's "The Subversive Languages of Carmen Ollé: Irony and Imagination." This chapter, on the poetics of a contemporary Peruvian, is also about reformulating barriers between public and private spheres, and between literature and the social sciences. Rowe shows that poetry communicates social knowledge, and often does so more powerfully than sociology, political science, or history. In the tradition of Sor Juana de la Cruz, Virginia Woolf, and Madonna, Ollé is a cultural revolutionary. She struggles against the great walls that societies construct around female artists and intellectuals. Like Shaw, Rowe discards any idea of an *escritura feminina* which lumps all women writers together. However, he suggests that women writers represent themselves differently from men, especially in their inventiveness of language and form, which in turn opens up spaces for political inventiveness.

Jean Franco continues the theme of making the personal political and the political personal by breaking the walls and silences surrounding gendered identities. In "From the Margins to the Center: Recent Trends in Feminist Theory in the United States and Latin America," she examines queer theory, in particular, the ways in which objectification is reworked through public performance into political agency. Her analysis emphasizes the precariousness of gender identities, which leads her to suggest that the frequently accepted distinction in feminist theory between sex (biological) and gender (social) is functionalist. Franco argues that gender is a frontier that people constantly cross over in one way or another; that transvestism, in particular, undermines the notion that sex is biologically fixed. Therefore, it throws into question the idea of a socially constructed gender constituted on the basis of "natural" sexual difference.

Drawing on examples from Chile, Franco shows how the abjection of transvestism and homosexuality was resignified into defiance through public performance. This development exacerbated tensions inherent in Pinochet's military regime, which advocated free markets on the one hand, while on the other it repressed the sexual revolution which was encouraged by capitalist competition in the market for art. In this milieu queer politics exposed the unfreedom inherent in capitalist freedoms. Franco concludes that queer politics might contribute to a revisioning of the utopian by moving to the center of political struggles "those bodies which were formerly marginalized as perverse."

In "Gender Politics: Luisa Valenzuela's *Cola de Lagartija,*" Claudine Potvin takes a novel as subversive text, and draws out the politics of language and of power. She shows how *The Lizard's Tail* is itself an act of political resistance. The novel presents a history of the era of President Isabel Perón in Argentina, a history that had been silenced. In showing how women speaking from the margins in the story disrupt the official voices, the male discourses of power, Potvin makes it clear that political categories are at the same time gender categories, that the institution of patriarchy is intertwined with the "art" of governing.

All of the chapters in different ways are about gender politics in Latin America. But, asks Nanneke Redclift in the conclusion, how do newer forms of gender politics relate to older questions about female emancipation? The earlier literature was explicitly about theoretical questions, about abstractions such as whether capitalism promotes or impedes the liberation of women. In "Post Binary Bliss: Towards a New Materialist Synthesis?" Redclift suggests that while much work has demonstrated that economic systems are constructed through gender, the economic sphere may not necessarily be the vehicle through which gender inequalities can be challenged successfully. In part this is because class, gender, and race do not simply intersect; in many ways they are, or stand for, each other. The reproduction of class depends on a sexual system which divides women into dominant and subaltern, and the reproduction of gender depends on the class system. Given this, Redclift argues, it may not make any sense to speak of "women's subordination" or "female emancipation." Analysis of how male-female identities are socially, economically, culturally, historically constituted in different societies, and challenges to those identities which threaten the political order, may be more subversive than attempts to explain the relative position of the sexes.

All of the chapters in this book were written in the middle 1990s, a time when the postmodern paradigm dominated political and scholarly discourse, and had done so for at least a decade. Each of us, explicitly or implicitly, wrote our chapters into or against a debate between postmodernism and Marxism. Although we do not all agree about the relative merits of the two paradigms, to varying degrees we all have drawn on both traditions. Therefore, in this introduction I analyze briefly the Marxism versus postmodernism debates. While my understanding of postmodernism has benefited considerably from the insights and arguments of my colleagues in the "Gender and Development in Latin America" research team (GENDLA) at the University of Portsmouth, the analysis below is not necessarily shared by them, nor by the other contributors to this volume.

The politics of what is loosely called postmodernism, post-Marxism—post-almost anything—share common ground. First, the emphasis on fragmentation and on the multiplicity of voices and meanings negates the possibility of any authoritative account of social reality.[1] Second, such politics neglect or reject the category of class and emphasizes individuality.[2] Class is criticized because it privileges a single side of social relationships—the social relations of production. Instead of class, which is based on a collective subject position vis-a-vis other social classes and their control of property, postmodernists stress individuals' unique subject positions as defined by their sex, race, age, nationality, class, community, sexual preference, marital status, and the like. As a consequence of privileging social diversity over social unity, advocates of postmodernism tend to de-emphasize relations of oppression and exploitation. They account for this in two ways. First, if, as they argue, everyone is oppressed in some way in relationship to someone else, then the political analysis of oppression and exploitation becomes either meaningless or simplistic. Second, if everyone occupies his/her own subject position which defines identity, then who are we (as scholars, feminists, political leaders, etc.) to impose upon them our view about who they are, such as whether they are oppressed. In other words, postmodernists argue that oppression—and all other social relationships—is subjective, not objective. Therefore, it is impossible for one person to analyze the oppression of another. And it is equally impossible to propose an authoritative account of social reality, as there is no such thing. There are only individual interpretations of the past and of the present, all equally valid. These currents in post-politics, with their emphasis on what I call the theories of social relativity, and their disregard for the unities of class and of gender oppression, have been a barrier in Latin America and elsewhere to building movements that are able to bridge identity politics.

The influence of postmodernism should hardly be surprising to anyone who believes, as do Marxists, that consciousness is explained from the conditions of material life. The 1980s and 1990s provided the economic and political underpinnings for post-politics. Economic restructuring, associated with high levels of unemployment, weakened the traditional working class and its social identity in Latin America as it did in many other parts of the world. This was accompanied by an ideological onslaught that extolled the freedom of the individual in the marketplace. Ronald Reagan in the United States, Margaret Thatcher in Britain, Carlos Menem in Argentina, Alberto Fujimori in Peru, Carlos Salinas de Gortari in Mexico, the ephemeral Fernando Collor de Melo in Brazil, all spoke in one voice. They said that collective action was outdated as the new free market economics rewarded the enterprise of unfettered individuals.

Postmodernism, notwithstanding the radical rhetoric in which it may be wrapped, shares great affinities with this neoliberal ideology. Both emphasize the freedom of the individual, or individual subjectivity, and both fail to recognize that capitalist freedoms mask unfreedom. The apparent freedom of individuals in the marketplace and elsewhere belies a reality in which economic and political freedoms lose much of their meaning within a social system where

15

people's lives are constrained by class exploitation as well as systemic gendered and racialized oppressions. In these reactionary times, when as intellectuals and political activists we should be unmasking the ideological underpinnings of the cult of the individual and the ever-widening circles of social atomization, instead there is great heat and light surrounding academics' efforts to develop a theoretical framework that is in danger of corroborating the underlying principles of neoliberal politics and economics.[3] In this climate, it is unfortunate, but not surprising, that, paraphrasing Jane Jaquette, class is disappearing as a category of analysis at the very moment when class differences are widening in Latin America.[4]

Despite their fundamental antagonism, post-politics has made some positive contributions to class politics. Marxist analysis tended to privilege class so much so that other forms of oppression were given insufficient attention; and when noticed, always were treated as derivative from and subordinate to class relations. Too often, Marxists argued that gender and race oppressions would disappear along with capitalism. Even more problematical, it was not uncommon for Marxists to suggest that with the end of class exploitation, ethnic differences would become a thing of the past. The postmodern critique has forced Marxists to reappraise those views.

On gender, the questions that Marxist-feminists posed were all related to how women's labor in the home and the workplace facilitated the accumulation of capital, and whether capitalism subordinated or emancipated women. Also, the Marxist tradition historically emphasized that class relations were the single key to understanding the reproduction of state power. More recently, it is accepted by Marxists that gender and race are important aspects of the complex of relations on which state power is based. One aspect of social control is the state's legitimation and delegitimation of what is feminine and masculine. For this reason, struggles that challenge state-sponsored gender oppressions may be as vital to revolutionary strategies as struggles against class exploitation.

The political fallout from an overly narrow focus on class was that the male leadership of political movements in Latin America always told women that their demands should wait until other, more pressing, conditions were resolved. Women's needs came last, as usual. This happened in the Cuban revolution; it happened in the Sandinista revolution. There is some hope, however, that future revolutions may be different. With the intensity of the gender wars it is possible that movements that envision major social transformation might accept the tenet of feminist politics that radical transformations in gender roles and identities will advance processes of social transition, not hold them back.

The postmodern critique of Marxism, and insistence that identities are multifaceted, has forced socialists to rethink their approach to gender politics. Most now agree that gender and race are fundamental social categories, and that under some conditions they could be more critical than issues of class. As Redclift says, "class, gender, and race do not simply intersect, in many ways they are/stand for, each other." This in no way contradicts the idea that the defining character of capitalism is a specific class system. It means that the class system is gendered and racialized and that the contradictions of capitalism are such that in particular times and places the political system might be challenged more successfully by targeting the gender or racial facets of oppression than the class nature of exploitation.

The postmodern emphasis on the multiplicity of identities and sites of struggle has expanded the spectrum of politics in Latin America, at the same time as it has tended to fragment it. Whereas past social struggles usually centered on class politics, more recent social movements in Latin America have mobilized around gender, race, indigenous, and environmental issues. Politics—including left politics—in Latin America once tended to be a predominantly male domain. By the 1990s this was changing—albeit very slowly and unevenly. In different ways gender politics won a measure of political legitimacy, even if this meant only that mainstream political parties found themselves forced to address gender issues. The threat of gender politics was reflected in the campaign launched by the Catholic church throughout the region, denouncing the notion that sex roles are socially constituted. Yet these struggles have opened up cultural spaces in which concepts of the family, gender, and sexuality are publicly challenged.

Finally, this collection of essays should dispel any notion that feminism in the United States and Europe is "more advanced" than in Latin America. That there is more published material about gender in the United States and Europe than in Latin America is a sign only that in the former there are more academics, who are paid more money, to publish more books on "sexy topics" than in Latin America. But gender politics is a vibrant and ongoing battle in virtually every region of the hemisphere.

NOTES

1. Jean-François Lyotard, *The Postmodern Political Condition* (Manchester: Manchester University Press, 1984) cited in H. Afshar and M. Maynard, eds., *The Dynamics of Race and Gender: Some Feminist Interventions* (London: Taylor and Francis, 1994).
2. For a brief and useful introduction to postmodernism as it applies to development, see "Introduction" in Jane Pappart and Marianne Marchand, eds., *Feminism, Postmodernism Development* (London and New York: Routledge, 1995).

3. The best Marxist critique of postmodernism is Ellen Meiksins Wood, *The Retreat from Class: A New 'True' Socialism* (London: Verso, 1988).
4. Jane S. Jaquette, "Introduction: From Transition to Participation—Women's Movements and Democratic Politics," in Jane S. Jaquette, ed., *The Women's Movement in Latin America: Participation and Democracy* (Boulder: Westview Press, 1994), p. 7.

WOMEN, WORK, AND EMPOWERMENT: ROMANTICIZING THE REALITY

SHARON McCLENAGHAN

The entry of women into the workforce and the impact of wage work on female status has formed the focus of a debate since the late 1970s. This follows the publication of Boserup's seminal work, *Women and Economic Development,* and the emergence of female employment as one of the highest priority policy issues during the UN Decade for Women (1975-1985).[1] During this time the expansion of world trade, characterized by global economic restructuring and the decentralization of production processes to developing countries, has seen employment opportunities increasingly open up for women. Many of these new jobs are in world market industries producing for export, such as garment manufacturing and electronics and provide important access to both formal and informal employment. While the restructuring of global industrial capital is differentiated regionally along gender, class, race, and ethnic lines, women remain central to this process.

In response to these global economic changes an expansive body of research has emerged on the subject of women and employment, part of which relates specifically to the growth of export-oriented industrialization. The parameters of the debate have broadened beyond an analysis of the structural determinants of labor force participation, in terms of supply and demand, to include consideration of the wide range of economic and symbolic meanings that wage work brings to women as well as its impact within the larger context of gender relations. While scholars disagree about the degree to which women's new working status can transform existing patriarchal relations, the general consensus is that formal employment represents an effective route for change from which women can develop the basis of autonomy and self-determination.

However, while women's entry into the workforce has become a global phenomenon, research has become dominated by case studies based on the export-processing industry, in turn creating the picture of a newly empowered (global) female proletariat. In the case of Latin America and the Caribbean, where the number of women entering the labor market more than tripled between 1950 and 1980, there has been considerably *less* female proletarianization than might have been expected given the number of new female entrants.[2] For these workers, their relationship to the international economy is defined less by the labor opportunities available to them and more by the creation of an economic environment which necessitates the acceptance of low-wage, low-skilled, and insecure employment.

Given the widely held view that pais work is an effective route for positive change in the lives of low income women, this calls for a reexamination and reevaluation of some important questions concerning the experience of such employment. Does waged labor offer the means to change oppressive relationships of power, and challenge existing values of the gender system? Can there be any *de facto* relationship between earning a wage and empowerment? Does the concept of a "female proletariat" have any currency in the context of short-term temporary employment in which the material basis for labor consciousness is slowly and continually being eroded? In light of these questions I argue that while women's increasing presence within the labor force constitutes a challenge to traditional gender ideology that places women at the center of the domestic sphere, the extent to which this represents a water mark of more fundamental change in power/gender relations is much less certain than previous research has indicated. What has emerged as a positive portrayal of women workers relates more to the implicitly "emancipatory script" of the theoretical framework employed than to the reality it seeks to describe.

The argument is developed in two stages. In the first section the global economic setting provides a backdrop to show that contrary to global trends,

Latin America and the Caribbean as a region does not conform to the feminization of labor thesis. Statistics show that changing global patterns have done little to change the rigidity of the labor market as a whole, where occupational segregation continues to characterize women's position at the bottom of the labor hierarchy concentrated in service sector and informal employment. In the second section I examine the thesis that wage work leads to empowerment through a critique of the household-based unit of analysis, which has evolved as a central theoretical framework for the study of women and work. I argue that such an approach can create a generalized and romanticized picture of the woman worker which obscures an accurate reading of the dynamics of power relations as well as screening out fundamental contradictions in the experience of work. This will be supported by findings from fieldwork in the Dominican Republic (1994-1995).

THE CHANGING GLOBAL BACKDROP: ECONOMIC RESTRUCTURING AND FEMALE EMPLOYMENT

A series of changes has occurred in the global economy which has facilitated the large-scale entry of women into the labor market and led to a significant redistribution in the gender composition of national workforces. In the discussion of these changes, two main factors are most commonly stressed: the growth of export-processing industrialization as a leading development strategy and the advances made in technology over the last three decades. The development of export-oriented industrialization is largely based on the exploitation of low labor costs and has become the favored strategy for a number of developing countries. In part this strategy has been successful due to technological development which has facilitated the decentralization of labor-intensive production processes to developing countries in the search for cheap labor with control of management retained in the core country.[3]

Capital has become "mobile," with the transnational corporation becoming a central protagonist in international trade relations and the creation of new capitalist patterns. Production processes are now characterized by the "global assembly line," made up of jobs which require short training periods and are ultimately flexible in the sense that they are not dependent upon one geographical location, nor one specific labor force. This, in turn, has led to what many consider to be a *"new international division of labor,"* and is regarded as integral to the economic successes of a number of countries, most notably the four East Asian "tigers," Taiwan, South Korea, Singapore, and Hong Kong.[4] Central to this division of labor is the employment of substantial numbers of women, who typically constitute 70 to 90 percent of the industrial workforce

21

in free trade zones (FTZs).[5] The demand for women workers relates not only to the "cheapness" of female labor, a fraction of what it would be in the home country, but to the belief among employers that women have a greater natural propensity for monotonous, repetitive factory work. A "nimble-fingered," docile, and inherently passive woman has become a stereotypical image of the factory worker.

More recently, since the late 1980s, the growth of export-oriented industrialization, has been further accentuated by the implementation of structural adjustment programs. These programs have been introduced in many developing countries under the control of the World Bank and the International Monetary Fund, as a means of meeting rising debt repayments incurred during the international economic crisis of the 1980s. In order to counteract the rising inflation and unemployment which occurred under import substitution industrialization, one of the prerequisites of structural adjustment is the outward-looking export-oriented development strategy.[6] In contrast to other industrialization strategies, namely that of import substitution, which provided relatively little employment for women, export-oriented industrialization is linked to what has been termed the "feminization of the workforce.'[7] Thus export-oriented industrialization has become a major focus in understanding the relationship between newly emerging patterns of industrial development and an increasingly female workforce. Countries which have most fully integrated their industrial sector into the international market through export-led industrialization have experienced the most rapid growth of female employment rates, leading Susan Joekes to state that industrialization in the postwar period has been as much female-led as export-led.[8] In response to these findings, much research attention has been directed to what has been termed the "new (global) proletariat" of young women and the demand for young single female workers that has emerged within the space of a generation.[9] Rather than providing a "labor reserve," which traditional labor market discourse implies, women are now widely regarded as a crucial and integral part of capital restructuring.

The case of newly liberalizing Latin American countries does not, however, fit easily within this model, which is not perhaps surprising given the heterogenous economic characteristics of the region as a whole. Its position within the world division of production is peripheral, with more than 70 percent of its exports made up of primary commodities. Although export-oriented industrialization has been heralded as a key developmental strategy by USAID since the 1980s and is currently supported by the World Bank, this has had relatively little significance for female employment in the region as a whole.[10] The provision of large-scale formal employment resulting from the "international division of labor" is restricted to relatively few countries, namely Mexico, the smaller countries of Central America, and the Caribbean.[11] Furthermore, as Ruth Pearson points out, the original hypothesis for women's increasing incorporation into the labor force as a result of export-led industrialization was developed from the Asian model. There, the dynamics of the labor force were significantly different than they were elsewhere, which places limitations on the hypothesis as it relates to the wholesale incorporation of women into the formal industrial labor market.[12]

However, trends since the late 1960s indicate increasing casualization within the organization of production, in the form of "sweatshop" subcontracting and homeworking, which means that a quantitative estimate of the impact of export processing cannot be wholly captured by formal statistics. Household-based studies reveal a diversity in production organization with many workers often involved in more than one type of work at any one time.[13] These activities range from factory-based formal work in specially constructed free trade zones under highly disciplined labor conditions, to home-based informal "piece work," where the worker undertakes production within her own home. As the informalization of industrial work becomes increasingly more common, the strength of the feminization thesis may lie more in its application to the informal sector than to the formal sector.[14] With accurate labor data notoriously hard to collect, it is impossible to confirm this thesis, but if it is correct, it may imply the need for a significant reorientation within the current debates on women and work toward a deeper analysis of the quality and conditionality of female employment "opportunities."

Women's position in the industrial labor market has never been secure. Even in countries in which women represent a significant percentage of the industrial labor force through export processing, employment is predominantly within "footloose" transnational companies or world market factories. These "flexible firms" can move production processes when there is the first sign of labor unrest or when an opportunity for cheaper production costs becomes a more viable alternative. Indeed, the success of export-led production strategies remains in part dependent upon the deregulation of the labor market, which curtails and erodes workers' rights in order to attract competitive foreign capital. Furthermore, while women remain the preferred workforce, export-oriented industries are becoming increasingly more male-dominated. This is partly related to the changing characteristics of global trade, which has increased the role of technology in both the globalization of products and markets.[15] The importance of skills is now becoming a key factor in the decisions of transnationals to invest or relocate; thus the importance of differential labor costs becomes less important in the new dynamics of capitalist development. This presents a major challenge to women's traditional labor market advantage of cost effectiveness, once conceptualized as the "comparative advantages of women's disadvantages," confirming that cheap labor in the abstract has never been sufficient in itself to guarantee women jobs.[16] At different periods of industrial development in Jamaica, Venezuela, Haiti, and Argentina, women have been replaced by male workforces, and in Ireland women were "removed" from the workforce via a series of policy disincentives.[17] In the case of the Border Industrialization Program in Mexico, women were important for establishing the "rules" of employment: employing a female-dominated workforce in an area of high male unemployment was instrumental in creating the "ideal worker"—docile, undemanding, nimble-fingered, nonunion, and unmilitant. After this had been established and accepted, men began to enter.[18] This move effectively necessitated the acceptance by the traditional male working class of low wages while simultaneously eroding the power of organized labor, or what has traditionally been called *class struggle,* demonstrating that gender characteristics are far from immutable.[19] The ideological rationale for employing women varies according to both economic and political goals.

A cursory look at labor market data shows that despite the growing integration of Latin America within the world economy, women's labor market position has not significantly changed. Between 1950 and 1980 the number of economically active women more than tripled, increasing from 10 million in 1950 to more than 32 million in 1980. These figures reflect a growth rate which outstripped the total growth rate of economically active women in the world.[20] Unlike a number of other regions where government policy was aimed specifically at the promotion of women's economic participation in productive work, the overall increase of women into the workforce in the period was not policy-led.[21] This increase becomes especially notable in the 1980s, commonly referred to as the "lost decade" for development in Latin America. Women entered the workforce to increase household incomes. Data show that during this period (1980 to 1990), the growth of economic activity in most countries in the region was a result of female economic activity.[22] However, in terms of women's share of the labor force, the 1980s represent the smallest increase within the last four decades (.5 percent). Since this figure is a measure of *formal* sector employment only, the disparity between the two sources of data shows that increase in female employment during the economic crisis was largely due to the rise in informal activity, confirming that women entered out of necessity.

The sectoral distribution of employment shows that global restructuring has not significantly altered patterns of occupational segregation but has reinforced them. The only sector to have shown significant growth within the period 1950 to 1980 is the service sector, which grew from almost 50 percent to over 65 percent.[23] In stark contrast, the female share of the industrial sector declined within the same period. As Draper points out, more than one in three women work as domestics in the service sector or in the informal sector, neither of which has a traditional history of organizing or any of the benefits of protected employment.[24] While women are becoming increasingly economically active, they remain disproportionately represented in these lowest paying sectors of employment, and are not keeping pace with men in terms of their relative labor market position.[25]

EVALUATING WOMEN'S WORK: IDEOLOGY, CONTINUITY, AND CHANGE

As increasing numbers of women enter the labor force there has been a consistent attempt within development studies to analyze changes resulting from women's new worker status and to evaluate the ways in which it can lead to empowerment. As opposed to studies which focus on the workplace, the household-based unit has emerged as a central theoretical framework in the evaluation of wage work on gender-power relations.[26] A number of these studies show that women have begun to achieve greater empowerment at a household level as a result of employment. This manifests itself in an increase in decision-making and bargaining power, increasing control over resources within the home which is shown to form the basis of personal autonomy and more egalitarian relationships.[27] Through the pay packet women workers are given the means to challenge male dominance at the household level.[28]

The importance of this body of research lies in demonstrating that wage work *can* provide the means to transform traditional gender relationships within the home. However, I propose that this approach provides only a partial indication of change and cannot be taken as framework for analysis of gender-power relations since it is grounded in an analytical separation of the household from its wider social and political context. By centralizing this theoretical framework, and promoting, unconsciously or otherwise, the idea that it is generalizable, we face the danger of assuming that, while remaining weak within the public sphere of the workplace and society in general, women are at least gaining power at a domestic level.[29] As my fieldwork shows, this is not always the case and depends on consideration of a larger number of variables than those contained within the small household unit. Furthermore, it encourages an interpretation that progress (here I refer to women's empowerment) is a unilinear process, the first stage of which is women's "entry" into the formal labor force.

As with any generalized picture of change there are a number of specific points which become problematic and must be deconstructed.[30] The male-headed household cannot be taken as an unproblematic, natural unit of analysis. As demographic trends show, the structure and characteristics of low-income households are not generalizable. Household and family size respond to socio-economic factors, an example being an increase in the number of women-headed households in urban areas as a direct result of migrant women moving to the city in search of work. In the context of Latin America and the Caribbean, the pattern of "visiting relationships" and the extended family are common, a direct antithesis to the mythical nuclear family assumed in traditional analysis.[31] In these situations the dynamics of domestic power relations are clearly outside the boundary of the imagined patriarchal household and challenge the implicit assumption that the internal dynamics of family life is generally known.

Another problem in the analysis of power relations within the home relates to the issue of male economic marginalization. While mentioned in a number of studies as a significant variable, it is generally greatly underplayed and relates more fundamentally to the problem of an absence of men from an analysis of gender relations.[32] This area is greatly undertheorized as a result of a lack of empirical data regarding men's changing economic status and how this rede-fines their social identities, as well as the implications this has for power relations.[33] What *is* known is that many women enter paid work as a result of male un- or under-employment in order to provide and supplement family incomes. While it is possible to say in these circumstances that male (patriar-chal) authority has been reduced, this has been at the expense of the economic "power" of the family unit as a whole, since net income is reduced. Within this context, increased economic responsibility for women throws up many more contradictions than the smooth picture of increased autonomy suggested by this theoretical framework. The association of male unemployment with absence from or desertion of the family unit, or with increases in aggressive male behavior manifest in higher rates of domestic violence, further complicates the picture.[34]

Prioritizing the household as the main area in which power relations are contested precludes an understanding of how power is mediated in society as a whole. As Diane Elson and Ruth Pearson point out, any change in power relations at the domestic level refers to "private power," which is by definition not collective and unlikely to be reproducible outside individual contexts.[35] Thus the household-based analysis is essentially problematic for a theory of empowerment because, as shown, there cannot be any *a priori* definitive relationship between earning a wage and fundamental change in power relations. The interplay between economic and ideological factors is considerably more complex than the above framework of empowerment/autonomy would lead us to believe.

The problems inherent in attempting to evaluate wage work from the perspective of the household are supported by findings from fieldwork (1994-1995) in the Dominican Republic.[36] The Dominican Republic boasts one of the highest percentages of industrialized female proletariat in the region, as a result of its export-oriented development policy. In response to the 1982 structural adjustment program, the peso was devalued to attract foreign investment and the Dominican Republic became one of the cheapest sites for investment in the region and, indeed, in the world. A number of free trade zones were constructed, which offered impressive financial incentives to overseas capital, and from the mid-1980s onward transnationals from North America and Korea have taken advantage of cheap labor and a deregulated labor market. The dismantling of the sugar industry, once the traditional agricultural base of the country, meant that women's entry into the industrial labor force has largely coincided with large-scale male unemployment and underemployment.

The town of Villa Altagracia, which was chosen as a case study, is considered a paradigmatic example of industrial restructuring, illustrative of the changes occurring in the country as a whole.[37] In response to the 1986 closure of the Ingenio Catarrey sugar mill, the principal source of male employment in the area, a free trade zone was established. Managed by the same public sector body (the CEA) as the ingenio, the zone has been predominantly financed by Korean capital and began operations in 1988.[38] The majority of the workforce are women, and as a result of widespread male underemployment, they have replaced men in the formal economy as the principal wage earners within the family.[39]

However, there is little evidence to suggest women have gained a sense of empowerment from their new working position in the *zona franca,* or that the patriarchal relationships both within and outside of the household have altered in any uniform or consistent way. In order to evaluate the role and impact of paid employment it is necessary to consider a number of interrelated issues: the context of the economic crisis, the position of women as mothers, and the concomitant changes occurring within dominant cultural ideology.

In contrast to the global norm of young single women workers in export industries, a defining characteristic of the Dominican labor force in this sector is that a majority of the women are mothers. Managers' preference for mothers derives from the belief that the additional responsibility of having a family to support will translate into greater labor market commitment. This rationale for employing women with children mirrors the dramatic changes of the last decade in attitudes toward paid work as gender roles have been continually renegotiated in response to the ongoing economic crisis.

As a result of rising inflation from the mid-1980s onward, the value of the minimum wage declined by 62.3 percent over six years from 1984.[40] The numbers living in absolute poverty have risen and the current minimum wage will not cover basic needs. The need to secure paid employment has become a fact of life for *all* family members. Female entry into the workforce has largely been in response to economic necessity: to compensate for the drop in real wages and family income, but more specifically to provide materially for their children. Within this economic climate both continuity and change characterize the ideological basis of traditional gender roles. Women now have a double role as mothers *and* breadwinners, and while significant changes are occurring in women's relationship to the production process, the fundamental core of gender roles remains the same. Identity as a mother now includes the ability to provide not only emotionally but materially for their children; thus women's *new* working identity, in as much as it exists, is forged *through* commitments to their mothering role.[41]

Thus while gender roles are changing as a result of waged work, this as yet poses no fundamental threat to the traditionally prescribed values of a gender system in which women remain responsible for the support and maintenance of the home. While wage work allowed the women to have more of a sense of control over spending patterns, such changes were negligible given the overall poverty of their economic situation. Furthermore, gender roles within the household had undergone no significant change. Working in the *zona franca* an average of ten hours a day, five and a half days a week, women remain responsible for (and committed to) the bulk of reproductive work.[42] In a marginalized area with erratic electricity supply the purchase and preparation of food and water, management of childcare, and the cleaning of the house is fitted around their long working hours, with many of the women rising as early as five in the morning in order to finish their tasks.

This "new" productive role is regarded as an extension of women's reproductive role, creating a double identity for women, a contradiction which capital can manipulate to its advantage in the labor process. When production quotas were not reached, a common means of pressuring women to work harder was to shout: "¡Vayase a su casa! ¿Qué clase de madre eres? [Go home, what sort of mother are you?]" Since women do not see themselves as workers first and foremost but as mothers whose economic circumstance forced them into the workplace, this was an effective psychological weapon. It plays on their guilt at leaving their children, as well as the inherent pride women take in fulfilling their duties. By conflating the responsibility of a good worker within the image of a good mother, at the core of their identity, this effectively negates any possibility of an alternative, more radical worker identity from forming. As the most viable economic option available to them, this mother-worker identity shames the women into working harder. Many women said they would rather have received *golpes* (slaps), preferring physical rather than mental punishment.

In general, women's relationship to the labor market is weak in terms of employment related demands. The instability of employment in the *zona franca* and the physical and mental exhaustion which characterize women's employment are accepted as part of the "natural" cycle of work in the context of few employment alternatives. Their weak worker identity is further compounded by a politically fragmented union movement, little or no former labor market experience, and a production process designed to undermine worker solidarity.[43]

The extent to which a new worker status can provide women with the basis to challenge traditional gender-power hierarchies is extremely limited. While the economic crisis has forced changes in gender roles, at an ideological level, "traditional" gender roles and identities are much more resilient. Rather than the "myth" of the male breadwinner having been dispelled there is evidence to show that patriarchal values are actually being reinscribed.[44] Even as the primary wage earners in the household, women continued to recognize the man as *el jefe* (the head); this was true despite the absence of the male partner—most men play little or no economic role in the family and in the woman's life—and even in cases where the male partner had deserted the family and was living with a new family (in four cases living in another country).[45]

Clearly, the entry of women into paid work cannot be taken as an unqualified indication of positive change at any level. While wage work offers access to economic "independence," this means very little in a context of poverty. Women are forging new identities for themselves, but the persistence of traditional ideological norms acts to curb the full potential for change. As long as the normative assumptions of the female role, continue to be reinscribed including responsibilities for reproductive work, so too do traditional patriarchal relations in the household.

CONCLUSION

The aim of this chapter has been to examine women's position in the labor market from a critical perspective, and question the idea that paid work leads to empowerment. Predictions that wage work provides the basis for increased autonomy or for improving patriarchal relations are as yet unsubstantiated. Many women enter the labor market out of economic desperation; for these women work represents an issue of survival rather than a means for self-improvement. While a flexible labor market can provide employment opportunities, the majority of women continue to move into low paid, unskilled work without acquiring marketable skills for future employment. Women remain a significant industrial labor force, but their position within the employment market is made increasingly vulnerable by the conditions of labor deregulation and casualization which characterize contemporary global economic trade relations. The international division of labor continues to realign itself in accordance with the exigencies of an international trade system in which new demands of increasing flexibility and technological skill are beginning to dominate.

An analysis of empowerment and gender relations requires a framework which can encompass all areas of life: the interrelation between ideological and economic factors within the private, social, and public spheres. Changing gender relations in the household must be located within the analysis of a wider nexus of power relations which can include the contradictions which arise as gender roles change. While gender relations are actively under renegotiation, "progress" is not the unilinear experience that some theoretical frameworks imply.

In an effort to counteract the essentialist and stereotypical view of women as inherently passive, feminist theorists have faced difficulties in confronting the negativity, contradiction and passivity which characterize many women's labor experience. In evaluating women's new working status it is largely ignored that for a majority of women, entry into the labor force is the means by which they can fulfill their mothering role. Identity, still largely absent in research on women and employment, is a key area if we are to understand how subordinate gender relations within the labor market come to be reproduced. For a majority of these women, what has been taken to be a direct correlation between employment, a wage, and "empowerment" at the household level, is nothing more than a "historical accident" where the gains made are not necessarily secure.[46] Analysis of employment (productive work) cannot take place without a concomitant analysis of reproductive work, and the value and meaning both come to occupy for the subject. This is the terrain in which ideology provides the rationale for substantiating women's secondary worker status. While the research on women and the labor market must occur within a structural context which includes consideration of the characteristics of gendered labor market and the economic climate, identity cannot be omitted.

The argument could be made that this is an overly pessimistic evocation of the current position of the Latin American woman worker, relating as it does in part to one of the lowest sections of the working class. However, while it is too early to venture conclusions regarding the very recent nature of women's incorporation into the industrial labor market, I believe it is a necessary corollary to the generalized picture which has begun to emerge of the newly empowered female proletariat, which bears little relation to a significant number of women who struggle through waged employment to feed themselves and their families.

NOTES

1. Ester Boserup, *Women and Economic Development* (New York: St. Martin's Press, 1970) was the first major text to highlight the need for a gendered analysis of the development process. For more recent approaches on the subject of women's economic position see K. Ward, "Women in the Global Economy," in B. Gutek, L. Larwood & A. Stromberg, eds., *Women and Work* (Beverley Hills, CA: Sage, 1988), pp. 17-48; Susan Tiano, "Women and Industrial Development in Latin America (review essay)," *Latin American Research Review* 21, no. 3 (1986): 157-170; and E. Draper, "Women's Work and Development in Latin America," *Studies in Comparative Economic Development* 20, no. 1 (1985): 3-30. For a discussion of the changes in policy focus during the UN Decade for Women see Caroline Moser, "Gender Planning in the Third World: Meeting Practical and Strategic Needs," *World Development* 17, no. 11 (1989): 1799-825.
2. I use the definition of proletarian labor to refer to workers engaged in full-time waged labor, as opposed to "semi-proletarian" labor where waged labor is combined with other economic activities. See David Broad, "Globalization and the Casual Labor Problem," *Social Justice* 22, no. 3 (1995).
3. See F. Froebel et al., *The New International Division of Labor* (Cambridge: Cambridge University Press, 1980); Diane Elson and Ruth Pearson, "Nimble Fingers Make Light Work, An Analysis of Women's Employment in Third World Export Manufacturing," *Feminist Review* 8 (Spring 1981): 87-107.
4. See F. Deyo, "Capital, Labor and State in Thai Industrial Restructuring: The Impact of Global Economic Transformations," in D. Smith and J. Borocz, eds., *A New World Order? Global Transformations in Late Twentieth Century* (Westport, CT: Greenwood, 1995), pp. 131-45.
5. See Sylvia Chant and C. McIlwaine, "Gender and Export Manufacturing in the Philippines: Continuity or Change in Female Employment? The Case of Mactan Export Processing Zone," *Gender, Place and Culture: A Journal of Feminist Geography* 2, no. 2 (September 1995): 147.

31

6. For a detailed explanation of what has been termed "the global hegemony" of export-led industrialization and its integral position in this present phase of "reformulated capitalism," see L. Sklair, *Assembling for Development: the Maquila Industry in Mexico and the United States* (Boston: Unwin Hyman, 1989), p. 157.

7. G. Standing, "Global Flexibilization Through Flexible Labor," *World Development* 17 (1989): 1077-1095.

8. S. Joekes, *Women in the World Economy: An INSTRAW Study* (New York: Oxford University Press, 1987), p. 81.

9. See S. Mitter, *Common Fate, Common Bond: Women in the Global Economy* (London: Pluto Press, 1986) and L. Lim, "Capitalism, Imperialism and Patriarchy: The Dimension of Third World Women Workers in Multinational Factories," in June Nash and María Patricia Fernández-Kelly, eds., *Women, Men and the International Division of Labor* (Albany: State University of New York Press, 1983), pp. 70-91.

10. See Helen Safa, "Women and Industrialization in the Caribbean," in S. Stichter and J. Parpart, eds., *Women, Employment and the Family in the International Division of Labor* (Basingstoke: Macmillan, 1990), pp. 98-136.

11. See D. Pantin, "The Role of Export Processing Zones in Caribbean Economic Development," in Stanley Lalta and Marie Freckleton, eds., *Caribbean Economic Development: The First Generation* (Kingston: Ian Randle Publishers, 1993).

12. See Ruth Pearson, "Latin American Women and the New International Division of Labor: A Reassessment," *Bulletin of Latin American Studies* 5, no. 2 (1986): 767-779.

13. See Lourdes Benería and Martha Roldán, *The Crossroads of Class and Gender* (Chicago: University of Chicago Press, 1987), and Sheila Rowbotham and S. Mitter, eds., *Dignity and Daily Bread: New Forms of Economic Organising Among Women in the Third World and the First* (London: Routledge, 1994).

14. See Rowbotham and Mitter, eds., ibid.

15. For reference to Mexico and the Dominican Republic, see D. Pena, "Tortuosidad: Shop Floor Struggles of Female Maquiladoras" in V. Ruiz and Susan Tiano, eds., *Women on the U.S.-Mexico Border: Responses to Change* (London: Allen and Unwin, 1987), and *World Survey on the Role of Women in Development* (United Nations, 1989), pp. 149-50. Also see Draper, "Women's Work and Development in Latin America": 1-30.

16. See Lourdes Arizpe and J. Aranda, "The 'Comparative Advantages' of Women's Disadvantages: Women Workers in the Strawberry Export Agribusiness in Mexico," *Signs* 7, no. 2 (1981).

17. See N.C. Hollander, "Women Workers and Class Struggle: The Case of Argentina," *Latin American Perspectives* 4, nos. 1 and 2 (1977): 180-193; Joekes, *Women in the World Economy;* R. Sauto, "The Female Labor Force in Argentina, Bolivia, and Paraguay," *Latin American Research Review* 15, no. 2: 152-161. For a discussion of the "gender tactics" of the capitalist process, see K. Hossfield, "Export-led Development and the Underemployment of Women: The Impact of Discriminatory Developemnt Policy in the Republic of Ireland," in K. Ward, ed.,

Women Workers and Global Restructuring (Ithaca, NY: Cornell University Press, 1986), pp. 149-78.

18. See Sklair, *Assembling for Development.*

19. The normalization of these labor relations is encapsulated in concept of *maquilization,* which refers not to the rules under which these export-oriented world factories operate, but to the social relations of production. See K. Kopinak, "Gender as a Vehicle for the Subordination of Maquiladora Workers in Mexico," *Latin American Perspectives* no. 84 (1995): 30-49.

20. See *ECLAC: Statistical Yearbook for Latin America and the Caribbean* (Santiago, Chile: United Nations, 1989). Statistics also show that the increasing rates of economic participation by women in most countries within the last twenty-five years has been a direct result of the rise in numbers of women entering the labor market. See *Statistical Abstract of Latin America,* Vol. 31, Part 1, pp. 384-85. For a general overview of women's employment position in Latin America, see Irma Arriagada, "Changes in the Urban Female Labor Market," *CEPAL Review* 5 (August 1994): 91-110.

21. Although deliberate cases exist of policy-led directives based on employment provision for women in Nicaragua and Cuba, this was not typical of the region as a whole.

22. Within a more recent period (1970 to 1995), half of the countries of the region record declining rates of male participation in contrast to increasing rates of female participation in all but one country. See Appendix: TABLE 1 *(ECLAC: Statistical Yearbook* 1992).

23. *Inter American Development Bank in Economic and Social Progress in Latin America: Special Section: Working Women in Latin America* (1991), p. 223.

24. Widespread research shows that opportunities exist for a "new class of female microentrepreneurs." See R. Lesser Blumberg, "Gender, Micro-enterprize, Performance, and Power," in Christine Bose and Edna Acosta-Belén, eds., *Women in the Latin American Development Process* (Philadelphia: Temple University Press, 1995). However, it should be noted this is a sector which is traditionally without a history of organizing in which women have always been represented in significant numbers. Within the Caribbean, women have traditionally worked as "higglers" and "tradeswomen" without any evidence to suggest that their labor position has improved. See Draper, "Women's Work and Development in Latin America," p. 18.

25. For an overview of women's global economic condition, see Kathryn Ward, "Women in the Global Economy," in *Women and Work* 3 (1988): 17-48.

26. For a discussion of how this framework has evolved see L. del Alba Acevedo, "Feminist Inroads in the Study of Women's Work and Development," in Bose and Acosta-Belén, eds., *Women in the Latin American Development Process;* and more specifically Helen Safa, *The Myth of the Male Breadwinner: Women and Industrialization in the Caribbean* (Boulder: Westview, 1995). Research which uses the workplace as a unit of analysis includes, J. Humphrey, *Gender and Work in the Third World: Sexual Division of Labor in Brazilian Industry* (London: Tavistock, 1987); C. Freeman, "Designing Women: Corporate Discipline and Barbados's Off

Shore Sector Pink Collar Sector," *Cultural Anthropology* 8, no. 2 (1993): 169-186; and Pena, "Tortuosidad: Shop Floor struggles of Female Maquiladora Workers."

27. See Benería and Roldán, *Crossroads of Class and Gender;* Nash and Kelly, eds., *Women, Men and the International Division of Labor;* Safa, *Myth of the Male Breadwinner;* Chant and McIlwaine, "Gender and Export Manufacturing in the Philippines"; P.D. Alfonso, *Women and Work in Chile: A Case Study of the Fish-Processing Industry on the Island of Chiloe,* unpublished Ph.D. thesis, University of Cambridge, 1993.

28. See Helen Safa, "The New Women Workers: Does Money Equal Power?" in *NACLA Report on the Americas* 27, no. 1: 24 -29. Safa refers to employment as a "weapon" to fight patriarchy within the home.

29. Safa defines patriarchy as male control over female labor, which is reflected at the levels of home, workplace, and state. Her thesis is that the primary locus of patriarchy has shifted with the development of industrial capitalism from the home to the workforce and the state, or from the private to the public; see *Myth of the Male Breadwinner,* p. 39.

30. For a full discussion of the household as a site for theoretical discussion see Naila Kabeer, *Reversed Realities* (London: Verso, 1996).

31. In the Dominican Republic, as in many other countries in the region, it is common for men to have sexual relationships with more than one woman. The number of children a partner "brings" with them to a relationship depends on the status of past and current relationships, all of which affect the power dynamics within the household.

32. See V. Stolcke, "The Social Impact of the Crisis of Development" in *The Crisis of Development* (CEDLA, 1991), pp. 87-103.

33. See Alfonso, *Women and Work in Chile.*

34. See R. Katzman, "Why Are Men So Irresponsible?" in *CEPAL Review* 46 (April 1992): 79-87.

35. Diane Elson and Ruth Pearson, "The Latest Phase of the International Division of Capital and its Implication for Women in the Third World" (Sussex: Institute of Development discussion paper, June 1980). See also Sylvia Walby, *Theorising Patriarchy* (Oxford: Basil Blackwell, 1990).

36. Fieldwork undertaken in Villa Altagracia was based on a comparative study of 100 factory workers in the local *zona franca* and 100 nonfactory workers. From this initial sample, fifteen women from each group were selected for in-depth interviews.

37. C. Baez, "Fuerza Laboral y Sector Informal," *Estudios Sociales,* Año XXV, 88, Abril-Junio 1992.

38. The report, *Rationalization of Free Trade Zone Policies in the Dominican Republic, Draft Final Report* (Vol II, Annexes, June 1991), submitted by the Services Group, shows that the opening of the FTZ by the CEA can be read as an essentially political move, its *raison d'etre* being the need to offset the local resentment for closing the sugar refineries. This is further substantiated by the decision made by the two main companies not to expand for "fear that labor problems could occur if the operations become too large" (p. 3). The fact that it employs women workers

in an area which is widely regarded as potentially disruptive and troublesome would seem deliberate and fits with Sklair's analysis of the BIP previously cited.

39. Although men worked only three months per year in the sugar industry, this was the main source of employment. The men were employed in the informal sector, in particular the construction industry which was booming as a result of President Balaguer's commitment to public sector development. This work was sporadic and usually meant that the men were absent from the home for substantial periods of time. Within Villa Altagracia, many men had jobs as taxi car drivers ("públicos") or motor bike drivers ("moto conchos").

40. Fundapec (Fundacion Apec de Credito Educativo), *Encuesta Nacional de Mayo de Obra* (Santo Domingo: Fundapec, 1992), p. 8.

41. See P. Pessar, "On the Homefront and in the Workplace: Integrating Immigrant Women into Feminist Discourse," *Anthropological Quarterly* 68, no. 1 (1995): 37-47; María Patricia Fernández-Kelly and Saskia Sassen, "Recasting Women in the Global Economy: Internationalization and Changing Definitions of Gender" in Bose and Acosta-Belen, eds., *Women in the Latin American Development Process* (1995).

42. This supports findings from other research in industrialized countries which show that despite advances made in women's formal labor market position, major changes have not occurred in the redistribution and division of domestic tasks.

43. One of the main sources of income is remittances from family members living in the United States, a large percentage of whom are undocumented immigrants.

44. See Safa, *The Myth of the Male Breadwinner,* for a full discussion of this.

45. While gender awareness was generally high in regard to women's rights. However, when it came to explaining the lack of equality in their own relationships or male behavior such as desertion, having other partners, or going to prostitutes, the interviewees identified the bedrock difference between the sexes as the cause. External forces such as state corruption was seen to reinforce and legitimatize men's "bad" behavior and irresponsibility. Although most of the women interviewed were the principal wage earners for their households and most of their partners were either unemployed or working in the informal sector, the women conceptualized their working role primarily in relation to that of the man. They would say: "I work to help him [Soy una ayuda para el]."

46. For a reference to this "historical accident," see Fernández-Kelly and Sassen, in Bose and Acosta-Belén, eds., *Women in the Latin American Development Process.*

NICARAGUAN WOMEN: LEGAL, POLITICAL, AND SOCIAL SPACES

ANNA M. FERNANDEZ PONCELA

> Intelligence galvanizes the world.... But is intelligence the sole preserve of men, or is it also a feminine trait? To affirm the former is to affirm an absurdity that repudiates both science and civilization. To recognize the latter is to give nature its due. It falls to female intelligence to galvanize the world as well.
>
> —*Benjamín Zeledón*

Throughout the 1980s in Nicaragua, the Sandinista National Liberation Front (FSLN), which advocated the struggle against women's oppression as one of its principles and policies, held power. The purpose of this chapter is to interpret and reflect on the political and organizational participation of Nicaraguan women in that decade, characterized as it was by broad social transformation. By examining new ideological constructs, legal reforms, and the creation of specific institutions, it exposes the true extent of women's presence. This chapter also includes an analysis of the opportunities and limitations involved in the development of more equal gender relations in Sandinista Nicaragua.

The methodology employed combines quantitative and qualitative analysis, including interpretation of documentary and statistical sources, and the conclusions of fieldwork carried out by the author. The voices of the women protagonists give context and meaning to the documental and statistical evidence.

HISTORICAL BACKGROUND

In Nicaragua, as in the rest of the world, women have been ignored and marginalized in politics, in history, and in the social sciences in general. Women's social and political role in Nicaraguan history has been reduced to "history as legend": the stories of individual women, elevated to the status of "national heroines." Examples range from the mythical Xochitl, daughter of the indigenous *cacique* Adiac de Subtiava of León, who committed suicide rather than submit to the domination of the Spanish *conquistadores*, to Rafaela Herrera, daughter of the superintendent of *El Castillo* at Río San Juan, who continued defending the fortress against English pirates after her father's death.[1] The genre survives in the twentieth century with stories of the female guerrilla commanders who fought against Anastasio Somoza's tyrannical dictatorship in the 1960s and 1970s.

These stories belong to the "official" version of history. However, obscured beneath the surface one can find another history: the history of the social and cultural resistance and readaptation of many anonymous women. Examples include the indigenous women who, during the conquest and colonial period, took the courageous decision not to conceive "Spanish slaves," thereby withholding their right to reproduce. Their stories are told in the Chronicles of the Indies.[2] Women were protagonists in the struggle for independence in 1811, in the civil wars of 1854 and 1856, and in the battles against North American intervention, from William Walker in 1856 to the historic uprising against the U.S. Marines led by Benjamín Zeledón in 1912. Women were present in Augusto César Sandino's war of 1926 to 1934,[3] the national strike of 1936, the 1944 struggle of the workers in the Patco textile factory, and the student demonstrations of 1956. Understood in this way, Nicaragua has a long and profound tradition of female social and political participation.[4]

In 1955, Anastasio García Somoza "granted" women the right to vote through a constitutional reform, suppressing articles 31 through 33 of the Nicaraguan constitution. The dictator sought a favorable international image, but beyond this he reasoned that the supposedly conservative female vote would serve his political purpose. However, it was precisely through the anti-Somoza insurrection that women began to assert themselves most visibly in the history of the nation. This was particularly apparent in the Association of Women Confronting National Issues (AMPRONAC), created in September of 1977.

A review of *La Prensa*, Nicaragua's best-known daily newspaper, shows that AMPRONAC worked in various ways to defend life and human rights. The conditions of mother, wife, sister, and daughter were brought together to express protests on behalf of disappeared and imprisoned relatives. Every denunciation of state abuse was used as a means to demonstrate dissent with the government. The objective of these activities, the organization stated, was "to achieve the participation of women in the study and resolution of the problems presented by the national situation; to defend the rights of Nicaraguan woman in all areas and aspects of her life including the economy and the social and political arenas; to defend human rights in general."[5]

An interview with Marina Madariaga, deputy mayor of León, in 1991, echoes this:

> AMPRONAC registered denunciations, carried out pot-banging protests and hunger strikes, and organized marches of women dressed in mourning. The objective was the downfall of the Somoza dictatorship, but they also related their struggle to the things women cared most about: children and family....

Nevertheless, women participated in only limited numbers in the uprising against the dictatorship which took place from 1977 to 1978. Only 7 percent of women were active, compared to 93 percent of men.[6] In fact, one of the few sources about women's activities during the 1970s, a survey done in some *barrios* of Managua, demonstrates the low level of female participation in their communities. For example, only 2.4 percent of women said that a housewives' group existed in their neighborhood, 71.7 percent claimed that no such organization existed, and 25.9 percent stated that they did not know if one existed or not.[7] While it would appear that women's presence in the anti-Somoza struggle was not as high as was claimed in official bulletins at the time, a distinction should be drawn between "combat duties," which these percentages represent, and "support duties." A greater degree of female participation would be found if participation is taken to include the support function.

Moreover, some women were active in the front lines of the Sandinista struggle. Like the individual heroines of old, their names have been recorded in the new history. Examples are the three women who participated in the FSLN's spectacular assault on Chema Castillo's mansion in Managua in 1974; the occupation of the National Palace in 1978 under the supervision of Dora María Téllez, one-time head of the FSLN forces on the Western Front; and the surrender of Granada to the FSLN forces led by Mónica Baltodano. These are some significant exceptions to the generally low level of female participation in the political struggle in Nicaragua in the 1970s.

WOMEN IN A DECADE OF CHANGE: PRINCIPLES, LEGISLATION, AND INSTITUTIONS

The FSLN took control of the government in July of 1979, signifying the transformation in many aspects of Nicaraguan life, among them, the treatment of women. Women became the "object" of new legislation, their specific problems were discussed and various interests coalesced to signal the need for concrete policy initiatives to reform and/or eliminate gender subordination. FSLN literature broached the problem of gender discrimination and the need for women's liberation, as an ideological principle, from the declaration that appeared in the first "Historic Program" of 1969 to the speeches of the First Congress of 1991.[8] At that time the FSLN recognized the intractable nature of the problem as well as omissions and errors made in relation to women's issues throughout eleven years of government.[9]

A study of party and government literature reveals a process of evolution from the level of propaganda toward a certain degree of sensitivity and awareness about the woman question.[10] When it became evident that the revolution alone would not be sufficient to combat gender inequality, a change of tone can be seen, including terms of self-criticism and the recognition of limitations. It should not be forgotten that the FSLN was the first political force within a progressive government in the American continent to not only endorse feminism, but also rapidly incorporate women's emancipation into its thinking.[11] Once in government, the FSLN introduced a body of new legislation and created a number of specific departments to give institutional continuity to its ideals. The party developed a two-pronged strategy: on the one hand, it attempted to mobilize political support for women's issues, and on the other, it initiated legislative reform.

The goal of legislation was to promote women's dignity and equality with men in particular areas of life. A stand was made with regard to the family, maternity, and childrearing. The Association of Nicaraguan Women Luisa Amanda Espinosa (AMNLAE), created days after the triumph of the revolution, and a member of the Council of State introduced proposals to counter sexist attitudes and practices, which the Council approved.[12] The broad spectrum of laws decreed in the early 1980s focused on protection of the family, and the woman within that unit. However, compliance with, and enforcement of, the legal reforms was uneven, either due to low levels of awareness or because of inconsistent judicial applications of those laws. Silvia Carrasco, coordinator of the Isnin Women's Center in Managua, reflected in 1992: "I always thought that all the laws and benefits for women, brought about through the revolution,

39

were not fully disseminated. Not all women had the interest or the facilities to take advantage of them."

Among the institutions created to deal with women's issues, the Women's Legal Bureau and the Women's Governmental Bureau stand out. The Women's Legal Bureau opened in 1983 in order to provide a legal channel through which to assert the rights of the Nicaraguan woman. Its major objectives were "to extend legal assistance to women, and to monitor the administration of justice in cases where women's rights and interests are at stake."[13] Cases included family conflicts and more general issues affecting women: subsistence pensions, divorce settlements, cases of abuse, custody and recognition of children, problems relating to housing, and so on. The Bureau was linked directly with AMNLAE, and was in charge of a team of specialists organized into the Judicial Group, the Psycho-Social Group, and the Judicial-Social Educational Group.

The Women's Governmental Bureau was organized as a dependent department of the Ministry of the Presidency at the end of 1982. Its principle objective was the coordination of projects concerning women's issues. Its Information Center was the first in the country and the only one to specialize in gender. Over time the Bureau established links between different institutions and organizations working in the field. Its objective was to achieve greater institutional emphasis for programs that would benefit women, and to effect a qualitative increase in female participation in those projects.

WOMEN'S ACCESS TO POLITICAL INSTITUTIONS: POLITICAL PARTIES AND STATE BODIES

In the sphere of formal politics, some women managed to attain posts within the state apparatus—the executive, legislative, and judicial branches—as well as within the political parties. However, according to data compiled by the Women's Governmental Bureau in the mid 1980s, female participation in national political parties was relatively low at the membership base level and within internal management structures.

Tables 1 through 4 present the findings of research at the Women's Governmental Bureau in 1984. In terms of party membership, the FSLN registered 21 percent female membership, although 56 percent of positions of responsibility within the party were held by women. These statistics can be understood in the context of the high numbers of male FSLN members occupying leadership positions in the armed forces and the government at that time. The Independent Liberal Party (PLI) and the Popular Social Christian Party (PPSC) both had 40 percent female participation. However, in other political groupings, female membership was less than 35 percent (Table 1).

Table 1: Female Participation in Political Parties, 1983 (by percent)

Party	Party membership	Official posts
FSLN (Sandinista Front)	21	56
PLI	40	5
PPSC	40	no data
PSN (Socialists)	20	5
PSD (Social Democrats)	24	38
PCN (Communists)	35	10
MAP (Popular Action Movement)	30	no data

In this same period (1984), 36 percent of executive positions within the government were filled by women. In the judiciary, women made up 27 percent of magistrates, 20 percent of judges in Employment Tribunals, 25 percent in District Courts, 40 percent in Local Courts, and 40 percent of attorneys (Table 2).

Table 2: Female and Male Participation in State Bodies, 1984 (by percent)

State Body		Women	Men
Executive Branch:	Senior governmental posts	36	64
Judicial Branch:	Magistrates	27	73
	Employment Tribunal Judges	20	80
	District Judges	25	75
	Local Judges	40	60
	Attorneys	40	60

By 1989, women held only 3 percent of important posts within the executive. In public administration, the figure rose to 49 percent, and 51 percent of positions in the service sector were held by women.[14] As is usual in these cases, women tended to succeed and acquire responsibilities in professions that extended their domestic role. Women's political participation in the Council of State—the parliament composed of representatives of political parties and popular organizations in the early 1980s—displayed a certain limited level of integration by 1983. Women made up 21 percent of delegates—representing political, popular, trade union, and women's organizations—and 23 percent of the Congress's alternate delegates. The Legislative Advisory Body was at that time made up of 60 percent women (Table 3).[15]

41

GENDER POLITICS IN LATIN AMERICA

Table 3: Female and Male Participation in the Council of State, 1983 (by percent)

Position	Women	Men
Delegate	21	79
Alternate delegate	23	77
Legal advisor	60	40

The FSLN won 67 percent of the votes cast in the 1984 general elections, followed at some distance by the Democratic Conservatives (PCD) with 14 percent of the vote. In the legislative chamber—created through those elections—13 percent of delegates and 13 percent of alternates were women, for a total of 96 seats (Table 4).

Table 4: Female and Male Participation in the National Assembly, 1984

Position	Women	Men
Delegates	13 percent	87 percent
Alternate delegates	13 percent	87 percent

In the electoral campaign of 1990, both the National Opposition Union (UNO)—a coalition of fourteen parties from the extreme right to the Communist Party—and the Central American Unionist Party had female presidential candidates. Violeta Barrios de Chamorro became the first elected female president in the country's history. In these elections, 16 percent of the 90 representatives elected to the National Assembly were women. The number of women elected to national parliamentary bodies has been steadily decreasing in Nicaragua since 1979 (Table 5).

Table 5: Female Participation in the National Assembly, 1990

Position	FSLN (by number)	UNO (by number)	Total	Women (by percent)	Men (by percent)
Delegate	9	6	15	16	84
Alternate delegate	8	2	10	11	89
Total	17	8	25	27	73

Source: Supreme Electoral Council, 1990.

In summary, women's participation was not equal to men's; the discourse and statements of principle promoting female "integration" in the framework of the revolution, the legal reforms, and the creation of institutions, were not sufficient to boost women's participation in the sphere of formal politics.

WOMEN'S PARTICIPATION IN POPULAR ASSOCIATIONS: TRADE UNIONS AND MASS ORGANIZATIONS

No less important to the ideological and social structure of the Sandinista revolution than the formal political arena was the political space created by the popular organizations. These included trade unions and syndicates, organized into concentrations of industrial workers (CST), health workers (FETSALUD), educators (ANDEN), professionals (CONAPRO), agricultural workers (ATC), and farmers (UNAG); mass social organizations (the Communal Movement, previously the CDS); and the sectoral organizations, the women's movement (AMNLAE) and the youth movement (JS-19J).[16] The membership of these organizations was mixed, with the obvious exception of the women's movement. And by the end of the 1980s, some of them had a relatively significant female presence (Table 6).

Table 6: Female Participation in Popular Organizations, 1989

Organization	Women		Leadership	
	by percent	by number	by percent	by number
FETSALUD	80	no data	90	no data
ANDEN	70	no data	30	no data
Communal Movement	57	no data	no data	no data
JS-19J	46	no data	40	no data
CONAPRO	40	no data	no data	no data
ATC	40	10,500	35	no data
CST	37	no data	40	485
UNAG	12	16,000	5	1,000

Source: Fundamental Bases of Power Conference, Resoluciones (Managua: Encuentro, 1989).

These statistics should not be accepted at face value, however. Besides being based on official figures, they refer only to a nominal presence, which does not automatically imply active or conscious participation. Nor do they signify that in the moment of participation, women act in the same way and with the same opportunities and rights as their male counterparts. Research into female participation in the aforementioned organizations during the same time period reveals a very low level of organization among Nicaraguan women. One survey indicates that by the end of 1989, only 15 percent of all women in the country were organized, compared to 85 percent who were not. Of the group that were organized, half were enrolled in popular organizations—trade unions, women's groups, and youth movements—and the other half belonged to groups of a religious nature. Religious organizations are essentially a female space (Table 7).[17]

Table 7: Women's Participation in Popular Organizations, 1989

Organization	percent
AMNLAE	12
FSLN	8
CST	2
ANDEN	16
FETSALUD	2
JS-19J	13
Religious Groups	43
Total	96

Source: Cenzontle, Encuesta Nacional (datos), Talleres Participativos (transcripción) (Nicaragua: Cenzontle, 1989-90).

To conclude, in all areas of political participation—official institutions and popular organizations—women's presence is low. The responsibilities and posts women do control tend to be secondary and there is little general awareness of the issue of women's subordination. However, women's groups and associations do exist, from the official body, AMNLAE, to Women's Sections in the various Sandinista unions, and independent feminist collectives. While the quality of representation and true extent of these collectives is open to question, they are proof of the existence of social sectors engaged in the struggle against gender discrimination.

AN EVALUATION OF WOMEN'S POLITICAL AND SOCIAL PARTICIPATION

It is evident that change favorable to women was promoted and developed in the eleven years of Sandinista government. This is especially apparent when compared to other periods in the history of the country, and to the contemporary situation in other Central American nations. Progress was made in terms of organization, legislation, employment, and education, and discrimination was confronted. However, the difficulties faced—sexist attitudes, traditional beliefs, the gender division of labor, domestic violence, paternal irresponsibility, problems regarding birth control, a shortage or time and energy, and a lack of skills and sometimes enthusiasm—were also very important.

Progress was often born of necessity, or the result of the socioeconomic context, rather than the fruit of deliberate political action. When women were the greatest beneficiaries of general social policies, it was because they were starting from a comparatively disadvantaged and precarious position, and not because effective policies were formulated and applied.[18] The Sandinistas inherited a country where men outpaced women in many social indicators. Women registered higher levels of illiteracy and less attention was paid to their specific health needs. Running concurrent to this was the fact that women traditionally bore the responsibility, within the family unit, for liaising with educational and health institutions—particularly with regard to the health and education of their children—and for housing construction, community organization, and municipal issues in general. In this context advances made in the fields of education, health, and housing had particularly positive repercussions for women.

Despite gains, women's social participation in the state structure and the popular organizations did not correspond to the expectations generated by the revolution, and did not reach the levels publicized by the Sandinista government. Massive female participation in the decade of the 1980s is a myth. In reality a chasm existed between women's daily experience and the progressive theoretical posturing of the party. This was reflected in a comment made by a teacher interviewed in a 1990 workshop: "I believe that there is a contradiction between what the Front wants us to be and what we want to be. It wants to perpetuate our dependence on men's political will; always to be governed by him, to do only what he says. Be that good or bad, for us its the same thing."

Evidence confirms that women's participation in formal politics was limited, and integration partial. Gender subordination persisted in every space and at every level. Women were confined by a complex conjuncture of material and cultural difficulties, ranging from the social system itself, to the perceptions and adaptability of women themselves. This was compounded by the socioeconomic constraints of eleven years of acute crisis in a militarized society with great infrastructural and technological deficiencies and a lack of adequate services. Of all the obstacles and difficulties blocking women's participation in formal politics, the structural bases of subordination—maternal and domestic obligations—stand out. Interviews with women from the popular sector underlined a lack of infrastructure and services which would allow them to participate, especially "lack of time," the "overburden of work," and the "scarcity of means and resources." Many of the women interviewed were holding down one or two jobs outside the home in order to generate extra income, as well as conscientiously involving themselves in community activities.

A further limitation to women's participation was provoked by the reproduction of the old traditional cultural model onto the new revolutionary ideological framework. The values and practices relating to the fundamental role of women within the home, and their passive participation in politics, seemed to evolve much more slowly than other aspects of society. And women themselves, as mothers, contributed to reproduction, which was the root of the discrimination they faced as women. The problem can be defined as the "weight of tradition" or the "power of custom." This recreation of old models affected organizational and political spaces. Agendas, needs, timetables, and work styles were not revised, and as a result they were not equal to the task of appealing to, or accommodating, the female population.

For their part, women had been conditioned through the process of socialization to conform to a determined role model. To free themselves from that model would require not only a certain level of awareness, but also the courage to break away from the norms and values reiterated and reinforced through cultural messages. Women had to confront their own identities and personal psychologies when they failed to fulfill the roles expected of them. The various women interviewed who revealed their feelings of "anguish" and "guilt" are evidence of this. All of these factors should be viewed within the context of a seemingly intractable economic crisis and a prolonged low-intensity conflict, intensified by the characteristic limitations of a small, peripheral country—including a lack of resources, infrastructure, services, training, and economic autonomy.

Women's limited participation in formal politics did not imply that they were nonparticipants in society. They did not penetrate a space created by and for men, to suit men's requirements: a space where those who did get involved had to overcome obstacles to survival, quite apart from the extreme effort that simply involving oneself represented. Politics, understood as a form of government or as formal institutions, are conceived of as male. As a consequence, they internalize and reproduce the structural forms and social functioning of men.[19]

Traditionally, the relationship between women and formal politics has been complex and problematic. From one perspective, politics have not been concerned with specifically female issues—in terms of their problems, needs, and interests; nor have they accommodated new ways of existing and working—in terms of timetables and working styles. But on the other hand, women themselves have maintained a distance, considering politics remote, dirty, other. One study of women's low participation in popular organizations in Nicaragua in the late 1980s reveals working styles and practices within organizations as key causes of the problem. Apart from a lack of time and interest, prohibition by a husband, or the belief that it is not women's place to go around organizing themselves, the most important obstacles were found to be organizational: the lack of internal democracy.[20]

Exactly what it means to be politically active as and for women should also be taken into account. This involves rethinking the organization of daily life to progressively eliminate the distinction between "the political (public) and the private (domestic), that stereotypically defines and sanctifies exclusive and rigid spheres of activity for men and women."[21] It is for this reason that there is a debate today in Nicaragua about new ways of being political, and strategies of analysis are being sought that allow women's multiple presences in the organizational processes of social life to be made visible.[22]

Certain conceptualizations of politics maintain that "democracy" goes beyond the state, involving organization within society as a whole. If politics is viewed as everything related to the authoritarian distribution of societal values, then power does not only lie in the public sphere of institutions, but is also present within the family, and in the pattern of neighborhood, friendship and extended family networks.[23] Understood as the capacity for, and the access to, decision-making, power arises at the level of social relations in public and private spheres. Thus politics represent the collective quest for the satisfaction of values and needs in line with our identities; politics involve the activities, relationships, and spaces of women as much as men.[24]

Women participate in the space of daily life: the structure of the family, the community, and the network of informal relationships within and between the two.[25] In this way, Nicaraguan women can be seen to have participated in politics. Women from the popular sector participated in the economy and in production, forming 1 percent of the economically active population in 1985.[26] Women were involved in wage labor and self-employment, particularly in the informal sector, making up 73 percent of that sector in 1992.[27] In 1992, 65 percent of families in urban areas and 82 percent in rural areas were headed by women.[28]

Women often participated in more than one area of work, holding down jobs in both the formal and informal sectors, with the aim of maximizing scarce income and resources in order to finance the survival of the family. Women were responsible for the administration of household funds, to which they were the major provider. They also invested the most time, commitment and effort in the maintenance of the family. Women participated, albeit at a relatively low level, in political groups and organizations, particularly those of a religious nature. They were also integrated in the formation, organization, and mainte-nance of the community, involving themselves as much in issues of community relations and social cohesion as in improving services and infrastructure.

Women took on this social work as a "natural" extension of their household duties and their responsibility for the family's residential needs, carrying out these functions as "mamas of the community."

In a society with an average of 5.5 children per family—7 in the rural areas, 4 in urban areas—and a low level of infrastructural and service provision in housing and domestic technology, it is clear that women participated in household and childcare work through fulfilling their roles as mother and housekeeper. Women were best integrated, and participated most, in the spaces they cared most about: the family and the community. However, these areas are extremely resistant to strategies to combat gender subordination. Such programs would be difficult to introduce, and the results would be shallow and ephemeral. The family and community spheres are territories hostile to new ideologies that reject their traditional vision of life and the world. Added to this is the fact that when material conditions are adverse, survival becomes an immediate, daily, practical gamble, and as a result it is always the highest priority. In spite of their extended participation in the aforementioned spaces, women did not have access to power in the public sphere, and they were often limited to the roles and issues assigned to them in the private sphere. It is clear that women do not participate in decision-making in the same way as men. Women move on other levels, establishing another type of relations, carrying out different activities; their skills and objectives in life are distinct.

In the 1980s, the Sandinista government promoted only nominal and formal equality between men and women. Through the transformation of the economic structures of production, the political system, and social organization, gender relations that linked women's reproductive functions to domestic subordination, and the symbolism that legitimated that connection, remained effectively intact. Changes in gender relations in the public sphere were peripheral and insignificant, limited in depth and extent, and often reversible. There was only a minimal transition in the social role of the Nicaraguan woman in a decade characterized by change. Perhaps only a small élite of intermediate leaders and women involved in the most politicized networks have effected changes in their lives. Although awareness of female subordination has been raised, in a time of acute economic crisis, anything not related to immediate, daily survival for the poor masses of the population, amongst whom women form the majority, is seen as "a kingdom not of this world."

NOTES

Translated by Grail Dorling, University of Wolverhampton, UK.

1. See Idelfonso Palma, *Rafaela Herrera o la niña de Nicaragua* (Managua: Academia de Geografía e Historia, La Nueva Prensa, 1948); Julián Guerrero and Lola Soriano, *Monografía León* (Managua: Editora Central, 1968).

2. Bartolomé de las Casas, *Brevísima relación de la destrucción de las Indias. De la provincia de Nicaragua* (Managua: Banco de América, 1976); Francisco López de Gomara, *Historia General de las Indias* (Barcelona: Orbis, 1985).

3. "There were very many acts of heroism carried out by women who collaborated with our forces, and the majority require their full stories to be told in order to comprehend the sacrifices that were made and the dangers that were confronted for the love of the *patria*. All of these women—peasants, teachers, nurses, housewives, even society *señoritas*—provided services without which our war would not have been possible." August César Sandino, *General Augusto C. Sandino. Padre de la revolución popular y antiimperialista 1895-1934* (Managua: ENN-IES, 1985).

4. See Anna Fernández Poncela, *De la construcción de la realidad a la transformación de la sociedad. Los diferentes ritmos entre la dinámica social y la recreación cultural en la participación de las mujeres de los sectores populares nicaragüenses* (Barcelona: Servicio de Publicaciones de la Universidad de Barcelona, 1992).

5. AMPRONAC, *La asociación de la mujer ante la problemática nacional* (Managua: AMPRONAC, 1978).

6. Carlos M. Vilas, *Perfiles de la revolución sandinista* (La Habana: Ciencias Sociales, 1984).

7. Reinaldo Téfel, *El infierno de los pobres. Diagnóstico sociológico de los barrios marginales de Managua* (Managua: El pez y la serpiente, 1978).

8. "The popular Sandinista revolution will abolish the loathsome discrimination that women have suffered with respect to men; it will establish economic, political and cultural equality between men and women." Frente Sandinista de Liberación Nacional (FSLN), *Programa Histórico* (Nicaragua: FSLN, 1969).

9. "The popular Sandinista revolution opened unquantified spaces to Nicaraguan women to redress specific wrongs as well as to advance in the struggle for complete equality. This was as much the result of the radically democratic nature of the revolution as it was the consequence of women's quantitative and qualitative participation in the revolutionary Sandinista struggle. However, apart from in moral and political terms, we were not able, for a variety of reasons including ideological problems, to articulate, as a party, an effective program of action consistent with the proposals which we had put forward in the declaration. A more systematic and coherent organizational structure relevant to the particular reality of women's problems and achievements would have allowed greater progress." Frente Sandinista de Liberación Nacional, *Informe Central de la Dirección Nacional* (Managua: FSLN, 1991).

10. This can be found in the following party and governmental documents: the Program of 1978; the First Proclamation of the Government of National Recon-

struction, 1979; the Statute of Rights and Guarantees for Nicaraguans, 1979; the 1981 ratification of the United Nations' Convention for the Elimination of all Forms of Discrimination against Women; the semi-official text, *Women and the Revolution,* by Tomás Borge, 1982; the Proclamation of the Twenty-fifth Anniversary of the FSLN, 1986; the Constitutional Policy, approved in 1987; and the Electoral Manifesto for the 1990 campaign. See also FSLN, *Plataforma electoral del FSLN* (Managua: DAP, 1984); FSLN, *El FSLN y la mujer en la revolución popular sandinista* (Managua: Vanguardia, 1987); FSLN, *Plataforma de lucha 1990-1995* (Managua: FSLN, 1989).

11. Maxine Molyneux, "Mobilization Without Emancipation? Women's Interests, State, and Revolution," in Richard R. Fagen et al., eds., *Transition and Development: Problems of Third World Socialism* (New York: Monthly Review Press, 1986).

12. The following legislation was initiated: the Parental Jurisdiction Law, which shared responsibility between women and men; the Adoption Law, which also shared responsibility between the sexes; the Mass Media Law, which prohibited the use of the female image as sex symbol; the Nationality Law, which protected women's independent civil status; the Breast Milk Production Law, which prohibited the commercial advertising of formula milk products; the Social Security Law, which recognized the widowhood of women in common law relationships, security in old age, extension of the antenatal and postnatal periods, and benefits for children born out of wedlock; the Cooperatives Law, which promoted women's participation in production and administration and recognized their right to hold property title; the Agrarian Reform Law, which promoted women's integration in agricultural and fishery enterprises; the Coffee Harvest Labor Standards, which gave equal rights; the regulatory Law of Mother, Father, and Child Relations, which gave joint authority over children to parents; the Nutritional Law, which shared responsibility between parents; labor legislation; and the Divorce Law, which recognized unilateral divorce by mutual agreement.

13. Oficina Legal de la Mujer (Women's Legal Bureau), *Qué servicios presta la OLM* (Managua: Oficina Gubernamental de la Mujer, 1986).

14. Consejo Supremo Electoral (Supreme Electoral Council), *Datos electorales* (Managua: CSE, 1990).

15. Another striking case is that of the Government Junta, which had an exclusively female legal advisory body between 1983 and 1985. See Oficina Gubernamental de la Mujer (Women's Governmental Bureau), *Evaluación del decenio de las Naciones Unidas para la mujer: Igualdad, desarrollo y paz, 1976-1985* (Managua: OGM, 1984).

16. CST: Central Sandinista de Trabajadores; FETSALUD: Federación de Trabajadores de la Salud; ANDEN: Asociación Nacional de Enseñantes Nicaragüenses; CONAPRO: Confederación Nacional de Profesionales; ATC: Asociación de Trabajadores del Campo; UNAG: Unión Nacional de Agricultores y Ganaderos; Movimiento Comunal, previously CDS: Comités de Defensa Sandinista; AMNLAE: Asociación de Mujeres Nicaragüenses Luisa Amanda Espinosa; JS-19J: Juventud Sandinista 19 de Julio.

17. Anna Fernández Poncela and Mercedes Olivera, "Subordinación de género en las organizaciones populares nicaragüenses," in Carlos M. Vilas, ed., *Democracia emergente en Centroamérica* (Mexico: CIIH-UNAM, 1993).

18. See Anna Fernández Poncela, *Mujeres, familias, comunidades. La vida cotidiana de la mujer en Nicaragua* (Barcelona: Historia y Fuente Oral, no. 8, 1992); and "The Disruptions of Adjustment: Women in Nicaragua," *Latin American Perspectives* no. 88 (Winter 1996).

19. Ana Sojo, *Mujer y política: Ensayo sobre el feminismo y el sujeto popular* (San José: DEI, 1985).

20. Fernández Poncela and Olivera, "Subordinación de género," in Vilas, ed., *Democracia*.

21. Julieta Kirkwood, "Mujer e identidad política," *Boletín Círculo de Estudios de la Mujer* 2 (1983).

22. Virginia Vargas, *Movimiento feminista en el Perú: Balance y perspectivas* (Montevideo: GRECMU, 1985).

23. See Carole Pateman, *Participation and Democratic Theory* (London: Cambridge University Press, 1970); and *The Sexual Contract* (Stanford: Stanford University Press, 1988). See also David Easton, *The Political System* (New York: Alfred A. Knopf, 1973).

24. Michel Foucault, *La microfísica del poder* (Madrid: La Piqueta, 1980); Teresina De Barbieri, *Sobre la categoría de género. Una introducción teórico-metodológica* (São Paulo: Taller de Derechos Reproductivos, 1990).

25. Agnes Heller, *La revolución de la vida cotidiana* (Barcelona: Peninsular, 1982); Norberto Bobbio, *El futuro de la democracia* (Mexico: FCE, 1986); Norbert Lechner, *Los patios interiores de la democracia. Subjetividad y política* (Chile: FCE, 1990); Eric R. Wolf, "Relaciones de parentesco, de amistad y de patronazgo en las sociedades complejas," in *Antropología social de las sociedades complejas* (Madrid: Alianza Universidad, 1990).

26. Instituto Nicaragüense de Estadísticas y Censos (INEC), *Encuesta Socio Demográfica de Nicaragua* (Managua: INEC, 1985).

27. Fundación Internacional para el Desarrollo Global (FIDEG), *El impacto diferenciado de género de las políticas de ajuste sobre las condiciones de vida en el área rural y concentraciones urbanas intermedias* (Managua: FIDEG, 1992).

28. INEC, *Informes* (Managua: INEC, 1992).

PUBLIC AND PRIVATE SPHERES: THE END OF DICHOTOMY

TESSA CUBITT AND HELEN GREENSLADE

The growth of new social movements in Latin America has attracted consider-able attention in recent years for a number of important reasons.[1] One of the most interesting characteristics of social movements in Latin America is the increasing participation of women. The analysis of women's presence in social movements has frequently been framed within terms of a public/private dichot-omy, with the suggestion that participation in social movements breaks the barrier between the two realms, releasing women "from lives that are 'naturally determined' to enter 'the socially determined world,' where they can be the subjects, not merely the objects of political action."[2] Recent theoretical and empirical work has revealed the increasingly blurred nature of the boundary between the two arenas, and dichotomous conceptualizations have come under increasing criticism, modifying the initial terminology in a variety of ways.

This chapter will assess this framework of analysis and its value in explaining and understanding the role of women in Mexico's urban social movements. The key issue addressed is the empowerment of women: Does the discourse of private/public realms help us to understand the process of empowerment? Does the breaking down of the traditional private/public divide empower women or merely lead to continued subordination, but of a different kind? In the first section we take issue with the conceptual terrain founded on an analytical separation of the public world of employment and politics from the private world of the family and interpersonal relations. In the context of a broad overview of literature which deals with women's entry into the "public" worlds of work and civil society we argue that the public/private divide is an abstraction which is mapped onto concrete settings and experiences and that this dichotomous framework produces an essentialized account of women's participation. The second section assesses this framework in relation to empowerment and subordination, and offers a guide to trends in analysis which point to a fuller understanding of women's social and political activities. We argue that the major strategic principle in the development of political empowerment is collective action. We propose that where blurring of the boundary between public and private spheres leads to collective action women's isolation in the domestic realm is reduced. In explaining the growth of collective action we suggest that an approach which sees the private sphere as public is more appropriate. It overcomes the essentializing tendencies that are implicit in a sharp public/private divide. In the last section we consider this approach in the specific context of the women's section of Mexico's CONAMUP (Coordinadora Nacional del Movimiento Urbano Popular), the umbrella organization established in 1979 to coordinate the various urban movements that emerged during the 1970s.

PUBLIC/PRIVATE SPHERES: BLURRING THE BOUNDARY

The distinction between public and private arenas of social life has been one of the core tenets of modern political thought and has been key to normative statements regarding the organization of social life.[3] While it is recognized that the public/private dichotomy is often used as an analytical distinction rather than a description of social reality, spatial metaphors embody a particular ideology. The mapping of gender around masculine and feminine polarities onto social relations has created a set of distinctions which associates politics and masculinity with the public world and women with the private, nonpolitical, domestic realm. This division enjoyed enormous currency in the political and social sciences, and has been a focus of feminist theorization of women's oppression and emancipation.[4] Reliance on this dichotomized framework has resulted in an essentialized version of women's subjectivity and reinforces the simplisitic equation "public man/private woman." This view has been subjected to a thorough critique. Carole Pateman holds that "a proper understanding of liberal social life is possible only when it is accepted that the two spheres, the domestic (private) and civil society (public), held to be separate and opposite, are inextricably interrelated; they are the two sides of the single coin of liberal-patriarchalism."[5]

Sylvia Walby also develops a critique of the usual public/private dichotomy, defining public and private in a particular manner: in terms of patriarchal strategies and spheres of action. She defines patriarchy as "a system of social structures and practices in which men dominate, oppress and exploit women."[6] In Walby's account, patriarchal structures operate differentially in the public and private spheres. The "private" is identified with an "exclusionary" strategy which entails women's subordination to a personal patriarch (husband or father). In the public realm a "segregationist" strategy operates to subordinate women to a "collective" patriarchy located in the spheres of the state and the labor market. The clarity of her approach is appealing but it serves to highlight analytical pitfalls. In Walby's scheme, public patriarchy offers the promise of a reduced subordination of women. However, even if women overcome the exclusionary mechanisms of private patriarchy, the move into the public world subjects them to a collective patriarchy.

Maxine Molyneux and, later, Caroline Moser developed the concepts of practical and strategic gender interests and needs to present a more dynamic approach to women's activities.[7] For them, the concept of "strategic" gender interests involves a positive challenge to women's subordination, whether in the private or public sphere. Demands for improved sanitation, housing, water are designated as "practical" and do not challenge gender inequality. On the other hand, "strategic" issues concern public challenges to the institutionalization of male domination. Yet they can involve such "private" issues as domestic violence and reproductive rights. This categorization reveals the ambiguity of what is considered "public" and "private." The conceptual analysis of the public-private spheres reveals that any dichotomy is culturally and historically constructed. In other words, what is considered public and private is subject to change. Nancy Fraser explains, "These terms are not simply straightforward designations of preexisting societal spheres; rather, they are cultural classifications and rhetorical labels. In political discourse, they are frequently deployed to delegitimate some interests, views and topics and to valorize others."[8]

In the Latin American context much of the discussion concerning women's participation in the "public" realm has placed great emphasis on the interface between domestic and public space.[9] Fiona Wilson underlines this point:

Cultural definitions of social space in Latin America are deeply gendered; but these never give rise to simple or exclusive spatial categories. At one level, social space is demarcated so as to underpin gender segregation. Domestic space is primarily associated with women's worlds and is the place of women's language, identity and visions. In contrast public space is considered men's domain.[10]

It is important to note that Wilson rejects the exclusivity of these spatial categories and points to the need for a more nuanced understanding of the relationship between domestic and public spaces. The state and labor market have been traditionally defined as constitutive of the "public" realm. Feminist politics have traditionally linked women's "entry" into these spheres of activity with strategies for improving women's social position. However, there are conflicting interpretations of women's involvement in "formal" sector employment, the effects this has on domestic power relations, and on women's self-perception.[11]

In the Mexican case, global economic restructuring, the economic crisis of the 1980s and the ensuing structural adjustment programs have given rise to two major trends affecting female employment. On one hand, there has been an increase in free trade zone employment and growth of the *maquila* industries; on the other hand, there has been an increase in homework, a move from factory-based production to home-based industrial activity.[12] To escape the costs for capital of working in the formal sector, workshop production increasingly takes place within the household, where family labor can easily be recruited. This growth of home-based labor has had mixed results for women. On the one hand earning an income provides women with a social identity and more say over the family budget, while on the other hand, isolation within the domestic arena discourages collective action.[13]

Research on export-processing workers in the *maquila* industries in Northern Mexico also suggests mixed results in terms of women's empowerment. Susan Tiano and R. Fialla indicate that participation in export processing has brought about a positive change in women's consciousness. Women's participation in the labor force has given them a world view that reflects personal autonomy and attitudes which favor gender equality.[14] However, Patricia Fernández-Kelly's 1983 study concludes that, while contributing to the family budget, women's work in the formal sector fails to increase either their independence or domestic power. Rather, the lack of financial security, job stability, and upward mobility perpetuates economic exploitation and structural subordination.[15] In broad terms, then, increasing impoverishment is forcing women into the labor market at a time when regular forms of work are scarce. Also, deregularization of labor practices resulting from neoliberal policies encourage the spread of insecure forms of work. In general women remain in the most poorly paid occupations and usually in a position subordinate to what Walby calls "collective patriarchy." Recent research conclusions suggest a need to reevaluate the definitions of public and private space, and the connections between empowerment and incorporation into the "public" realm.

In Latin America, discussion of women's political participation often has been split between "formal" politics, and associations and movements that comprise civil society.[16] In recent years there has been a profusion of material on the increasing participation of women in social movements. Much of the research suggests that concerns associated with "private" space (rising food prices, lack of access to piped water, poor sanitation, anxiety over missing children, etc.) prompt women to participate in the public arena.[17] Logan asserts that women's participation in the public arena "arises not from consciousness of a new role, but rather from a desire to perform their traditional roles well. [Thus]... what is familial and communal becomes political." In other words the "personal becomes political."[18]

It is all very well to claim that the personal is political but the stress on "motherhood" as the primary causal factor in women's collective action is problematic.[19] The suggestion is that women are redefining politics, that so-called private issues are colonizing the "public" realm of politics. As a spatial metaphor, women are depicted as "moving" into a "space" which was previously occupied predominantly by men. In the case of military regimes, the imagery of this is potent. The military regimes removed the usual (masculine) agents (trade unions/parties) leaving a vacuum into which women moved. This spatial abstraction underlines the transformative impact that women's activities have had on politics, and on our understanding of political processes. However, these views support the "public man/private woman" discourse and reinforce essentialist views of women's social and political identity.[20] Women's mobilization and the demands they express are generally explained as reflections of moral and familial commitments, in other words, "private" roles. This approach creates a stark vision of Latin American women's activities as it detracts from other important aspects of political identity.[21] The key point is that the binary definition of public and private spheres, the gendered associations of these definitions, and the differentiation of activities proper to those spheres often are uncritically replicated by many scholars attempting to theorize women's participation in social movements.

EMPOWERMENT AND SUBORDINATION?

The considerable body of research that shows a more complex picture of modern social settings than the dichotomized separate spheres model has important implications for understanding women's political action and con-sciousness. The material which indicates growing empowerment suggests women's awareness of gender subordination is gained through participation in social movements.[22] Women's actions are not undertaken simply to defend the domestic sphere against the increasing intervention of the state and the market. As citizens, women are demanding incorporation into the state, confronting the state directly rather than going through traditional, male-dominated intermedi-aries, such as unions and political parties. Women's political consciousness grows with the awareness of their public persona. Elizabeth Jelin argues that personal self-awareness can expand within the context of participation in social movements, from the personal to the social.[23]

But changes in traditional gender roles do not necessarily or automatically result from participation in social movements. For one thing, while women form the backbone and numerical majority of many of these movements, the leadership is usually male. In cases of movements centered on collective consumption and resource mobilization, often women took an active part in the formation and development of a movement, but once it started to gain some achievements, men began to take over the key roles.[24] The transformative potential of female participation in social movements can only be realized, then, if women create a "space" for themselves in which they are able to express their specific concerns in dialogue with others and define solutions to their prob-lems.[25] Finally, it is important to point out that much of the research on social movements exaggerates the differences between men and women, invoking women's relationship to the private sphere, but not men's.[26]

As the above argument makes clear, any analysis based on a dichotomy of public-private spheres is specious. The approach adopted by Nikki Craske, who conceptualizes the public and private as a continuum, is more useful. This allows for thinking in terms of different degrees of participation between the two spheres and accommodates the many activities that sit between them. For instance, as a site of political action, the neighborhood, once identified with the domestic sphere, can be seen as a public arena of political struggle.[27] However, we suggest that a dialectic approach to the analysis of women's political action and consciousness is more suitable than approaches framed in terms of the public-private dichotomy.[28]

Anthony Giddens's theory of structuration seems to be a useful point of departure in this respect. Giddens rejects the mutual oppositions of structure and agency, arguing that people's actions can alter relations of production.[29] At the same time, however, he recognizes the importance of class structures, asserting that attention must be given to the ways in which "structures enable behavior, but behavior can potentially influence and reconstitute structure."[30] The advantage of this approach is that it allows for a theorization of the mutual constitution of structure and agency. It provides the possibility of a move beyond the increasingly false dichotomy of public and private spheres.

BEYOND DICHOTOMY: CREATING SPACES OF EMPOWERMENT IN MEXICO'S URBAN MOVEMENTS

Giddens's approach can be useful in analyzing the development of the women's section of CONAMUP, Mexico's first national network of urban popular movements. CONAMUP provides an example of how structural change leading to collective action has a transformative potential. The organization provided a space where different urban popular movements could criticize official politics and challenge the traditional monopoly on the political system of the Institutional Revolutionary Party (PRI).[31] For more than seventy years, the PRI-dominated political structure of Mexico has controlled almost all forms of protest and potential opposition through clientelism, offering short-term favors for political support.

Since 1970, rural migration and the spread of squatter settlements in Mexico City have given rise to a number of urban popular organizations. These movements challenged the state by occupying empty land on the outskirts of the city and making demands for property rights and public utilities. In 1979 urban movements from thirteen different states came together to form a network of neighborhood organizations that became known as the CONAMUP. Worsening economic conditions brought about by the 1982 crisis and the 1985 earthquake in Mexico City brought a new urgency to urban problems and acted as a spur to the growth of grassroots neighborhood and regional organizations. Most of the participants in these movements were women, who suffered the immediate consequences of the economic crisis. They campaigned for property rights and basic household services: sanitation, water, schools, health centers. Out of these struggles the women's regional councils of CONAMUP were born.

Irene Flores, director of the women's regional council of CONAMUP in Mexico City, identified two issues as crucial in the development of a gendered group within CONAMUP—democracy and domestic violence. The first issue related to the gendered hierarchy which operated throughout the movement. The vast majority of members of neighborhood movements were women; however, leadership was predominantly male. The creation of a separate women's movement was seen as the means of women achieving a more active role. Second, as women became more involved in popular movements, tensions within the home became increasingly apparent. Women's participation in the movement frequently brought confrontations in the private sphere. Eugenia Flores Hernández states "Women were beaten just for going to meetings. There was a real need to deal with these types of issues. That's why we decided to have that first national meeting just for women."[32] Confronting domestic violence became an issue in itself and women wished to address this collectively. In this way women began to shape their own political agenda.

Another crucial step in the growing consciousness of the women's section of CONAMUP was the collectivization of domestic work, suggesting that the most profound change in women's thinking comes when they begin to collectivize domestic work. This occurred when collective kitchens were set up in different districts of Mexico City to distribute government subsidized breakfasts to children. Women began to realize the value of cooking in the home through the general acclaim the same task received in the public arena. The women of CONAMUP saw this as a step toward recognizing and financially compensating domestic work.

The way that different structures influence people's behavior can be seen in Craske's study of two neighborhood organizations in Guadalajara.[33] The first was a PRI organization, the other an independent organization linked to CONAMUP. Craske found that women in the latter were more politically aware, exhibited greater self-confidence, had a greater sense of empowerment and generally felt patriarchal constraints less than their counterparts in the PRI organization. The PRI emerged as a far less enabling structure within which to operate than the independent neighborhood organizations of Guadalajara. CONAMUP provided women with a structure within which to press for specific issues in the framework of the broad objectives of its movement. The creation of the CONAMUP's women's section provided a space for the recognition of women's issues in which they could give voice to their grievances.

Through the manipulations of the PRI, societal structures have for the best part of this century prevented political mobilization of opposition forces. However, the economic conditions of the "lost decade" of the 1980s in Latin America and the declining popularity of the PRI provided fertile conditions for the opposition. The women's sections of CONAMUP defined their own political agendas. For example, "Las mujeres del valle de México," one of the women's sections, listed their main aims as: to fight from within the framework of the class struggle in Mexico; to fight for services within their communities (including such demands as piped water, better housing, healthcare, etc.); to examine the role of women in the family and the community and to address the oppression that women within these communities face; to examine the role of women within the social/popular urban movements; to analyze the specific problems women face within the movements themselves as well as the limitations placed upon them with specific reference to their participation in politics; and to gather the experiences of women organizers specifically inside CONAMUP.

Clearly there is no perception of a dichotomy between public and private interests here, nor is there the sense that activities should be delimited to one sphere or another. In the lived reality of poor women, public and private spheres merge into one continuous relationship which reflect their lives in the intimate, political, material and cultural spheres. Social problems are not conceived of in dichotomous terms, nor in a differentiation between strategic and practical issues. These abstractions cannot account for a reality which is complex and diversified.

Where the PRI's co-optive strategies have often marginalized women, viewing them as non-participants in the political field, women's participation in social movements is bringing large numbers of women into explicitly political action. In Lynn Stephen's view, "It is out of these spaces that popular feminism is emerging in Mexico and other parts of Latin America."[34] The women's sections of CONAMUP have had some impact on the Mexican state. Strengthened by a coalition with unions, political parties, and feminist organizations, the women's sections have pressed for legislation on women's issues. In response, the government set up its own department of women's issues.[35] However, pressures from deteriorating economic conditions, exacerbated by adjustment policies have prevented greater achievements. Nevertheless the women's sections achieved enormous symbolic power in the perception of its members.[36]

CONCLUSIONS

This chapter suggests that a conceptual public-private divide is inappropriate in the analysis of gender in Latin America. First, economic restructuring has brought about a conceptual blurring of boundaries between domestic space and the labor market. Second, women's participation in social movements made them agents of collective action in the political arena. Walby argues that greater participation in the public sphere brings reduced levels of subordination, as well as a change in the nature of subordination from personal to collective patriarchy. However, in Latin America, there is evidence of both continued subordination and increased empowerment. There is no smooth path from "private" to "public," nor a clear progression of empowerment from practical to strategic actions. Instead, through the dialectic of agency/structure women have shown themselves to be active subjects in the political landscape rather than passive recipients of state policy. The notion that social life can be divided into public and private realms cripples our capacity to analyze women's participation in civil society. These divisions are ideological constructs which reinforce the normative gendered patterning of people's lives.

NOTES

1. Popular mobilization throughout Latin America in the 1970s and 1980s raised questions about the nature of politics beyond narrowly defined institutional settings. The emergence of movements based on resource mobilization, collective consumption, and human rights has given rise to the creation of collective identities based on categories other than class. See Introduction in Arturo Escobar and Sonia E. Alvarez, eds., *The Making of Social Movements in Latin America* (Boulder: Westview Press, 1992); Joe Foweraker and Ann Craig, eds., *Popular Movements and Political Change in Mexico* (Boulder: Lynne Reinner Publications, 1990).

2. Jane Jaquette, ed., *The Women's Movement in Latin America: Feminism and the Transition to Democracy* (London: Unwin Hyman, 1989), p. 188. The chapter by Perrelli is especially useful.

3. In liberal thought, the public/private dichotomy is key to the principle of maintaining a private sphere free from the intervention of the state. See John Keane, *Democracy and Civil Society* (London: Verso, 1988); Benn and Gaus, eds., *Public and Private in Social Life* (London: Croom Helm, 1983). Marxist thought seeks to overcome this division based on the critique that it masks domination. See Eugene Kamenka, "Public/Private in Marxist Theory and Marxist Practice" in Benn and Gauss, *Public and Private in Social Life*, pp. 267-79. Hannah Arendt argues that the blurring of the boundaries in modern social life is detrimental to politics and to human emancipation. She asserts the need to restore the rigid separation of public and private spheres in order to maintain the complementarity of separate spheres. See Arendt, *The Human Condition* (Chicago: University of Chicago Press, 1958).

4. See, for example, Jean Betke Elshtain, *Public Man, Private Woman: Women in Social and Political Thought* (Princeton: Princeton University Press, 1981); Susan Moller Okin, "Gender, the Public and the Private" in David Held, ed., *Political Theory Today* (Stanford: Stanford University Press, 1991).

5. Carole Pateman, *The Disorder of Women: Democracy, Feminism and Political Theory* (Cambridge: Polity Press, 1989) pp. 121-22. See also Pateman, "Feminist Critiques of the Public/Private Dichotomy" in Benn and Gaus, *Public and Private in Social Life* (1983).

6. Sylvia Walby, *Theorising Patriarchy* (Oxford: Basil Blackwell, 1990), p. 20.

7. Maxine Molyneux, "Mobilisation Without Emancipation: Women's Interests, the State and Revolution in Nicaragua," *Feminist Studies* 11, no. 2 (1985): 227-254; Caroline Moser, "Gender Planning in the Third World," *World Development* 17, no. 11 (1989): 1799-1825.

8. Nancy Fraser, "Politics, Culture, and The Public Sphere: Toward a Postmodern Conception," in Linda Nicholson and Steven Seidman, eds., *Social Postmod-*

ernism: Beyond Identity Politics (Cambridge: Cambridge University Press, 1995), p. 294.

9. Sarah A. Radcliffe and Sallie Westwood, eds., *Viva: Women and Popular Protest in Latin America* (London: Routledge, 1993).

10. Fiona Wilson, "Workshops as Domestic Domains. Reflections on Small Scale Industry in Mexico," *World Development* 21, no. 1 (1993): 69.

11. Sylvia Chant, "Family Structure and Female Labour in Queretaro, Mexico," in Janet Momsen and J. Townsend, eds., *Geography of Gender in the Third World* (London: Hutchinson, 1987); Helen Safa, *The Myth of the Male Breadwinner: Women and Industrialization in the Caribbean* (Colorado: Westview Press, 1995). See also McClenaghan (this volume).

12. Wilson states, "the definition and protection of domestic space can be seen to dovetail remarkably well with the way industrial activity strives for physical concealment and uses a household identity so as to avoid legislation." "Workshops," p. 69.

13. See Lourdes Benería and Martha Roldán, *The Crossroads of Class and Gender: Industrial Housework, Subcontracting, and Household Dynamics in Mexico City* (Chicago: University of Chicago Press, 1987).

14. R. Fiala and Susan Tiano, "The World Views of Export Processing Workers in Northern Mexico: A study of women, consciousness, and the new international division of labour," *Studies in Comparative International Development* 26, no. 3 (1991): 3-27; Tiano, "Women's Work in the Public and Private Spheres: A Critique and Reformation," in M.P. and P.S. Abraham, eds., *Women, Development and Change: The Third World Experience* (Bristol: Wyndham Hall Press, 1988), pp. 749-87.

15. María Patricia Fernández-Kelly, *For We Are Sold, I and My People: Women and Industry in Mexico's Frontier* (Albany: State University of New York Press, 1983).

16. By "civil society" we refer to the space of social interaction which is (relatively) autonomous from the state, and the organizations and association which comprise it. See A. Arato and J. Cohen, *Civil Society and Political Theory* (Cambridge MA: MIT Press, 1992). For a discussion of women's incorporation into "formal" politics in the Nicaraguan case, see Poncela (this volume), and for an examination of the more recent phenomenon of state feminism, see Matear (this volume).

17. See, for example, Jaquette, *The Women's Movement in Latin America;* Radcliffe and Westwood, *Viva;* Elizabeth Jelin, *Women and Social Change in Latin America* (London and Geneva: UNRISD, 1990); Katherine Logan, *Haciendo Pueblo: The Development of a Guadalajara Suburb* (Alabama: Alabama University Press, 1984); Jo Fisher, *Out of the Shadows: Women's Resistance In Politics in Latin America* (London: Latin American Bureau, 1993).

18. Katherine Logan, "Women's Participation in Urban Protest," in Foweraker and Craig, eds., *Popular Movements and Political Change in Mexico,* p. 152.

19. Maier's study of EUREKA, the mothers' group seeking the disappeared in Mexico supports this view. See Maier, "La madre como sujeto político," *Estudios Latinoamericanos* (México: Centro de Estudios Latinoamericanos, UNAM, 1990), p. 70.

20. This view then serves to reinforce the traditional definitions of men and of women which bolster patriarchal structures. As Beneria and Roldan state, "current inequalities of gender power are embedded in the very structures which define men and women." Benería and Roldán, *Crossroads of Class and Gender,* p.12.

21. Recent research which has focused on the cultural construction of motherhood identifies the contradictions inherent in the socially defined motherhood role. Schirmer, for example, describes how the mothers' groups in El Salvador and Guatemala became aware of the conflict in the meaning "motherhood" when mothers were abused and raped by soldiers. Challenging the traditional submissive cultural construction of mothering, women made the connection between human rights and women's rights. Jennifer Schirmer, "The Seeking of Truth and the Gendering of Consciousness: The Comadres of El Salvador and the CONAVIGUA Widows of Guatemala," in Radcliffe and Westwood, eds., *Viva.*

22. See Helen Safa, "Women's Social Movements in Latin America," *Gender and Society* 4, no. 3 (1990): 354-369; Logan, *Haciendo pueblo;* Vargas, "The Women's Movement in Peru. Streams, Spaces and Knots," *European Journal of Latin American and Caribbean Studies* 50 (June 1991): 7-50; Sonia E. Alvarez, *Engendering Democracy in Brazil* (Princeton: Princeton University Press, 1990).

23. Elizabeth Jelin, ed., *Ciudadanidad e identidad: las mujeres en los movimientos sociales latinoamericanos* (Geneva: Instituto de Investigaciones de las Naciones Unidas para el Desarollo Social, 1987).

24. Jaquette, ed., *The Women's Movement in Latin America;* Lynn Stephen, "Women in Mexico's Popular Movements: Survival Strategies against Ecological and Economic Impoverishment," *Latin American Perspective* 19, no. 1 (December 1992): 74; Logan, *Haciendo pueblo;* Craske, "Women's Political Participation in Colonias Populares," in Radcliffe and Westwood, eds., *Viva.*

25. Stephen, "Women in Mexico's Popular Movements," p. 74.

26. Ernesto Laclau's theorization of Latin American social movements points to a shifting relationship between the demands made on the state and the groups making those demands. This position enables us to destabilize the connections between women and so-called "private" issues. Men too have taken part in struggles for human rights, health centers, sanitation, lighting. Is this ascribed to their private "fathering" roles? For the theory underpinning this approach, see Laclau, "New Social Movements and the Plurality of the Social," in David Slater, ed., *New Social Movements and the State in Latin America* (Amsterdam: CEDLA, 1985).

27. Craske, "Women's Political Participation in Colonias Populares."

28. This is an approach adopted in Schirmer's study of women seeking the disappeared in El Salvador and Guatemala. She states that "in the seeking of truth and justice for their families, women can gain a gendered consciousness of political women/motherhood and a responsibility of collective citizenry that is being passed on to their daughters and sons. They may also allow us to understand how the transformative process of gaining a gendered consciousness is dialectic, not binary—that is, dependent upon both what the women bring to the struggle, as well as how the state constructs them and their actions externally." Schirmer, "The Seeking of Truth," p. 62.

29. Anthony Giddens states that the duality of structure is "the essential recursiveness of social life as constituted in social practices: structure is both medium and outcome of the reproduction of practice. Structure enters simultaneously into the constitution of ....social practices and 'exists' in the generating moments of this constitution." See Giddens, *Central Problems in Social Theory* (London: Macmillan, 1979), p. 5.

30. P. Cloke et al., *Approaching Human Geography: An Introduction to Contemporary Theoretical Debates* (London: Paul Chapman, 1991), p. 98. This approach has been adopted by Naila Kabeer's study of women's entry into the export-oriented garment industry in Bangladesh to show how out of economic necessity women have modified the institutionalized practices that have served to define and marginalize them. See Kabeer, "Cultural Dopes or Rational Fools? Women and Labour Supply in the Bangladesh Garment Industry," *European Journal of Development Research* 3, no. 1 (1991).

31. See V. Bennett, "The Evolution of Urban Popular Movements in Mexico between 1968 and 1988"; Judith A. Hellman, "The Study of New Social Movements in Latin American and the Question of Autonomy," both in Escobar and Alvarez, eds., *The Making of Social Movements in Latin America.*

32. Quoted in Lynn Stephen, "Popular Feminism in Mexico: Women in the Urban Popular Movement," *Zeta Magazine* (December 1989) p. 104.

33. Craske, "Women's Political Participation in Colonias Populares."

34. Stephen, "Popular Feminism in Mexico," p. 106.

35. Mexico's National Commission for Women, created in 1983, had as its main aim the incorporation of women into the development process rather than dealing with specifically political demands. The Commission ceased to function in 1992. See Carmen Ramos Escandón, "Women's Movements, Feminism and Mexican Politics," in Jaquette, ed., *The Women's Movement in Latin America,* pp. 199-221.

36. See Escobar and Alvarez, eds., *The Making of Social Movements* for a discussion of the political significance of symbolic challenges to authoritarianism.

ENGENDERING HUMAN RIGHTS

ELIZABETH JELIN

Two stories run parallel through the history of the last two decades. The first is women's struggle for their liberation and for their rights: the story of feminism. The other is the development and expansion—through nongovernmental networks, governments, and societies—of the demand for human rights, including the key role played by women in the struggle to defend human rights. But can the two be put together, and if so, where do they meet?

There is no single solution, no uniquely correct way of relating women to human rights. With this as its point of departure, this chapter pursues two objectives. First, it presents a theoretical-conceptual exercise, exploring how women are situated vis-à-vis human rights and how human rights can be conceptualized from a gender perspective. Subsequently, it grounds the argument in the context of contemporary Latin America, reviewing the history of the relationship between feminism and the human rights movement in the region, and exploring the possibility of interpreting women's demands in terms of the human rights paradigm.

HUMAN RIGHTS: WHICH RIGHTS? WHOSE RIGHTS?

Historically, human rights appear in the West as an issue raised by modernity, specifically by the bourgeoisie (and its philosophers) confronting the power and privileges of monarchies. Both the French Revolution's Declaration of the Rights of Man and the American Constitution reflect concepts grounded in natural law. The U.S. version—based on the perception of the English subject's freedom and rights—implied the recognition of man's "natural" freedom and of its potential, with the intention of reducing to a minimum the interference of political power. Natural rights, inherent in society, were expected to operate without inhibitions. In contrast, the French version is a manifesto against a hierarchical society and against privilege, a universalizing bourgeois pronouncement grounded in the general will of "the people," establishing the distinction between man as depository of natural rights, and the citizen, who enjoys rights because he is integrated into a political system. In the latter view, political citizenship is a condition for the recognition of man's freedom.[1]

Since these beginnings in the eighteenth century, the history of human rights is long and complex, in terms of both political and ideological struggles.[2] Historical and comparative analyses go to considerable lengths to explain the changes in the notion of rights. The mandatory reference here is T.H. Marshall, who shows the interconnection between the development of the English nation-state and the expansion of citizenship rights. Marshall presents a historical progression: first, the extension of civil rights; second, the expansion of political rights; and finally, it is the turn for social rights. In this view, for instance, the development of the welfare state can be conceived as the public face of the process of expansion of the socioeconomic rights of citizens.[3]

Marshall's hypothesis of the historical expansion of rights also corresponds to the terminology used in the United Nations, which refers to generations of rights.[4] As a historical rule, however, this is not universal. At times, rather than complement and expand civil rights, the development of social citizenship rights through the welfare state can replace the ideal of the responsible citizen with the reality of the "client," turning in fact into a kind of boycott against the development of the citizen as a subject of rights.[5]

In Latin America, the preeminence of populist regimes and of social and political authoritarianism during this century has fostered a culture in which awareness about citizens' rights is weak. The expansion of labor and social rights in the region has not always been the outcome of full enforcement of civil and political rights, and in the 1980s, the recovery of political rights in the transition to democracy coexists with widespread violations of civil rights.[6] In general terms, until the 1980s, a decade characterized by adjustment policies and economic restructuring, socioeconomic rights were more prevalent than political ones, which in turn were more prevalent than civil rights, although there were some significant variations among countries in the region.

Before analyzing concrete historical realities, let us insist on some theoretical considerations. The notion of citizenship is a good place to start analyzing this subject, provided one does not indulge in what Habermas calls a "positivization of natural right."[7] The danger lies in reifying the concept and identifying citizenship rights with a group of concrete activities—voting, enjoying freedom of speech, receiving public benefits of any kind, or any other specific activity. Even though these practices are key features of the struggles for the expansion of rights in specific historical situations, from an analytical perspective, the concept of citizenship implies power and conflict—namely, a struggle about who can participate in the process of defining common problems and how they are to be faced.[8] Citizenship, like rights, is always in the process of construction and transformation.

This perspective implies a specific premise: the basic right is "the right to have rights."[9] In this framework, citizens' action is conceived in terms of its self-sustaining and expanding qualities: "the actions pertaining to citizens are only those that tend to maintain and, as far as possible, increase the future practice of citizenship."[10] The important element in the tradition of human rights in the West is the absence of transcendental referents, thus generating the democratic debate.[11]

Without sacred powers or superhuman reference points, there is no authority above that of society itself, no "transcendent judge" to settle conflicts. Consequently, justice has to be grounded in the existence of a space for public debate, and participation in the public sphere becomes a right and a duty. In the words of Hannah Arendt:

> The fundamental deprivation of human rights is manifested first and above all in the deprivation of a place in the world [a political space] which makes opinions significant, and actions effective. ... We became aware of the right to have rights ... and a right to belong to some kind of organized community, only when millions of people emerged who had lost and could not regain those rights because of the new global situation. ... Man, as it turns out, can lose all so-called Rights of Man without losing his essential quality as man, his human dignity. Only the loss of a polity expels him from humanity.[12]

This self-referential perspective of the notions of rights and citizenship has important consequences for the struggle against discrimination and oppression: the contents of the demands, the political priorities, the scenarios for the

67

struggle can change, if and when the right to have rights and the right to a public debate of the contents of both norms and laws are upheld.[13]

The Universal Declaration of Human Rights, adopted by the United Nations in 1948, established the basic framework for concrete action. The statement that "all human beings are born free and equal in dignity and rights ... with no distinction based on race, color, sex, language, religion, political, or any other opinion, national or social origin, economic position, birth ..." expresses a universal ideology that upholds equality and freedom. In contemporary history these principles have led to constant struggles and actions aimed at expanding the social base of citizenship (for instance, extending voting rights to women or to the illiterate), at including minorities and dispossessed social groups as members of the citizenry, and at demanding equality before the law.

How do we interpret women's demands within the framework of the struggle for universal human rights? Which is "The Law" to which the demands for equality are directed?[14] The feminist critique of the predominant "androcentrist" view of equality has been quite clear and explicit, as has its demand for reconceptualization:

> [...] the reconceptualization of equality not only implies the redefinition of the concept of citizenship, but the very concept of "human being," because when one speaks about "equality" of the sexes, one is generally thinking about "raising" women's condition to that of man, paradigm of humanity.[15]

The difficulties with the notion of equality do not end here. A related issue is the tension between the universality of rights and the cultural, gender, and class pluralism which generates diversity. Modern history, including the colonialism and racism of the past two centuries, was the ideological backdrop for the Universal Declaration. Proclaimed in the postwar period, the Declaration was part of the efforts to prevent new horrors. The ideology of universal human rights was therefore intended to serve as a protection of potential and actual victims. However, the implicit tensions soon began to surface, producing a lively academic and political debate. How is it possible to reconcile cultural relativism with the defense of universal human rights? Universal equality or the right to be different? The Universal Declaration began to be criticized on the basis that its underlying notion of human rights was individualistic and Western, and that the will to extend it worldwide was an act of an imperialistic, discriminating, and ethnocentric power.

Today, after years of debate and dialogue, cultural diversity and the comparative parameters can be approached in a different way. If the original idea of universal human rights responded to an individualistic view of rights, it now pivots on communities. To speak of cultural rights is to speak of groups and communities: the right of societies and cultures (self-defined as such) to live their own lifestyles, speak their own languages, wear their own clothes, pursue their own objectives, and receive fair treatment from the laws of the nation-state in which they happen to be living (almost invariably, as "minorities").

In these cases, individual human rights can even contradict collective rights.[16] The prevalence of universal human rights does not guarantee the prevalence of people's collective rights, while conversely, the right of a people to live its own lifestyle may imply the denial of basic human rights and cruelty toward certain categories of people within that culture. The emergence of demands for indigenous peoples' rights based on ethnicity is one significant field of discussion of these issues. To think about the agenda of ethnic rights implies a profound revision of the original notion of human rights, so far conceptualized in an abstract way, with a bias toward universality and individual subjects. The statement that indigenous peoples and minorities have rights implies that the very notion of "human rights" can acquire meaning only in specific cultural circumstances, which thus become requisites for, and part of, human rights.[17]

In this framework, to speak about human rights of indigenous peoples or of traditionally oppressed or marginalized groups of the population (to which women obviously belong) implies the recognition of a history of discrimination and oppression, and an active commitment to reverse this situation. To advance on this point entails acknowledging the inevitable tension between individual and collective rights. Rodolfo Stavenhagen argues that there may be cases where individual rights cannot be fully enjoyed if collective rights are not granted. Where the two are in conflict, he concludes, "Group or collective rights must be considered human rights insofar as their recognition and practice in turn promote the individual rights of the members." He adds that "collective rights that violate or curtail their members' individual rights cannot be considered human rights."[18] Beyond the critique of the individualistic and universalistic definition of human rights and their identification with Western and masculine values, the analogy between the discussion of human rights of indigenous peoples and of human rights of women take different routes. Further analysis of women's rights implies thinking about rights in the context of gender relations as well as reconceptualizing the relationship between what is public and what is private.

69

THE LOGIC OF DIFFERENCE: RIGHTS AND RELATIONS

From a legal point of view, there are various ways of approaching the issue of difference. A first approach conceives difference as inherent in some persons, becoming significant when identified with inferiority. Persons who are different cannot enjoy rights and are seen as "dependents" and "noncitizens." A second approach strives to secure "equality before the law," but defines equality in terms of a single set of (masculine?) traits, which implies overlooking, and even denying, many traits which indicate differences. But since differences do exist, this approach eventually leads to a search for the "real" differences, that is, those that deserve a "truly differentiated" treatment. In a third approach, difference is a function of social relations, and therefore cannot be situated in categories of individual persons, but in social institutions and in the legal norms which rule them.[19]

Social demands on the part of the "different" (inferior) actor, in our case women, express themselves first in a call for equality. In recent decades, this has meant demanding access to places and positions previously out of bounds for women (from exclusive clubs to traditionally male jobs), and condemning both discrimination (for instance, barriers for access to high level positions in work or in politics) and inequality ("equal work, equal pay").

Much remains to be done to attain equality for women before the law. However, a literal interpretation of equality can be misleading or insufficient in many situations. For instance, in cases of workers' pregnancies, is equality— in the sense of denying the difference between men and women—called for? Or should the law recognize the need for "special" treatment? To pose the issue in a different area, what does equality of educational rights mean for a disabled child? Or for one whose "mother tongue" is not the language used in public school?

Emphasis on the norm of equality reinforces a conception grounded in universal natural law; it reasserts that all human beings are naturally equal. This is politically effective insofar as it allows opposition to certain forms of discrimination, asserts individualities, and limits the exercise of power. However, there is another side to social reality: not all individuals are equal, and hiding or denying differences eventually serves to perpetuate the implicit notion that there are two essentially different kinds of people—those who are "normal" and those who are "different" (which always implies "inferior"). Maintaining the notion of equality and stating it in universal terms entails risks: it may lead to an excessive formalization of rights, isolating them from the social structures in which they exist and acquire meaning. The passage from the universal to the social, historical, and contingent then becomes difficult.

One of the major contributions of feminism has been its profound critique and unmasking of the assumptions implicit in the dominant paradigm that takes (Western) men as the universal reference point and makes women (and others) different or invisible. By so doing, feminism has moved on contradictory grounds: on the one had, it has claimed equality of rights and equal treatment vis-à-vis men; on the other hand, it has demanded the right to a differentiated treatment and to the social recognition of women's uniqueness. This implies an unavoidable tension between the principle of equality and the right to difference. Recognizing this tension stimulates debate and creativity, and helps avoid dogmatism.

Rather than talking about the "woman," we are talking about women, aware of the enormous variety of experiences and viewpoints, of differences according to race, class, and nationality. The critique of the claim to universal equality implies the incorporation of the perspectives and social positions of different women and men, considering also the intersections of differences and of the power relations inherent in those differences.[20]

Feminist legal theorists are currently debating whether to pose the issue in terms of women's rights or in terms of gender relations. Demands stated in terms of rights make reference to a paradigm of equality, yet this is increasingly difficult to maintain in light of all the progress that has been made in the recognition of difference. Demands posed in terms of rights cannot be abandoned, however. Such an abdication may entail strategic and political costs, since demands presented in terms of human rights have a very high moral and emotional legitimacy.[21] A possible resolution, strategic as well as theoretical, is to combine the critique of the assumptions of the discourse on rights with a permanent conceptualization of rights in systems of social relations, especially gender relations. The case of domestic violence is particularly relevant.

PRIVATE SPHERE AND PUBLIC LIFE: DOMESTIC VIOLENCE

The human rights paradigm rests on an implicit differentiation between public and private life: civil and political rights of individuals are located in public life, but these rights are not recognized in the private sphere of family relationships.[22] Unlike the structures of political domination and inequality among men, domination of men over women is socially and economically established before the intervention of law, without explicit state actions, often in intimate contexts defined as everyday life. In fact, the dichotomization of life into public and private spheres leads to a mutilation of women's citizenship.

Mistreatment of women is often described as an emotional outburst of an enraged man, or as a symbolic manifestation of power resulting from men's

71

need to display masculinity. Furthermore, insofar as it curtails the freedom of women and creates a climate of terror and submission that accentuates gender inequality and women's economic dependency, domestic violence reinforces the structural limitations on women's options. The privacy of family life appears as a justification to limit the intervention of the state in this sphere.

We are faced with an inescapable tension between respect for privacy and intimacy on the one hand, and public responsibilities on the other. This tension demands a redefinition of the distinction between public, private, and intimate. This distinction has operated on a symbolic and ideological level, but not in practical terms, for the modern state has always had the power to police the family.[23] Due to the social recognition and moral indignation caused by domestic violence in recent years, it becomes clear that when human rights are violated in the private realm of family life, respect for privacy in the family context cannot justify legal impunity for violence.[24]

If at this juncture the issue of women's rights can no longer be presented as a matter of equal rights and is framed in terms of demands related to an anti-subordination principle, the role of the state is due to change. Whenever a contradiction appears between respect for privacy and defense of the victims of violence, the affirmative obligation of the state to protect the basic human rights of its citizens becomes the final criterion for defining state responsibility.

This does not solve the tension or the contradiction. State intervention in the private sphere may be justified as a defense of the victims and the subordinate people in the patriarchal system. Under authoritarianism, however, such intervention may imply arbitrary intervention, control, and even terror, on the part of the state. Thus it may be desirable to protect from state interference all those domains associated with arbitrary intervention, but not those which strengthen (gender) subordination.

In summary, the solution to the questions posed is not to be reached through the unyielding confrontation of the discourse of equality and the discourse of difference, but through an approach which poses the issue of equality of rights in contexts of social relations in which differences, including those of power, marginalization, and gender, can be explicitly stated.

WOMEN'S STRUGGLES AND FEMINISM

What are the most important demands put forth by Latin American women today, and how should priorities be established? How is it possible to take advantage of the legitimate spaces opened up by the debate about human rights, and at the same time promote a basic change in the way of conceptualizing the very notion of rights? To begin to answer these questions requires a look at the recent history of women's struggles as well as specific fields of action in terms of human rights.

When feminist movements reappeared at the end of the 1960s, they confronted a dual challenge. On the one hand they sought to understand and explain the various forms of women's subordination, and on the other they aimed to propose strategies for overcoming that condition. Women had to subvert the theoretical and conceptual order; they had to undermine power relationships at the macro and the micro social levels. The struggle necessarily had to take place on several fronts simultaneously.

What was (or is) the nature of gender subordination? How is it best understood, not only in theory but also in the context of efforts to design practical responses? There is no single conceptual approach or unified strategy. The debate within feminism has been intense, reflecting the permanent hetero-geneity and theoretical and tactical conflicts of the movement. New perspectives and new themes are constantly discovered, while old ones are recovered and redefined. Without pretending to offer an exhaustive history, what follows pinpoints some key moments and turning points.

A landmark was the discovery of the social invisibility of women: in the hidden realm of domestic work, in the active background of historical moments of struggle, "behind" great men. During the 1960s several influential books sought to make visible the invisible. Recognition and naming bestows social existence, and existence is a prerequisite for self-esteem and for revindication. It was necessary to reveal and acknowledge the social value of everyday life, of anti-heroism, of the social web that supports and reproduces social existence. This coincided with a theoretical debate. What do women produce when they dedicate themselves to their families and their homes? Who appropriates their work? In the 1970s, the recognition of the housewife as a "worker" and the demand for a definition of her labor rights became major topics of debate and controversy.

The next stage of the struggle was for women to abandon the private sphere, to leave the house to participate in the public world, which was, until then, a masculine world. Historical trends were already bringing this about: increased educational levels for women, higher rates of female participation in the labor market—were evident all over the world during the 1970s. In Latin America, the participation of women in the labor market increased dramatically. Yet, when women go out into the labor market, occupational segregation and discrimination are the rule: there are few opportunities to get access to "good" jobs, and women suffer from wage discrimination and from social definitions of "typically feminine" tasks. These occupations reproduce and expand traditional domestic roles (domestic and personal services, secretaries, teachers, and nurses), where female employment is concentrated. This second dimension of visibility, anchored mostly in access to the world of work and, to a lesser degree, to other forms of participation in public spaces, promotes a specific form of struggle: the fight against discrimination and for equality vis-à-vis men.

To struggle for more favorable conditions for women without challenging the traditional sexual division of labor was clearly inadequate. Thus, by the 1970s the goal was to transform those conditions: the sexual division of labor is oppressive in itself, implies subordination and lack of autonomy on the part of women who remain the "property" of the pater-familiae. Theoretical discussions of the history of patriarchy—a concept that links relationships within wider social processes, focusing on power relations—were important landmarks in the 1970s. Liberation implied a transformation of patriarchy as a social system.[25]

Women have always been in charge of reproductive tasks within the family. Given the need to rely on collective consumption and on public services for performing such tasks, women of the urban popular classes have participated actively in neighborhood organizations and in local public activities demanding collective services from the state. As the state became unable or unwilling to respond, self-managed community provision of these services was promoted. This collective dimension of the domestic role had also been socially invisible and without recognized social value. A feminist analysis of the reproductive roles of women implied recognizing the domestic tasks of women as socially necessary, and considering participation in neighborhood activities as a training ground for action in public spaces.

The movement of women out of their homes and into the workplace, along with their increasing participation in organizations and in collective action with other women, seemed to promise liberation, especially for women in popular and marginal quarters. If oppression was grounded in the domestic-patriarchal domain, breaking the divide between the private and the public world and learning to express their needs and demands in work and in collective action could become the means of shattering it.

Experience showed that at times these practices were liberating, but that they could also reinforce subordination. Women's community work in collective dining halls, in cooperative childcare efforts, or in neighborhood activities is not renumerated. Nor is it evidence of autonomy or power in decision-making and management. Indeed, it often ends up reproducing subordination and clientelism. And entering the world of paid work generally means a double (or triple, if there is also community work to do) day's work, which suggests not liberation but rather exhaustion, fatigue, and overwork. Badly paid and precarious jobs, without access to social benefits or the recognition of labor rights, implies segregation and the strengthening of discriminatory practices.

The struggle against explicit and implicit forms of discrimination against women and their segregation in the labor market and elsewhere represents an important fight for equality of opportunities and of life conditions. It is a struggle in which much remains to be done. Since the 1980s, the effort to achieve equality vis-à-vis men has taken place in a context of growing social inequality and income polarization, with privilege on one side and increased misery and marginality on the other. The crisis affects both genders, although in an unequal way.

The past two decades of struggle against discrimination have had contradictory results. The demand for equality has gained increasing legitimacy and social visibility. Although Latin America has not yet managed to create a social consensus and a political will to change, it has made some headway in that direction. Yet there is little evidence of a reduction in the profound gaps separating the conditions faced by men and women in the region. On the contrary, women are carrying a disproportionate share of the social costs of economic crisis and adjustment. The crisis of the welfare state, diminished public services, and the trend toward the privatization and mercantalization of services all complicate tasks of domestic reproduction. At the same time, while neoliberalism implies a reinforcement of duties and responsibilities on the part of the family, it also erodes the capacity of households to command the resources necessary to meet domestic needs. Traditional solutions to the social tasks of reproduction, be it through placing demands for services on the state and/or through the invisible extra work of women in the domestic world, are no longer viable. Community organizations, which were seen as alternative ways to cope with these tasks, are also showing their limitations, lacking resources and the efficiency needed to survive in the neoliberal environment. Thus there is the challenge to rethink the social tasks of reproduction in this new context.

The issues discussed above concern some of the most noteworthy invisibilities, but there are numerous others. Only recently, for instance, have sexuality and reproduction become separated and differentiated, and only now are women beginning to enjoy a voice in their definition. The story is well-known: because life originates in the bodies of women, the ability to exercise power over reproduction requires the appropriation and manipulation of women's bodies, whether privately or publicly (e.g., population policies,

75

ideologies, and desires of paternity). The wishes of women can be taken into account or not. And something similar happens with the history of sexuality: the pleasure is man's, the woman "serves."

To transform this cluster of ideologies and practices is not an easy task. Culture counts: machismo in all its forms combines with the cult of the dedicated and suffering mother, and with the horror caused by the sterile woman. And all this is linked with the taboo against naming, talking about, or mentioning sexuality. Concealed and forbidden in words, but real and everyday in practice, to make sexuality visible and to expose the sexual oppression suffered by most women has been one of the feminist movement's significant achievements. Public and political recognition of this form of oppression and of the changes which are necessary have been slower and more controversial. The strong presence of the Catholic church and of ideological traditionalism, and the entrenchment of practices and ideologies that blame the victim ("Could she have incited the rape?"; "If she was careless about her sexual relationships, she must suffer the consequences"; "It is irresponsible to have so many children") have made it difficult to enact legislative change and implement programs of public health and education.

And then there is the other, invisible and complex, taboo: domestic violence. The victims of violent practices within the family—also protected by the mantle of privacy—are almost invariably women, although children and the elderly have surfaced as visible victims in the 1980s and 1990s. It would seem that in Latin American culture it is harder to speak about domestic violence than about sexual violence, and that this silence is sustained by considerable complicity on the part of both victims and culprits.

During the last two decades, there has been a great deal of tension between feminism—the movement of women oriented to liberation—and movements of women within their communities (a difference conceptualized as the tension and contradiction between women's strategic and practical interests). Women active in the struggle for family survival at first glance seem far removed from the women who denounce, for instance, the identification of sexuality and reproduction, demanding the right to a free sexuality based on pleasure. Given the strength of traditional culture and its "progressive" identity, feminists often practiced a kind of self-censorship; they had to show that their struggle focused on what "really mattered," and not on frivolities. Legitimacy also depended on not imposing bourgeois concerns and values on women from the popular sectors. Only when women from the popular sectors started demanding sexual education and family planning (in Brazil, for instance) did the feminist movement explicitly take up these issues.[26]

76

WOMEN AND THE HUMAN RIGHTS MOVEMENT

If violence against women and the curtailment of their freedom are taken into account, human rights violations have a long history. However, the human rights movement emerged in relation to massive violations of rights by dictatorial regimes. From the outset, women were at the forefront of this movement. Their commitment rarely stemmed from a democratic ideological conviction or from strategic calculations in the struggle against dictatorship. It was not a political position, but a practical one, as women were directly touched by repression—as mothers, grandmothers, relatives of victims, of missing or tortured people, asking and demanding for their children. The names of the organizations speak of the predominance of the family bond: mothers, grandmothers, relatives, widows, godmothers, women, who having lost their fear were willing to face any risk to satisfy their personal need to learn something about their relatives, to recover the victims. Their actions multiplied and expanded the feminine role of lovingly and devotedly caring for the family. What came afterward is another matter.

However, the presence of women *in* the human rights movement did not imply that what was at stake were primarily the rights of women. The expectation among feminists that since activists of the human rights movement are women, they spontaneously express the "intrinsic" or "specific" demands of women, turned into a position—often a dogmatic one—that complicated and even blocked dialogue with the human rights movement.

The women who left their homes in search of information about their children did so as part of their personal family drama. The histories, well-known and yet still devastating, converge: desperation and bewilderment, the search for help, the effort to set up contacts in order not to lose hope, encounters and mutual recognition with other women in the same circumstances, meeting and later joining activists from the human rights movement. In this way the private search for a son or daughter gradually was transformed into the public and political demand for democracy.[27]

A peculiar historical circumstance marked the relationship of women in the human rights movement with feminism: the dictatorships and human rights violations of the 1970s coincided with the moment in which women began to place their interests on the international agenda. In 1975, the International Decade for Women opened with a large international meeting in Mexico City, where the subordination of women gained worldwide attention. These were also the years when women, particularly in popular neighborhoods, began to present social demands to governments, which were not prepared to meet them.

Let us take the case of the Mothers of the Plaza de Mayo, who generated enormous concern and solidarity in first world countries, becoming an international symbol of the struggle for human rights in Argentina. The remaining organizations, militants, and activists in the Argentine human rights movement received much less coverage abroad. The Mothers symbolized women who, emerging from deep pain and suffering and from their traditional role as mothers, subvert the social and political order, thus revealing the revolutionary potential of women.[28] From a feminist point of view, the ensuing question is obvious: Does public action originating from private grief transform these mothers into women aware of gender demands? Does it encourage them to fight for these new demands? The limited available evidence shows that, in relation to gender demands, women active in the struggle for human rights display the same range of differences as members of the movement as a whole: their objectives are diverse and they pursue a wide range of strategies and political alliances. They will endorse as much (or as little) of the feminist ideas as the rest of the people in the milieu in which they act.

In each country where the military regimes ruled, female victims were systematically humiliated, raped, and tortured; in many cases, they joined the ranks of the disappeared.[29] Differences begin to surface when we look at the practices of oppression of women who, although experiencing similar state violence, occupy different social spaces. Thus in Guatemala, indigenous peoples' issues overlap with those of human rights: the tradition of raping Indian women takes on a political meaning when practiced on activist women.[30] Similarly, the exploitation and wage discrimination against political widows in agricultural work is a clear case of the interaction between class, ethnicity, gender, and politics. In Argentina, on the other hand, femininity and maternity became part of a strategy of resistance: beyond having lost their fear, and acting with the conviction that one has "nothing to lose," the Madres felt that their status as mothers protected them from physical violence.[31] In rallies and protests, they were convinced that they were less exposed to danger than men or the young. In Chile in contrast, the tradition of political socialization fostered a women's movement in which personal experiences as direct or indirect victims of repression were converted rapidly into political demands against the regime.[32]

Today, in most countries in Latin America, although accounts with the past are still not settled, democracy has replaced the terror-based regimes in which state organizations engaged in massive violations of human rights. In this context, should issues related to the subordination of women be posed in terms of human rights? The transitions to democracy have left a considerable degree of social awareness of human rights, although not always with progressive implications. The challenge is to transform that social sensibility into a strategy that would avert violations, deter violence, and confront the diverse forms of subordination and marginalization in daily life.

Meanwhile violations of human rights continue in more or less covert ways in several countries. The network of women active in the human rights movements plays an important role in denouncing abuses and expressing solidarity. In this regard, acts of international recognition, such as the Nobel Peace Prize awarded to the Guatemalan indigenous leader Rigoberta Menchú, are exemplary in that they publicize rights violation and confer legitimacy upon those who resist them. In sum, the combined effects of the various dimensions of subordination—gender, race, class, political orientation—create historically specific circumstances which resist simple generalizations.

CONCLUSIONS

Analysis of human rights and women requires recognition that demands change historically. This in turn implies abandoning the idea that there are natural, transcendental, universal references, free of the constraints of time and space. Thus it is not possible to draw up a list of "basic human rights," from which to locate and denounce violations against women; nor is it possible to set up a "basic agenda for women," and then present the demands around each of its items in terms of human rights. The process of debate, dialogue, and struggle is more flexible, more dynamic, and more varied.

The recognition of the contingent nature of struggles and demands should not, however, imply abandoning ideals and utopias. It requires a more humble approach, the acknowledgment that there are no "absolute truths." And in the quest for partial and contingent truths, to seek the materialization of ideals: the elimination of suffering and oppression, the promotion of solidarity and of concern for others. If there is no single way of solving the basic tensions and contradictions which permeate the relationship between women and human rights, what becomes important is to make visible these tensions, and to recognize their implications for a gender perspective of human rights:

- The tension between individual rights and collective rights.
- The tension between the principle of equality and the right to be different.
- The tension between a perspective rooted in universal rights and a perspective grounded in systems of social relationships.
- The tension between public responsibilities and the respect for privacy and intimacy.
- The tension between opening up the space for the development of wishes and subjectivities, and the realization that there are cases in which these wishes

and subjectivities, historically and culturally formed, block democratization and equity.

The challenge for feminism is to combine the struggle for recognition of women's rights as human rights within the current paradigm, while at the same time actively participating in the permanent redefinition of the very notion of human rights, toward one which goes beyond the male-Western frame which originated the definition in the first place, without abandoning the ideals of freedom and equality which inspired it.

NOTES

1. See Waldo Ansaldi, "La ética de la democracia. Una reflexión sobre los derechos humanos desde las ciencias sociales," in Waldo Ansaldi, ed., *La ética de la democracia* (Buenos Aires: CLACSO, 1986); Claude Lefort, "Los derechos del hombre y el estado benefactor," *Vuelta* (México), July 1987.

2. Ansaldi, "La ética de la democracia"; Luciano de Oliveira, "Derechos humanos y marxismo: Breve ensayo para un nueva paradigma," *El Otro Derecho* 4 (1989).

3. T.H. Marshall, *Citizenship and Social Democracy* (New York: Doubleday, 1964); Claus Offe, *Contradictions of the Welfare State* (Cambridge, MA: MIT Press, 1985); Claude Lefort, "Los derechos del hombre."

4. Rights of the first generation are basically civil and political. The second generation rights include economic, social, and cultural rights, which require active participation of the state in order to secure the material conditions required for the operation of the previous rights. These two types refer mainly to individual rights. The third (peace, development, environment) and fourth (people's rights) are of a different nature, since they refer to global and collective phenomena. This sequencing of rights refers to the history of the discussion within international agencies, and should not be interpreted as a statement about priorities or history.

5. See Habermas, "Derecho y moral (Dos lecciones)," in David Sobrevilla, ed., *El derecho, la política y la ética* (México: Siglo XXI, 1991); Fabio Wanderley Reis, "Cidadania, Estado e Mercado," paper presented at the seminar "Modernization, political democracy and social democracy" (México: El Colegio de México, 1990).

6. See Ruth B. Collier and David Collier, *Shaping the Political Arena* (Princeton: Princeton University Press, 1991); Teresa Caldeira, "Crime and Individual Rights: Reframing the Question of Violence in Latin America," in Elizabeth Jelin and Eric Hershberg, eds., *Constructing Democracy: Human Rights, Citizenship and Society in Latin America* (Boulder: Westveiw Press, 1996).

7. Habermas, "Derecho y moral." Habermas is referring to the reduction of citizenship to a set of specific activities, thereby potentially excluding the progressively emancipatory potentials bound up in the concept of citizenship.

8. Herman van Gunsteren, "Notes on a Theory of Citizenship," in Pierre Birbaum, Jack Lively, and Geraint Parry, eds., *Democracy, Consensus and Social Contract* (London: Sage, 1978).

9. See Hannah Arendt, *The Origins of Totalitarianism* (New York: Harcourt, Brace and World, 1973).
10. van Gunsteren, "Notes on a Theory of Citizenship," p. 27; see also Norbert Lechner, "Los derechos humanos como categoría política," in Ansaldi, ed., *La ética de la democracia.*
11. As Lefort states: "The naturalist conception of law concealed the extraordinary fact that the declaration was also a self-declaration, that is, a declaration in which men ... were at the same time the subjects and the objects of the statement ... and by so doing, they became the witnesses and judges of each other." Lefort, "Los derechos del hombre": 39.
12. Arendt, "The Rights of Man: What are they?" *Modern Review* 3, no. 1 (1949), cited in Elizabeth Young-Bruehl, *Hannah Arendt: For Love of the World* (New Haven: Yale University Press, 1982), p. 257. Also, in *On Revolution* (New York: Viking Press, 1965), Arendt refers to the public nature of the notion of freedom in the French Revolution, and to public happiness (the right of the citizen to gain access to the public sphere, to participation in public power) in the American Revolution. Later on in history this disappearance of the "taste for political freedom" can be considered as the retreat of the individual into an "intimate sphere of consciousness."
13. See Lefort, "Los derechos del hombre," especially p. 40. To recognize that there are no final criteria for the selection between alternative values implies the need to acknowledge the contingency of our own beliefs and values, but simultaneously, the urgency of an ethical-political commitment in agreement with the central issues of our times. Avoiding suffering, expanding the bases of solidarity, widening the spaces for public and responsible action, as well as promoting tolerance, respecting autonomy and difference, and giving voice to the excluded and silent: all these may not have a final transcendental justification. They are therefore in this sense contingent, but not less necessary. See Theodore E. Downing and Gilbert Kushner, eds., *Human Rights and Anthropology* (Cambridge, MA: Cultural Survival, 1988), especially Jennifer Schirmer, "The Dilemma of Cultural Diversity and Equivalence in Universal Human Rights Standards"; Zygmunt Bauman, *Modernity and the Holocaust* (Oxford: Polity Press and Blackwell Press, 1991); Richard Rorty, *Contingencia, ironía y solidaridad* (Barcelona: Paidós, 1991); Agnes Heller, "Rights, Modernity, Democracy," *Cardozo Law Review* 11 (1990): 1377-1391; Emmanuel Levinas, *Ethique et infini* (Paris: Librairie Artheme Fayard, 1982).
14. See Alda Facio, "El principio de la igualdad ante la ley," *El Otro Derecho* No. 8 (1991); Charlotte Bunch, "Hacia una revisión de los derechos humanos," in Ximena Bunster and Regina Rodríguez, eds., *La mujer ausente. Derechos humanos en el mundo* (Santiago de Chile: Isis International, 1991).
15. Facio, "El principio de la igualdad": 11.
16. See Rodolfo Stavenhagen, "Indigenous Rights: Some Conceptual Problems," in Jelin and Hershberg, eds., *Constructing Democracy;* Stavenhagen, *The Ethnic Question: Conflicts, Development and Human Rights* (Tokyo: United Nations University Press, 1990).
17. "The principle of cultural relativity does not seem to excuse us from exercising

judgement about the function, meaning, or utility of a given practice. Rather, it is a warning that this judgement must be made in terms of the cultural context in which it is embedded.... As long as the context is taken into account, any practice can be evaluated or judged against a stated expectation or goal." Clifford R. Barnett, "Is there a Scientific Basis in Anthropology for the Ethics of Human Rights?" in Downing and Kushner, eds., *Human Rights and Anthropology.*

18. Stavenhagen, "Indigenous Rights."
19. Martha Minow, *Making All the Difference: Inclusion, Exclusion and American Law* (Ithaca, NY: Cornell University Press, 1990) p. 9.
20. See Celina Romany, "Ain't I a Feminist?" *Yale Journal of Law and Feminism* 4, no. 1 (1991); Minow, ibid.
21. See Celina Romany, "Women as Aliens: A Feminist Critique of the Public/Private Distinction in International Human Rights Law," *Harvard Human Rights Journal,* 1993. Caldeira, in "Crime and Individual Rights," shows how in present-day Brazil the identificatio n of the human rights movement with the rights of marginalized and victimized groups is leading to a paradoxical reaction: large sectors of public opinion reject the case of human rights because they identify the movement with the defense of criminals and other transgressors.
22. Domestic violence is a widespread phenomenon, kept silent until very recently. In countries where they are registered, the rates of domestic aggression against women go from 40 to 80 percent. See Verónica Matus, "Derechos humanos, derechos de las mujeres," in José Aylwin, ed., *Derechos Humanos: desafíos para un nuevo contexto* (Santiago de Chile: Chilean Human Rights Commission, 1992).
23. Jacques Donzelot, *The Policing of Families* (New York: Pantheon, 1979); Elizabeth Jelin, *Familia y unidad doméstica: mundo público y vida privada* (Buenos Aires: Estudios CEDES, 1984).
24. See Minow, *Making All the Difference.* Romany, in "Women as Aliens," argues that states are responsible for men's systematic private violence against women, and shows that when the state systematically fails to provide the necessary protection, it could be declared an accomplice of the "private" actor who violates women's rights to life, freedom, and security. The state can also be considered responsible for discriminatory treatment towards women, since by failing to prevent and punish violence against women, it is denying them equal protection before the law.
25. Teresa Valdes, *Mujer y derechos humanos: "menos tu vientre,"* FLACSO Working Paper, Social Studies Series, no. 8 (Santiago de Chile: FLACSO, 1990).
26. Carmen Barroso, "Sexo y Crisis" in *Mujeres y Movimiento: America Latina y el Caribe* (Santiago: Isis International-MUDAR, 1987).
27. See Jennifer Schirmer, "The Seeking of Truth and the Gendering of Consciousness: The Comadres of El Salvador and the CONAVIGUA Widows of Guatemala," in Sarah A. Radcliffe and Sallie Westwood, eds., *"Viva!" Women and Popular Protest in Latin America* (London: Routledge, 1993).
28. Maria del Carmen Feijoo and Mónica Gogna, "Las mujeres en la transición a la democracia," in Elizabeth Jelin, ed., *Ciudadania e identidad: las mujeres en los movimientos sociales lationoamericanos* (Geneva: Instituto de Investigaciones de las Naciones Unidas para el Desarollo Social [UNRISD], 1987).

29. Ximena Bunster, "Sobreviviendo más allá del miedo," in Bunster and Rodríguez, eds., *La mujer ausente.*

30. The rape of human rights activists as a form of repression was a relatively frequent experience and similarly became a means of social control. At the height of the counterinsurgency campaign in Guatemala, gender-specific terror in the form of rape and other sexual abuse was an integral part of army operating procedure. See A. Aron et al., "The Gender Specific Terror of El Salvador and Guatemala: Post Traumatic Stress Disorder of Central American Refugee Women," *Women's Studies International Forum* 14, nos. 1-2 (1990).

31. Feijoo and Gogna, "Las mujeres en la transición a la democracia."

32. Valdes, *Mujer y derechos humanos.*

"DESDE LA PROTESTA A LA PROPUESTA": THE INSTITUTIONALIZATION OF THE WOMEN'S MOVEMENT IN CHILE

ANN MATEAR

Throughout the 1980s, major political debates on Latin America revolved around the transitions from military to civilian regimes and the nature of the emerging democracies. Because of the central role women played in the opposition movements, as well as Latin American feminists' analyses of gender oppression within a global context of political repression, the "women question" occupied a prominent position in those debates, which in recent years have been considerably less vociferous. While the silence may represent a much-needed period for reflection on the movement's future role, it is unnervingly reminiscent of the withdrawal from politics which followed the suffrage campaigns once the right to vote had been won. Was the return to democracy an end in itself? I believe it was not, but the transitions have thrown up new challenges for social movements in general and the women's movement in particular.

Chile was one of the last countries in Latin America to return to civilian government. This chapter analyzes the impact of the women's movement on the political process during the transition to democracy in Chile. It then examines how gender politics have become institutionalized as élite sectors of the women's movement have entered the state and formal politics. In so doing it endeavors to show how, and with what success, gender has been incorporated into the political agenda in the period of democratic consolidation.[1]

Women's political mobilization is nothing new in Chile. Throughout the nineteenth and twentieth centuries women struggled for equal rights and opportunities in the law, education, employment, and suffrage.[2] The movement for women's emancipation demanded access to formal education that would enable women to enter the universities and professions which had previously been denied to them. Female political and economic participation is often considered an indicator of modernization, yet the process of women's enfranchisement in Latin America bore little relation to the developmental stages of particular countries. Women first gained the vote in 1929 in Ecuador, a country characterized by poverty, low levels of urbanization, and no democratic tradition. Argentina and Chile, by contrast, modern urban societies with high per capita incomes and literacy levels, did not grant women the vote until the late 1940s. Women found tactical political allies in unlikely quarters; in Chile, they were enfranchised in municipal elections by a conservative government which hoped that women, molded by the ideology of *Kinder, Küche, Kirche,* would automatically lend them political support.

Despite their success in achieving formal incorporation into the democratic process, the institutional structures of power have remained largely unchanged for women. Women's representation in the state, political institutions, and civil society is abysmally low, and women continue to be subordinated to men politically, socially, and economically.[3] Clearly this situation is not unique to Latin America, but is a common feature of political systems worldwide, raising the question of whether a political and social system which has been structured to serve the interests of one half of the population can be a mechanism into which the other half of the population can be incorporated on equal terms.[4]

The experience of authoritarian bureaucratic regimes of the 1970s and 1980s in many countries of Latin America revealed a fundamental paradox. While within open democratic systems women and men were formally incorporated with the same political rights, in practice they did not have equal

85

representation or access to positions of power. By contrast, the closed systems of the military dictatorships produced high levels of female mobilization in noninstitutional politics. The women's movement brought together diverse organizations in terms of social class, political ideology, and approaches to gender issues, all of which had become disaffected with left-wing politics and the left's inability or unwillingness to address gender issues.[5] The experience of exile was also important for those women who entered the movement on their return, bringing ideas and lessons from the feminist movement in Europe and the United States and linking the debate on women's rights to the global issue of human rights. In this way, gender oppression in the private and public spheres became intrinsically linked to the political and economic repression in the nation and throughout the region.

In country after country, the dismantling of political parties meant that the locus of political organization shifted from the national arena to the neighborhood, and from élites to the base. Social movements provided one of the few channels for the popular sectors to express political demands and dissent. Traditionally, women have been more active in local than national politics because the community is viewed as an extension of their role as caregivers. Women are the interface between local government and the household for the use of public services, including health care, education, housing, and other support networks. State welfare provision was sharply reduced during the military regimes, whether for ideological reasons or because of the economic crises. Women responded to these crises by participating in popular economic organizations and as a result, their roles as community organizers became politicized.

Some of the popular women's organizations progressively moved beyond the specific issues of human rights and economic survival which had initially characterized their actions, to increasingly gender-based demands. The 1980s witnessed the emergence of "popular feminism" within the women's movement. This current addressed the nexus between class oppression and gender oppression within a Latin American context, and provided a much-needed alternative to what had been perceived as middle-class feminism imported from first world countries. The class divisions within the women's movement as a whole were also exacerbated in the return to democracy. At regional feminist conferences *(encuentros)* in Valparaíso (1991) and in Concepción (1992), women from the popular sectors *(pobladoras)* organized a parallel meeting for working class feminists *(mujeres feministas de sectores populares)* which aimed to link discrimination by social class and by gender.[6] There is a degree of mutual mistrust between the two camps: the middle-class feminists perceive the *pobladoras* as not challenging traditional gender roles and the *pobladoras* feel exploited by the middle-class women. This comment from a *pobladora* active in grassroots politics and the popular feminist movement illustrates this suspicion:

> The feminists should not kid themselves. We're not stupid—working class women are not stupid. They should watch out if we see that they are out to use us, because ... we've been through this before. Working class women have experience of politics, and we're not going to hand over our votes to just any feminist.[7]

THE POLITICS OF TRANSITION: FROM DICTATORSHIP TO DEMOCRACY, FROM MOVEMENT TO...?

The experiences of the social movements under the military regimes provided glimpses of ways in which other forms of social and political participation might be possible. These alternatives emphasized involving those directly affected in the process of decision-making, and increased representativeness and accountability. The challenge was to envisage how these experiences could be translated into post-dictatorship politics at local, regional, and national levels, thereby constructing a "more democratic" democracy, rather than simply restoring the formal democracies which had existed prior to the coups. The women's movement was faced with the dual challenge of incorporating gender demands into the political process and of making political spaces representative of gender interests.

Jane Jacquette has proposed that transitions from military to civil regimes represented a period of political uncertainty and contained within them the potential for change.[8] In Chile, this juncture provided the opportunity for the women's movement to develop a dual strategy. First, the movement could generate public awareness (and support) for women's concerns at a political juncture where mainstream politicians required their political backing. Second, if women's interests and demands could reflect and complement national interests in terms of increased democratization or the redistribution of resources, they were more likely to be incorporated into policymaking. Arguably the most significant advance for the women's movement during this period was its ability to move beyond protest action and toward a strategy—however tenuous—for political and social change for women within the national project of democratization. The "Feminist Manifesto: Feminist Demands for Democracy" identified areas of discrimination against women in society, including female political participation and representation, work (employment, unemployment, domestic labor), the welfare state, education, family relations, legislation and violence against women. The document called for the decriminalization of abortion and adultery, and changes to divorce legislation.

The feminist movement recognized that political, economic, and legislative changes would not be sufficient to end women's subordinate position in society: "It is essential that we promote real changes in culture and behavior, within the framework of a truly democratic society."[9]

In 1985, the Movement for the Emancipation of Chilean Women, MEMCH '83, elaborated "The Principles and Revindications which Constitute the Chilean Women's Platform," which called for the restoration of democracy and for women's demands to be taken up by the political parties as issues of national importance.[10] This document clearly linked women's subordination to the political, economic, and social conditions in Chile, and proposed that women's participation was essential for democratization and development. Moreover, it countered the argument traditionally put forward by the left-wing parties that the struggle for women's rights was a bourgeois concern and a potentially divisive issue. In 1986, the Women's Document *(Pliego de las Mujeres)* was presented to the Civil Assembly *(Asamblea de la Civilidad),* which was composed of more than 200 social organizations.[11] This document reaffirmed women's commitment to the restoration of democracy but reiterated the need to actively incorporate women, to end their subordinate position within society, and to link their struggle for emancipation to the nation's struggle for freedom from the dictatorship.

Most of the mobilization against the military regime was urban based. However, in 1986, union women from the rural sector formulated the Rural Women's Demands *(Demanda de la Mujer Rural),* which called on rural women to organize and mobilize for democracy. Five years after its first declaration, the feminist movement outlined the "Women's Demands for Democracy" *(Demandas de las Mujeres a la Democracia),* which demanded the ratification of the UN Convention on the Elimination of all Forms of Discrimination against Women (CEDAW), the creation of an institution with ministerial rank and specialist staff to channel the demands of women and their organizations, to study, propose, and evaluate sectoral policies. The document proposed affirmative action as a tool to eliminate discrimination by allocating 30 percent of government posts to women and imposing a quota of 50 percent for representation in trade unions and political parties.

While the document specifically addressed women in their triple roles as citizens, mothers, and workers, significantly it did not call for divorce legislation or the decriminalization of abortion. This climbdown was due to increasing pressures from the political parties, as it was becoming increasingly likely that General Pinochet would be rejected in a national plebiscite and the democratization process was underway.

The fate of the women's movement in the transition did not depend only on their ability to organize and influence the emerging democracies but also on the larger political process. The transition process in Chile was negotiated between the military and the mainstream political parties. While the presence of female political élites within the women's movement enabled them to incorporate many of their demands into the newly elected government's political program, the negotiated transition also meant that to preserve the unity of the democratic opposition *(Concertación)* and minimize that of the right-wing parties, the most divisive issues, including legislative changes affecting the family—notably divorce and abortion—were sidelined.[12] The bill outlawing domestic violence struggled through parliament for four years of the government of Patricio Aylwin (1989 to 1993) until it was finally passed in a watered-down form in 1994. Despite support from prominent male politicians for legislative change, the political parties have demonstrated reluctance to take up gender as a political issue.

Although women had united as political actors in opposition to the military, their cohesion and identity was precarious and vulnerable to the reopening of factionalism along party lines.[13] Women from the Communist Party and the Movement of the Revolutionary Left (MIR) who had participated in the women's movement were excluded from the Women's Alliance for Democracy *(Concertación de Mujeres por la Democracia),* just as these parties were excluded from participating in the mainstream opposition, the Alliance of Parties for Democracy *(Concertación de los Partidos por la Democracia).* Equally significantly, fissures widened between women along class lines and, in 1988, these divisions were made explicit as different factions formulated demands and proposals for inclusion in the future democracy. Women from the base organizations linked up with political independents and feminists to form the Women's Coordination of Social Organizations *(Coordinación de Organizaciones Sociales de Mujeres),* while party activists, academics, and some independents formed the *Concertación de Mujeres por la Democracia.*

The issue of female representation at all levels—from the popular sector or the middle class, professionals or housewives, in human rights organizations, political parties, nongovernmental organizations—remains problematic. To date, the effort to transfer the voice of the diverse women's groups within the movement to the power structures of the state and the political system has not been successful. After International Women's Day in 1989, many of the women's organizations disbanded or simply ran out of steam as the democratization process became increasingly focused on formal party politics.

The fate of the social movements, and of the women's movement in particular, in the Chilean transition has led many to question the nature of these movements, how they are inserted into the political process, and their future under democracy. The diversity and heterogeneity of the women's movement makes it difficult to analyze, and some have even come to question its very existence. Adriana Muñoz has opted instead for "women in movement," a term which accurately conveys the dynamic nature of the organizations involved, their diverse objectives and forms of action.[14] However, it also suggests that the movement was not a cohesive social force, capable of effecting lasting changes. While diversity may give voice to a broad spectrum of women with widely different experiences and demands, unity is more prized in political practice. Citizens, faced with the increasingly complex task of deciphering a barrage of information from the media, prefer political parties to present a united front and a coherent party line. This approach is likely to result in little debate, narrow policies, and simplistic solutions; worse, it obscures the complex origins and manifestations of gender inequalities.

The women's movement in Chile is autonomous and, in most instances, it has no formal links with political parties. Like all social movements, however, it does not operate in a void; many women have allegiances and interests in both camps and are active in both formal and movement politics *(doble militancia)*. Moreover, specific women's organizations within the movement may be directly or indirectly connected to the political system. During the transitions to democracy, fear of co-option placed great emphasis on the movement's need to retain autonomy. However, in political systems which are characterized by the power of formal institutions, autonomy can be a double-edged sword. On the one hand it can provide a space for women to debate, analyze, and elaborate strategies without becoming co-opted or ghettoized into a women's section of the political parties. On the other, it can also result in isolation, if the women's movement becomes marginalized from mainstream political debate. This is an increasing danger in the post-transition democracies, as the hegemony of the political parties is fully restored. More than ever, therefore, it is imperative that female representation in parliament be increased. It falls to those women with *doble militancia* in the movement and the political parties to campaign for women's concerns and to push for the inclusion of gender issues into government and party policy.

Moreover, there may have been unreal expectations of the transition period for many social groups. The fixation on removing the military and the emphasis on democracy from a technical perspective—the mechanics of government, establishing channels of communication and institutions—meant that insufficient attention was paid to the substance of the political system they hoped to create. There were hopes that the new democracy *per se* would facilitate equality of opportunity, representation, and participation in which a wide range of social actors could be involved, and this expectation clearly has not been realized. In this regard, it is necessary to distinguish between the processes of social democratization and political democratization vis à vis women's role in the transition.[15] While social democratization refers to the ability of the women's movement to form a pressure group within the transition process, political democratization implies the creation of institutional spaces which could incorporate gender into state policy. The transition challenged women to question their role as political subjects, no longer in unified opposition to the military, but in terms of constructing a political program which encompassed diversity on the basis of social class and individual life experience and unity on gender-specific issues.

The greater challenge, particularly for women in the political parties *(políticas)* and feminists *(feministas)* was to exploit the shifting political opportunities before the patriarchal state once again normalized gender rela-tions. It is by now widely accepted that "women" cannot be defined as a social and political category. Instead, gender acts as a filter along with race, class, education, age, and employment to break down social categories into diverse sectors with their specific interests. If we accept that women (like men) do not form a homogenous group, this raises the question whether they can organize and participate politically as *women,* on similar terms as other interest groups such as business, workers, or the military. Despite their diversity, women do have certain gender-specific interests which vary according to culture and time. Democratic politics are conducted through representation of interests, bargain-ing, and negotiation yet, if women are to organize as a social sector with specific interests, what would be their bargaining power? Unlike the business sector, they cannot threaten to take investment elsewhere; unlike the trade unions, they cannot strike; unlike the military, they cannot threaten a coup. Women's capacity to pressure the state and influence the decision-making process as a unified social group became limited once the critical need for their support in the transition had passed.

The transition to democracy in Chile emphasized the re-establishment of institutional democracy over the processes of social democratization. Conse-quently the women's movement, which had played a central role in the opposition to the Pinochet dictatorship, found its role as an autonomous pressure group circumscribed. They sought to construct a political program around gender-specific issues which could encompass the social diversity of the movement at the same time as political élites deemed it necessary to contract civil society in order to consolidate democracy. The dynamic of the transition emphasized the return to institutional politics and consensus on the political and economic models rather than debate. The very mechanisms which had contributed to ending support for the dictatorship could easily lead to civil unrest if not demobilized. The memories of women's destabilizing role in the later years of the Allende government continued to weigh heavily as the opposition became the government and their enthusiasm for social movements, alternative grassroots politics, and popular mobilization quickly evaporated.

As the transition progressed, the business of "doing politics" shifted from the social movements, and these became increasingly associated with protest and single-issue politics. They were assigned a limited role in the emerging civil society and instead, the locus of political activity has once more returned to the political parties. The élites within the women's movement perceived clearly that their access to political power was contingent on abandoning the movement for the political parties and the state. It could be argued that by doing so, they became less representative of women. Furthermore, by entering formal politics they may have limited their ability to criticize, to lobby, to constitute a relatively autonomous political force. Conversely, they are now better placed to influence political outcomes and promote political, economic, and social changes which can benefit women.

FROM MOVEMENT TO STATE INSTITUTION

Several Latin American countries, including Chile, Paraguay, Uruguay, Costa Rica, Peru, Argentina, and Venezuela, have established state institutions to plan and implement specific policies affecting women. These institutions seek first to improve the condition of women in society by addressing practical gender needs, such as women's access to employment, housing, education or credit, and second to improve the relative position of women in society by addressing strategic gender needs, such as eliminating institutional forms of discrimination, alleviating women's responsibility for the home and childcare, and ending the sexual division of labor.[16] Certain sectors of the women's movement (party activists, academics, professionals, women in nongovernmental organizations) successfully breached the gap between the noninstitutional politics of the social movements and the formal political process. They demanded that women be incorporated into the process of political, economic, and social participation, and that policies for women should complement public policy on national development. They proposed that appropriate mechanisms should be created to coordinate and plan policy at national, regional, and local levels. They considered that while women should not be ghettoized into a separate unit, gender issues could not be left to the individual institutions and departments for whom gender planning was not a priority.

Despite opposition from right-wing parties in parliament, the *Servicio Nacional de la Mujer* (SERNAM), outlined by the *Concertación de Mujeres por la Democracia* in the Women's Program *(Programa de la Mujer),* was created on January 3, 1991. SERNAM attempted to adopt a coherent and integral approach to policy-making in order to redress gender inequalities, looking at employment, legislation, education, housing, and health with the aim to promote long-term social change in attitudes and behavior. SERNAM was composed of approximately 300 women who had been active in NGOs and social movements working on women's issues during the dictatorship, who pooled their experience and analysis of the pertinent issues.[17]

Since it has nonministerial status, SERNAM cannot implement its own policies or programs, but can propose measures to various ministries which may be accepted or rejected. While this has allowed SERNAM to approach the structural factors which discriminate against women in an integrated, multisectoral manner, its disadvantages in terms of lack of institutional muscle resulted in limited success.[18] In its first four years of operation, SERNAM implemented short-term programs which may have been positive developments in themselves, but which remained marginal to national policy. It was less successful in developing a long-term strategy to hold the ministries to greater accountability on their incorporation of gender perspectives into the political process.

SERNAM's programs targeted violence against women, women's rights, childcare provision for women in paid employment, and affirmative action to encourage women to enter nontraditional fields of employment. They sought to address the complex causes of social and economic disadvantage for female heads of households. These measures challenged the patriarchal structures of the Chilean state, society, and the judicial system. Not surprisingly, they have met with considerable opposition from politically and socially conservative sectors of society, such as certain elements in the Christian Democrats, and the right-wing parties, and the Catholic church, with the result that key areas affecting women including divorce and abortion were not addressed, and sexual violence was excluded from the bill on domestic violence proposed by members of parliament. Although abortion is illegal, it is estimated that there is at least one abortion for every three live births, and that abortion accounts for a quarter of all maternal deaths.[19] The laws on rape have not been amended and it continues to be an offense, not against the woman, but against the family and public morality. While democracy will not crumble if divorce legislation is introduced or women can terminate pregnancies legally, these issues expose

93

the hidden social and political structures of power in Chilean society, revealing areas of conflict between political parties within the Alliance—between Church and State, the government and the people. There has been no debate on divorce and abortion within SERNAM, nor has the organization attempted to bring the issues into the public arena.

These issues, perhaps more than any others, link the personal and the political. Many of the women in key positions in the SERNAM have close links with the political class, either as party activists or through family ties. Hence for them to declare their personal views on issues which are still political dynamite in Chile could be highly prejudicial for their own political future, as well as that of their families. In its politicization of the private sphere, SERNAM has not been exempt from political maneuvring and pressure from the church and right-wing forces.[20] As a state institution, SERNAM must be seen to agree with government policy, and it has therefore effectively self-censored internal debate on vital issues which affect women. Except for the director of the SERNAM who had ministerial status, women were entirely excluded from the executive branch of government. They represented only 5.8 percent of deputies and 6.4 percent of senators, and they continued to have low levels of representation within the political parties. Controversial issues affecting women risk being sidelined unless they are taken up by the political parties and included in the government's program. Male politicians have initiated bills and supported legislation benefiting women—the most prominent example is the bill on domestic violence—but in general, it is left to female politicians to raise gender-specific issues in parliament. While simply having more women in politics does not guarantee progressive policy-making, increased female representation particularly in the center and center-left parties is essential to put women's issues firmly on the agenda. The lack of female representation in national politics is likely to hinder change for many years to come.

Among feminists and academics in Latin America and elsewhere, there was particular optimism that women's experience in the social movements might significantly alter the political arena as the new democracy became consolidated. In particular, there were expectations that women might do politics differently from men and that this difference could be incorporated into the new democracy. Despite such hopes, SERNAM proved to be no exception to the rule of appointments by party quota; a cursory glance at the political sympathies of those in the top jobs indicates that the distribution bears more than a passing resemblance to the distribution of power within the coalition. SERNAM has rapidly distanced itself from the women's movement and the

94

proposals which it had elaborated and neither of the two directors to date have had any links with the women's movement.

During the dictatorship, women mobilized in defense of their traditional roles through the popular economic organizations and protested against the economic crises. These actions brought pressure on the state or were self-help initiatives to alleviate poverty. Women mobilized around practical gender interests which, through organization, became transformed to encompass strategic interests also. This form of organization has not disappeared since the return to democracy, but the state has resumed welfare provision to some degree.

SERNAM's actions have focused on income generation, poverty alleviation, and groups within the female population which have been identified as particularly vulnerable, such as female headed households. Such actions support paternalistic state welfare policy, which has a long tradition in Chile, rather than gender policy to promote social change. A commitment to focus on low-income women is likely to advance short-term practical gender interests which improve their material conditions and quality of life. Yet this may be at the expense of long-term strategic gender interests which promote women's emancipation. SERNAM's interventions in defense of motherhood and women's traditional role in the family have done little to end poverty for poor women and their families, yet they have effectively depoliticized women's organization to meet practical gender needs. SERNAM's inability to foster links with popular women's organizations at the base level has meant that women are not being empowered by pressuring the state. Instead, they have become passive recipients with minimal input to the services provided for them.

As a result of the military's intervention in the universities, alternative academic research centers mushroomed during the dictatorship and played a key role in civil society which emerged in opposition to the dictatorship. Many of the women now involved in the political parties or in the SERNAM were also involved in NGOs and academic research into women's issues during the dictatorship. Despite the reduction in foreign aid after the return to democracy, in 1991 there were fifteen research-NGOs specializing in women and gender issues, and twenty-nine research-NGOs with a women's program.[21] Much of the economic assistance from foreign governments now goes directly to the government and is then channeled to the NGOs via contracts for services. The NGOs' loss of financial independence and new relationship with the state as a provider of services has meant a reduction in their autonomy and critical perspective on state practice. This does not mean that the NGOs are uncritical of SERNAM's performance, but the research is commissioned by SERNAM and as such will reflect the biases of the institution. The limited pool of NGOs specializing in women has led to a lack of competition for contracts between the NGO sector and the state. SERNAM has tended to use those organizations which are tried and tested and, in some cases, has even permanently transferred certain functions to external personnel, resulting in a form of subcontracting: for example, training in gender planning for civil servants has gone to the University of Chile.

The close levels of collaboration between a select number of NGOs, university departments, and SERNAM has produced a form of insider trading. Since the same NGOs have collaborated with SERNAM in designing, implementing, and evaluating programs and research, they have knowledge of the criteria by which SERNAM judges applications for future contracts and are therefore in an advantageous position over outsiders. An example is the Equal Opportunities Plan, commissioned by SERNAM and elaborated by an external consultant.[22] Despite its claim to respond to the women's proposals and demands, drawing on the experience and knowledge of different sectors of society and institutions, the Plan was based on input from women in the political parties and women in SERNAM, active in the political parties which make up the Alliance. The women's organizations and social organizations were not consulted.

The return to democracy profoundly altered the political expectations of international donors and their policies on funding NGO activities have changed accordingly. Their aim is no longer to foster opposition, but to promote political stability. New criteria for granting funding and evaluating the projects places less emphasis on social benefits such as autonomy and empowerment, and more on market values such as efficiency, targets, and quantifiable results. The NGOs which survived the transition have undergone a process of "professionalization," and working class women who staffed them have been replaced by "experts," who are often closely linked to the political parties. Radio Tierra is an all-women feminist radio station linked to the NGO Casa de la Mujer "La Morada." The project is funded from overseas donors, originally contingent on there being a cohort of twenty women in the shantytowns to cover issues of concern to working class women. However, interviews with women who participated in this project reveal frustration and humiliation over marked differences in the treatment given to the popular correspondents (*correspon-sales populares*) and the professional journalists. The *pobladoras* were not given payment for their work, and received only basic expenses for bus fares and batteries for tape recorders. Their time was deemed to be an elastic resource which had no market value, in contrast with the "journalists" who did the same work for full pay at market rates. The lack of solidarity between working and middle class women, combined with the radio's desire to professionalize and market itself to attract advertizing revenue, gradually squeezed the *pobladoras* out. One woman said she feared losing "the space which is mine by right."[23] The experience of the Casa Sofía, a center for *mujeres pobladoras* in the periphery of Santiago, was similar. Originally run by nuns in conjunction with the women themselves, the center was taken over by La Morada with a new team of young, paid professionals, in contrast to the *pobladoras* who were mainly middle-aged volunteers. One woman who had been involved in both the Casa Sofía and the Radio Tierra commented, "The professionals have taken over the space which we had achieved for ourselves."[24]

CONCLUSIONS

Any analysis of the relationship between social movements and the state needs to be located within the specific political and historical context. The women's movement played an important role in the opposition movement but their gender-specific demands were only a part of the global demand for democracy. The objective of ending the dictatorship temporarily obscured fundamental divisions within the movement based on social class, political ideology and different approaches to feminism. The transition process fragmented the women's movement and challenged political identities which had been forged in unified opposition to the military. The future of the women's movement really only became an issue once democracy was clearly returning; then the questions about autonomy, integration, class differences, and relationship with the state and the political parties were raised.

The women's movement in the 1980s was not simply campaigning on behalf of women—it was an expression of political opposition, and therefore was associated with the center and the left. Research conducted in the early 1990s into women's political allegiances and voting behavior indicates that 47.5 percent of women ideologically identify themselves with the center and 22.8 percent with the right; only 17.3 percent identified themselves with the left.[25] The transition to democracy marked the end of a particular stage in the movement's life cycle.

The democracies that have emerged in the postmilitary period are restricted versions of liberal democracy, in which stability is valued over social transformation and consensus is valued over debate. While the transition to democracy saw the politicization of gender, the period of consolidation in Chile has witnessed a curious gendering of politics. The consensus between the renovated left, the center, and the right on the benefits of democracy as a political model and of the free market economic model have left few distinctions around which to conduct political debate. The debates have shifted to the family, morality, divorce, legislation on domestic violence. However, the ways in which the issues are treated has been largely determined by the male-dominated parliament (94 percent).[26] In this sense, the fate of gender politics will be affected by the actions of women within the state (SERNAM and other ministries) and by civil society (the ability for women to lobby through the political parties and the women's movement).

If we assume that improving the access of marginalized groups to the political institutions is an essential part of democracy, some form of incentive must be available. The institutions must consider that the participation and representation of marginalized groups (in this case, women) constitutes a key part of democratic practice. Women must also believe that their input will influence the political outcome, and that their representatives will indeed represent their interests. However, the reality of representative liberal democracy in Latin America is that the political parties do not represent the diverse interests of the electorate but serve the interests of the political and economic élites. The marginalized groups (the urban poor, the peasantry, women, indigenous peoples, youth) may organize through the social movements, but in a system based on competition between political parties they remain essentially isolated from political power and the decision-making process.

In national and local elections in Chile, political disaffection is most clearly marked by age. Young people are the group most disenchanted with democracy and have the lowest levels of voting. In surveys, women claim less interest than men in politics, yet they consistently demonstrate higher levels of voting than men. Women are actively involved in political parties; on the right, female membership exceeds male. They continue to be actively involved in diverse social organizations and politics at the municipal level. The historical context of transition politics may explain why in Chile many women were able to transfer from movement politics to the state. When the opposition became the government they simply flowed with the tide. Does this suggest that women in a sociopolitical movement have succeeded in subverting gender barriers and gained entry into political institutions? The Chilean case suggests that female élites did indeed overcome the gender barriers and use the social movements to gain entry into the political parties and the state. The more lasting barriers to institutional politics therefore may be based not on gender, but on social class.

In Chile, therefore, the issue is not so much political participation as representation. Women's voices in all their diversity are missing from a wide range of political debates, not only on gender issues. Compared to the levels of female mobilization during the military regime, the circle has narrowed considerably, leaving working class women and the popular organizations on the periphery of the political debate. The focus has shifted to the female political class who are present in the political parties, the government, and state institutions, and are supported by the women's academic network. Certain sectors of the women's movement have thus become institutionalized, thereby gaining greater access to political power. While these women are now well positioned to act on behalf of others, they have failed to maintain the essential links with the women's movement and the popular women's organizations, and as a result are less representative. We may see the emergence of a false consensus, based on political self-interest. The democratic ideals pursued by the women's movement during the 1980s may have far exceeded the reality of the 1990s.

NOTES

1. Although I refer to "democratization" and the "consolidation of democracy," I consider that the political systems which emerged after military rule have been restricted forms of liberal democracy. The political process in Chile was determined to a significant degree by the "binding laws" laid down by the military before handing power over to civilian rule, and by the 1980 Constitution.
2. Felicitas Klimpel, *La mujer chilena (El aporte femenino al pogreso de Chile) 1910-1960* (Santiago: Editorial Andrés Bello, 1962); Teresa Valdés and Soledad Weinstein, *Mujeres que sueñan: Las organizaciones de pobladoras en Chile* (Santiago: FLACSO, 1994); Diamela Eltit, *Crónica del sufragio femenino en Chile* (Santiago: SERNAM, 1994).
3. *Mujeres Latinoamericanas en Cifras* (Santiago and Madrid: FLACSO/Instituto de la Mujer, Ministerio de Asuntos Sociales de España, 1992).
4. This is not to suggest that all men benefit from liberal democracy in the same way; indeed, citizen equality is meaningless if class-based interests are not represented. Carole Pateman, *The Disorder of Women* (Cambridge: Polity Press, 1989); Anne Phillips, *Engendering Democracy* (Cambridge: Polity Press, 1991).
5. Jane Jaquette, *The Women's Movement in Latin America: Feminism in the Transition to Democracy,* (Boston & London: Unwin Hyman, 1989); *Transiciones: Mujeres en los procesos democráticos* (Santiago: ISIS International Ediciones de Mujeres, No. 13, 1990); Valdés and Weinstein, *Mujeres que sueñan.*
6. "Documento Síntesis Segundo Encuentro de Mujeres Feministas de Sectores Populares," 29 December 1992, Casa de la Mujer "La Morada" (Santiago: unpublished).
7. Interview with a *pobladora* involved in the feminist radio station Radio Tierra and the women's center Casa Sofía.
8. Jaquette, *The Women's Movement in Latin America.*
9. "Manifiesto feminista: demandas a la democracia," Movimiento Feminista, December 1983. Reproduced in Edda Gaviola, Eliana Largo, and Sandra Palestro,

99

Una historia necesaria. Mujeres en Chile: 1973-1990 (Santiago: Akí y Aora Ltda., 1994).

10. "Principios y reivindicaciones que configuran la plataforma de la mujer chilena," Coordinadora de Organizaciones Femininas MEMCH '83, 1985. Reproduced in Gaviola, Largo, Palestro, eds., *Una historia necesaria.*

11. Reproduced in ibid., and in Jaquette, *Transiciones: mujeres en los procesos democraticos.*

12. Ann Matear, "The Servicio Nacional de la Mujer (SERNAM): Women and the Process of Democratic Transition in Chile, 1990-93," in David Hojman, ed., *Neoliberalism with a Human Face? The Politics and Economics of the Chilean Model* (Liverpool: University of Liverpool Monograph Series, 1995), pp. 93-117.

13. This was apparent among other social movements as well. See Adriana Muñoz D'Albora, "El movimiento de mujeres en Chile: una realidad deseada" (Santiago: unpublished, 1986).

14. Ibid.

15. Natacha Molina, Lilian Mires, and María Elena Valenzuela, *Cambio social, transición y políticas públicas hacia la mujer* (Santiago: Instituto de la Mujer, 1989).

16. Caroline Moser, *Gender Planning and Development: Theory, Practice and Training,* (London: Routledge, 1994); Kate Young, "Reflexiones sobre cómo enfrentar las necesidades de las mujeres," *Una nueva lectura: Género en el desarrollo* (Lima: Centro Flora Tristán, 1991).

17. After the elections, many of the women who had participated in the Women's Program went on to collaborate in the Political Working Group (*Grupo de Trabajo Político*) within the Aylwin government, headed by Soledad Larraín, who was to become SERNAM's subdirector.

18. Matear, "The Servicio Nacional de la Mujer."

19. Mariano Requena, "Aborto inducido en Chile, 1990," (Santiago: Sociedad Chilena de Salud Pública, 1990). Therapeutic abortion, if the mother's health was threatened, was legally available in Chile until 1989, but this law was revoked by the military government before they left power.

20. This vulnerability became apparent with the removal of Soledad Larraín as subdirector of SERNAM, following public disagreement with a senior church figure in 1992.

21. *Mujeres latinoamericanas en cifras.*

22. Rosalba Todaro, from the Centro de Estudios de la Mujer.

23. Interview with a *pobladora* who was head of her Neighborhood Association, local leader of the Partido por la Democracia, and *corresponsal popular* for Radio Tierra.

24. Interview with a *pobladora* previously active in Casa Sofia women's center and Radio Tierra.

25. Marta Lagos & Ema Lagos, *Estudios y encuestas: Mujeres chilenas 1992* (Santiago: Centro de Estudios de la Realidad Contemporánea, 1992).

26. *Mujeres latinoamericanas en cifras.*

THE HOLY FAMILY: IMAGINED HOUSEHOLDS IN LATIN AMERICAN HISTORY

ELIZABETH DORE

As we totter toward the millennium, conservative crusaders across the globe decry the breakdown of the traditional family. Their apocalyptic pronouncements about a rising tide of female- headed households that is undermining society as we know it contain great truths, yet greater falsehoods. The truth is that the gendered social order is changing in many parts of the world. The falsehood is that this alteration is rooted in a breakdown of the traditional family. Rupture of "the traditional family" is greatly exaggerated; in many societies such a family is more ideological than historical.

Throughout the world, traditionalists have embarked on an ideological battle to roll back the gender revolution.[1] This backlash has united around two articles of faith: first, male-headed households have been universal and transhistorical; second, the patriarchal family is the centerpiece of social stability. I call this the myth of the traditional family. Like most myths it is a simple moral tale woven out of half-truths and dominant ideologies. It tells a story of how people should live, not the history of how they did live. The myth of the traditional family was, until recently, a central tenet of popular—as well as academic—history in Latin America. Historians believed that the patriarchal family, in which a senior male controls and protects everyone in his household, male and female, has been virtually universal. This patriarchal family became a paradigm which transcended boundaries of time, space, class, and race.[2]

In the 1980s, sociologists discovered a high proportion of female-headed households in Latin America. With the prevailing stereotype of the family, they concluded that such households were a new phenomena. This research attracted the attention of politicians searching for a simple explanation of crime and poverty. As in the United States and Europe, Latin American policymakers cast the blame for an array of social ills on female-headed households, stigmatized as "nontraditional."

Female-headed households in Latin America are not nontraditional—in the sense of being historically rare. While male-headed households generally were more numerous, they were far from universal. In many areas and social strata, female-headed households were the norm. In the last twenty years historians of the Latin American family have discovered that female-headed households were common, particularly since the early nineteenth century. This produced a shift in paradigm, but a quiet one. With family history relegated to a subordinate status within the academy, these major discoveries largely have been overlooked by the historical mainstream. Instead of sparking widespread debate over what the new family history means for our understanding of political and economic change, household studies have been shrugged off as having relevance only to some private world of the family. And if historians have been slow in grasping the importance of the new Latin American family history, policymakers have ignored it. Its discoveries are threatening; they subvert the cosy picture of a natural family type.

The intention of this chapter is to debunk the myth of the traditional patriarchal family. It analyzes patriarchalism in nineteenth-century Latin America in elite discourse, in law and in family headship. I argue that dominant currents in religious and political thought institutionalized and universalized the patriarchal family. But for many people in all social strata life did not conform to this ideal. For the purposes of this analysis the patriarchal household is defined by one aspect—headship. I assume that for a household to qualify as patriarchal, whatever else it is, it must be male-headed. Male headship is not the only characteristic of the patriarchal family, but I take it to be the indispensable condition. The argument applies to Latin America as a whole, and is supported by evidence throughout the region.

102

Within this general framework the case of Nicaragua is examined in more detail, as it is the focus of my research on historical transformations in class and gender, and of E. Bradford Burns's *Patriarch and Folk: The Emergence of Nicaragua 1789-1858,* an insightful analysis of elite patriarchal discourses.[3]

For analytic purposes, the chapter treats only the nineteenth century. Practically, there is more abundant information on headship and discourse for the nineteenth century than for previous periods. Strategically, I feel compelled to check any temptation to replace one totalizing paradigm with another. The discovery that male-headed households were not a characteristic feature of the nineteenth century does not mean the same is true of other periods. Analytically, the nineteenth century is particularly pivotal in family history, as it is seen as embracing a transition from patriarchalism to liberalism—and from "feudalism" to capitalism—with implications for rights, duties, and patterns of authority within households.[4]

The argument is developed in four parts. Part I analyzes changing paradigms in gender history, with a focus on the Latin American family, and defines key terms. Part II draws on case studies to shed light on the ideological representation of patriarchy in nineteenth-century Latin America. Part III analyzes the patriarchal nature of Latin American law in the same period. Drawing from recent literature on family history, Part IV argues that family arrangements in the nineteenth century diverged significantly from the model of classic patriarchy set out in elite discourse and the law and draws out the relevance of the shift in paradigm for historical and contemporary analysis.

I. GENDER, FAMILY, AND HISTORY

There are significant differences between Women's History and a Gender History. Gender history begins with the hypothesis that the ways in which societies perceive and reproduce sexual difference are the result of social processes, not biology. Therefore gender history examines the way in which social institutions that usually are considered political or economic, such as taxes, property law, and labor systems, materially and ideologically reproduce power relations that are gendered. Gender history does not—or should not—constitute a separate field about women and the family. Until recently, many historians classified gender history as a sub-field that was "just" about women. As it was about the half of the population that had little power and visibility, the profession fenced off gender history from the big concerns of economic and political change. For the most part, feminist historians went along with this, content that the history of women and "her" spheres at last was accepted as a legitimate research field. This approach institutionalized gender history as a separate field that was about "private" spheres as opposed to the "public" arena. That view has changed.

Theorizing gender was crucial to broadening the field of enquiry. While the chronology of debates over gender theory was not linear, originally "gender" was taken to be a synonym for women, used to display some kind of political correctness, or conversely, to eschew the militancy associated with the terms *women's studies* or *feminist studies*. As gender studies developed, so did the recognition of the transformative potential of gender theory. By the middle 1980s, there was a consensus that gender is a social category; sex a biological one. Like class, gender is, among other things, a political and economic relation.[5]

Within this broad agreement, debate continued over the interrelationship between gender and sex; specifically over how much nature (mostly women's reproductive capacity) has influenced meanings and practices associated with womanhood and manhood in different periods, classes, races, and so on. Recently, the biological determinism of sex has been challenged, which erodes the sex/gender divide that had been a mainstay of gender theory.[6] The idea that gender is a social category makes the study of politics and power central to research in the field. Feminist theorists questioned the validity of a binary divide between private and public spheres, a notion that once underpinned much work on gender (see Cubitt and Greenslade in this volume). Historians documented the extent to which what appeared to be private, such as the family, sexuality, even the body, was a product of state and church policy, and therefore was public. The indivisibility of public-private domains was emphasized more than their separation.[7] The critique of a divide between public and private domains marked a watershed in the evolution of gender studies; one that more or less coincided with Joan Scott's call for feminists to examine how the category of gender (not the category women) alters political, economic, and social analysis.[8]

By the 1990s there was a new consensus that dictated a new research agenda: the consensus was on the importance of gender in the constitution of political power; the research agenda examined the myriad ways that societies reinforce and undermine attitudes and practices regarding sexual difference. In summary, gender history evolved in important ways. When it began as "women's history" its objective was to make women visible.[9] Ten years later, no longer focused on fitting women into history, it was about why conventional approaches to history did not fit women's past.[10] At the turn of the millennium, gender history is still about these things, but they are subsumed within a broader framework which focuses on how state building, class exploitation, and racial oppression construct power relations that are gendered.[11]

The theoretical shift refocused family history. It exposed the stereotype of the family as a natural and private institution, and emphasized interrelationships between social policy, economic systems, and family patterns. Until the late 1970s, Latin American historians paid little attention to family headship because it was taken to be self-evident that the family was a patriarchal domain. Questions about the timing of the change from extended to nuclear families, about households' political and economic roles, and about gendered power relations in the interior of the family were studied, but not headship.[12] The male-headed household was represented as transhistorical, cross cultural, and characteristic of all classes.

This conceptualization of patriarchy was hardly unique to Latin America. Scholarship on the family, almost regardless of region, traditionally emphasized the universality of the male-headed domestic group.[13] More recently, however, studies from different continents have suggested that family forms varied more widely than previously imagined, in particular that male-headed households were not as prevalent as once believed.[14] The lesson to be drawn from these shifts in academic thought is not to dismiss classic patriarchy as fiction, but to investigate disjunctures among patriarchy as ideal type, patriarchy as law, and patriarchy as household practice.

Before proceeding, some key words require clarification. The first is patriarchy, a term that has been used in many contexts and has a myriad of definitions. For the purposes of this chapter I use the term in its orthodox historical-anthropological sense, as a particular family/household type in which the senior male controls and protects everyone in the household—male and female. This coincides with its discursive and legal meanings in nineteenth-century Latin America. To assess the historical prevalence of this prototype I reduce it to its essential element: headship.

Two additional terms requiring definition are family and household. The first refers to kin groups constituted by blood and/or marriage; the second to residence units. As my inquiry centers on the incidence of female- and male-headed living arrangements, I am more concerned with residence than kinship.

II. THE DISCURSIVE REPRESENTATION OF PATRIARCHY

Colonial Latin America was organized as a hierarchical assemblage of corporate bodies, which included the state, church, army, merchant guilds, and Indian communities. Many scholars argue that in the prolonged interim between the disintegration of this corporate structure and the maturation of a civil society composed of heterogeneous individuals, society's basic social unit was the patriarchal family. Certainly in the eyes of the law and the state the patriarch represented the entire family. Nineteenth-century Latin America was a world in which, for the most part, only men with property or a profession were citizens of the nation, with rights to participate in formal politics. However, all male household heads (with the exception of slaves) exercized legal authority over their wives and children, and represented family members in the public domain. For practical and ideological purposes, the new nation-states were hierarchies of patriarchs, a few of whom had extensive political and economic powers, while most had little authority outside the bounds of their homes.

In that era of political upheaval, with its shift from monarchical to republican rule, Latin American leaders justified their exercize of power by appealing to the traditional authority of the family head. In the process of nation-building, elite discourses conceptualized the nation as a family ruled by a supreme patriarch. Like all male householders, he had the obligation to control his children. Fruto Chamorro, one of Nicaragua's early presidents, clearly articulated this patriarchal philosophy; he defined his presidential role in the framework of patriarchal duties. Chamorro likened himself to the good father and husband, obliged to rule over the nation in the same way as the patriarch ruled his household. Nicaraguans were "his children," to whom he had to be strict and benevolent, from whom he expected obedience and respect.[15] Nicaragua's leaders inculcated the idea that upholding patriarchal authority could preserve the social order.[16] In 1851 an anonymous pamphlet circulated in León, addressed to the city's youth. It reminded young men and women that a father's "will is law in domestic society" and warned that "public order rests on the respect due the father and on the subsequent peace and tranquillity of the family."[17]

The historical context sheds light on why what otherwise might have been seen as a relatively mild challenge to the established order was considered highly subversive. This marriage of patriarchy and social order occurred soon after the political system was threatened from below, as rural rebellion swept the country from 1845 to 1849. Peasants and Indians looted and burned haciendas, killing members of the political elite.[18] This may explain why public appeals to the authority of the father figure were extreme in form, even when they addressed such issues as the disobedience of the children of the elite. Nicaraguan leaders articulated their worst fear: that popular respect for the nation's patriarchs was shattered.

When peasants were challenging the authority of their patrons, and children the prerogatives of their fathers, domestic patriarchy was in decline.[19] Large numbers of people cohabited outside of marriage and many households were headed by women.[20] With the society and polity in disarray, civil and religious leaders beseeched their flock to respect the patriarchal order. In 1846 Father Agustín Vijil, curate of Granada, sounded the alarm. Writing in the year that Indians of his parish were tearing down fences to defend communal rights to land, Vijil declared that "only marriage can preserve society." He reminded Nicaraguans that the patriarchs were the bulwarks of a peaceful society, and warned that only by upholding their authority would the chaos subside.[21]

That Vijil and his ilk should worry about marriage and parental permission in the midst of peasant insurrection might seem bizarre. Yet to them, disregard for the institutions of patriarchy represented a fundamental challenge to the established order. The state, the church, the courts all rested on the legal and moral authority of the patriarchs. In addition, the patriarchs, in their public and private personas, were responsible for enforcing the laws of the land. It is much more bizarre that present-day social analysts, such as Charles Murray in the United States and Peter Lilley in Britain, uphold a belief system grounded in nineteenth-century patriarchalism. Unlike Fruto Chamorro and Father Vijil, Murray and Lilley have little legal or material basis for their ideology. Nevertheless, they both think that modern-day insurrections, in the form of crime, drugs, and urban riots, are caused by a decline in patriarchy.[22]

Bradford Burns proposes that the depth of patriarchal politics in Nicaragua may reflect the country's chronic instability. Its elite failed to convince the population to accept the legitimacy of its rule through peaceful means, and lacked the repressive apparatus to impose its rule through force. Therefore, he argues, its political leaders had no alternative but to confide in the power of patriarchal authority to preserve order. While it is true that the Nicaraguan oligarchy experienced great difficulties in imposing some sort of collective elite rule, its appeal to the traditional authority of the father figure to justify state power was no more extreme than in other countries, but was merely a variant of the political discourse that prevailed throughout Latin America in the nineteenth century. In Argentina, struggling to forge nationhood in the first half of the nineteenth century but vastly different from Nicaragua, there was also a strong link between domestic and political or "public patriarchy." As in Nicaragua, Argentine's political institutions were weak or absent, and patriarchy embodied the principle of collective authority. Politicians' legitimacy and relations of civil society were constructed along patriarchal or familial lines and articulated as a relation between the "domestic" and the "political" estates. Argentinians fought over the contours of the emerging nation. Yet within discord there was consensus, among elite politicians and between elites and plebes, that patriarchy underpinned social stability, however elusive that stability might be.[23]

Patriarchal rhetoric echoed throughout Latin America. Over the course of the nineteenth century, political and familial discourses about stability, patriarchy, and nation-building were intertwined. The political elites generally took it for granted that families were patriarchal, which meant, at a minimum, male-headed. In their appeals to the authority of the father-figure, public and domestic, rarely did they acknowledge that many people did not, in fact, live in households that included an adult male. Elite discourse about patriarchy hid the reality that patriarchalism was not a seamless system which integrated all households within the nation. That society was patriarchal there is little doubt; that it rested on a universe of male family heads is a myth.

III. THE LAWS OF PATRIARCHY

Patriarchy was not simply some discursive invention, but was the law of the land throughout Latin America in the nineteenth century. Patriarchal authority was a central tenet of the Spanish colonial legal system and of the civil codes enacted by the newly independent countries. Wide-ranging legal powers of the father figure—the father-husband-patron trinity—remained intact until the Liberal reforms of mid-century, and in the main survived well into the twentieth century. The centerpiece of patriarchal law was *patria potestad*—power of the father. With extensive authority over his wife, children, and dependents, the patriarch was the state's representative within the household. In law, society was governed at its most basic level by male family heads.[24] For 400 years Hispanic patriarchal law changed little; *patria potestad* was a central element of Spanish legal doctrine since the fifteenth century.[25] But as Patricia Seed and others show, there were great temporal changes in how patriarchal laws were interpreted. Also, enforcement varied dramatically in different class, ethnic, and national contexts. As a consequence, family practices were not static.

Patria potestad legally bound sons and daughters to obey their father and wives their husband. The father/husband was both guardian and legal representative of every member of the household; only he was empowered to enter into contracts and control property. Unmarried children remained subordinated to paternal authority throughout their father's life, unless he specifically "emancipated" them—granted them independence. If a child, even as an adult, disobeyed her/his father, the latter could call upon the state to enforce his authority. Failure to obey one's father or husband could, in extreme circumstances, result in imprisonment. Marriage, or a father's death, liberated adult sons and daughters from paternal control. Yet for daughters marriage brought little freedom, as it transferred guardianship from father to husband.

The justification for women's juridical subordination to men was that females were inferior to and weaker than males, hence they needed to be protected by them. In law protection took the form of restricting married women's rights and codifying male authority. Legally, wives were treated like children. This was spelled out in the preamble to Nicaragua's civil code of 1867, which explained that wives "like minors were obliged to submit to the tutelage of their husbands."[26] Married women's rights were limited, as were those of criminals and the insane. If a woman brought property to a marriage she continued to own it, but she had to relinquish control to her spouse. Wives, however, had legal channels for the redress of abuses. Should her spouse mismanage her affairs, she could ask a judge to withdraw his authority over her property, and request appointment of another man to administer her affairs.

If in life Hispanic property law perpetuated gender oppression, in death it was virtually sex-neutral.[27] A widow could control her property. If acquired during her marriage, it was jointly owned and divided equally upon the death of either spouse. In general, half passed to the survivor, the other half was distributed in equal shares among all the deceased's legitimate children, regardless of sex or order of birth. A widow acquired the same rights as men to administer property and enter into contracts, rights she probably never had before, unless prior to marriage she had been emancipated by her father. The rights of widows and of emancipated single, adult women were similar to those of men. In one important regard, however, widows and single mothers remained legally inferior to men. Neither could exercize *patria potestad*. They had the legal responsibility to support their children, but not the authority that, for men, went with it.

The law did not cast women as a homogeneous group; yet only two differences among them were legally significant. A woman's juridical status depended on her conjugal state and her behavior. She was decent if she was a virgin before marriage, monogamous and obedient to her husband when wed, and chaste if widowed. The law offered some women protection from sexual violence, but only if she was "decent," and if the perpetrator was not her husband or father. The delineation between decency and immorality was a matter of life and death for women, as a husband was allowed to kill an adulterous wife; no woman had a parallel right to take the life of an unfaithful husband. However, if a female was raped, her family was permitted to kill the man if the court decided that she was "honest." As decency and honor were categories conditioned by class and race, in practice the courts infrequently protected lower-class, Indian, and mixed-race women against sexual assault, especially when perpetrated by men of the upper social strata.[28]

In one regard, however, all Latin American women were equal—equally excluded. No woman enjoyed political rights; no female, regardless of class, race, or age, was a citizen of the country in which she lived; none could vote or hold public office. In mid-nineteenth-century Latin America only propertied or professional adult males were citizens and eligible to participate in formal politics. Patriarchalism stratified even this masculine elite. In Nicaragua, as in other countries, the constitution of 1858 suspended a man's rights of citizenship if he showed ingratitude toward his father.[29] This underlined the interconnection between the domestic and the public spheres, and fortified the authority of male elders throughout society.

Liberal legal reforms, gradually enacted in most Latin American countries in the mid-nineteenth century, tended to expand individual rights at the expense of patriarchal authority. In Mexico, the Civil Code of 1870 reduced the power of the patriarch. Upon reaching adulthood, unmarried children no longer were subject to their father's control. Also, single mothers and widows who did not remarry were granted *patria potestad*. However, a married woman's legal status vis-à-vis her husband did not change. Moves to permit wives and husbands to share authority over their children were rejected. Consequently, as Silvia Arrom points out, in a relative sense women's marital subordination deepened. By reducing patriarchal domination over children, and leaving it intact for wives, the state underscored married women's dependence. Reformers were wary of expanding wives' independence from their husbands; evidently they feared the empowerment of married women would destabilize the patriarchal system.[30]

Liberal legal reforms came late to Nicaragua. When change came, however, it was radical in form. Laws of 1904 granted married women legal independence from their spouses and curtailed husbands' domestic policing powers. Wives could administer property and sign contracts without their spouses' consent. Also, to a degree, liberalism privatized sexuality within marriage; state control over the marriage bed declined. The amended civil code nullified the provision that granted husbands recourse to the police to force their wives to have sex with them. Slowly, the exclusivity of patriarchal authority over children was dismantled in Nicaragua. Although like their Mexican counterparts, jurists refused to give wives a share in *patria potestad,* in 1904 the state moved a small step in that direction. An amendment to the civil code provided that *patria potestad* passed to the wife in the event the father was mentally incompetent or died. This enhanced the domestic authority of some wives at the same time that it underlined the extent of most married women's powerlessness. The sea change in re-gendering paternal authority came to Nicaragua in 1940, when the law granted father and mother shared authority over their children.

Strongly indicative of the power of patriarchy was the legal status of adultery in Nicaragua. The 1904 amendments to the civil code finally nullified a husband's right to kill his adulterous wife; a wife's adultery instead became grounds for divorce. But the law did not establish gender parity on this issue; a husband's infidelity was not made illegal. The law of 1904, as well as the 1940 amendments to the civil code, officially sanctioned informal polygamy, as long as it was not particularly flagrant.[31] Under such a system, many if not most married men may have, at any moment in time, more than one long-standing sexual relationship. Informal polygamy was and still is customary in Nicaragua, and if it is not officially tolerated, it is still widely accepted as inevitable.[32] Thus gendered jurisprudence regarding adultery has had far-reaching effects on family mores in Nicaragua, where social practice has mirrored the law, and vice versa.

IV. HOUSEHOLD HEADSHIP IN AN ERA OF SOCIAL CHANGE

Nineteenth-century Latin Americans imagined one community; they lived in quite another. The elites spoke and wrote about a world in which the male head of household was ubiquitous. The family law they inherited from Spain rested on their male-centered notion of their world. Yet the society around them was considerably different from their idealized community of patriarchs. Depending on region, class, age, and ethnic groups, anywhere from one-fifth to one-half of all households were matrifocal, or female-headed.

When research on Latin American household composition began in the 1970s, historians discovered that a high proportion of households had no adult male. The earliest studies focused on the region's urban centers, and found that in the first half of the nineteenth century about one-third of households in Mexico City, and between one-third and one-half of households in two Brazilian cities (São Paulo and Vila Rica, the provincial capital of the state of Minas Gerais) were headed by women.[33] That in 1985 such discoveries were called "surprising" by specialists in the field suggests the degree to which *our* society has naturalized the patriarchal family.[34]

The dramatic discrepancy between the homogeneous world created by elite discourses and the heterogeneity of the households in which people lived was explained in different ways. In Mexico City Arrom found that female household headship was more common in the higher and lighter social strata than in the lower and darker in the first half of the nineteenth century. From this she concluded that female headship was more of a European feature than an Amerindian or Amer-African one, and that along with other characteristics such as late marriage, a high incidence of female headship set apart the marriage behavior of the metropolitan elite from that of the masses.[35] Other historians turned that proposition upside down to explain family arrangements in Brazil and Argentina in the same period. Some suggested that female headship, more prevalent in the lower and darker social strata than in the higher and lighter ones in urban Brazil and Argentina, was a feature of non-European and nonelite family patterns. In particular, it is widely believed that the high incidence of matrifocality in Brazil was a feature of its slave society.[36] Although these analyses are apparently contradictory, it is probable they are valid explanations for female-headship in urban Mexico on the one hand, and Brazil and Argentina on the other. The association of matrifocality with elite and non-elite cultures, with European and non-European customs in different settings supports the thesis that there is no such thing as a natural family form. Rather, a complex of contingent factors conditions household composition, including politics, economics, gender ideologies, class relations, and racial hierarchies.

More interesting in some ways than the specifics of the explanations is that historians continued to feel obliged to justify high rates of matrifocality. If research had revealed nearly universal male-headed households, it would not have been considered worthy of comment. The one issue on which historians agreed was that the prevalence of female-headed households was an aberration which needed to be explained. This consensus stemmed from the unarticulated presumption that the male-headed household is the natural type. It took some fifteen years and more than forty studies before specialists in the field were convinced that a prevalence of female-headed households was the norm in nineteenth century Latin America.

In 1991, in the *Journal of Family History*, which might be considered the gatekeeper in the field, Robert E. McCaa wrote, albeit with some caution, that "female-headed households were widespread—sometimes as frequent as those headed by couples, married and unmarried combined...."[37] Each article in that journal issue is about the fact that female-headed families were commonplace and why.[38] Some of the authors expend effort in showing that female headship was marginally higher in the lower social orders in some countries; other writers, studying different regions, demonstrate the opposite. Certainly, the idea that emerges from a collective reading of the articles is that female headship was prevalent throughout society: in all class, race, ethnic, and geographic groups. McCaa implies that historians now should expect that Latin American societies in that period were characterized by a high rate of female-headed households, and that they should turn their attention to how this feature varied over time and place, and how it affected politics, economics, and people's perceptions of their world.[39]

The special issue of the *Journal of Family History* points to a paradigm shift. That it was traditional for females, and for males, to head Latin American families in the nineteenth century is significant for historical as well as contemporary analyses of the family. Ironically, however, its announcement is accompanied by a discussion that underlines how deeply naturalized are our conceptions of what constitutes a normal family. McCaa, a major family historian of Latin America, calls unmarried couples, illegitimacy, and child abandonment "family pathologies," and seems to put female-headed household arrangements in the same category. In other words, those normal abnormalities, as he calls them, were a social disease.[40] But were they? Elite political and religious leaders certainly considered such practices deviant and sick, but it is not clear that most people shared their moral stand. After all, now we know that female-headed households, non-marrying behavior, and illegitimacy were aspects of most people's lives.

The rural household is among the last of the sacred cows of the nineteenth-century patriarchal family. Notwithstanding the consensus that female headed-ship was common in urban areas, leading scholars in the field continued to maintain that the rural family was different; it really was traditional.[41] Recent studies have shown, however, that the ubiquitous patriarchal household was not a general feature of agrarian society. In rural Mexico, Nicaragua, and Paraguay, female-headed households were common.[42]

Throughout Latin America historians have overturned the paradigm of the universal male-headed household. In the nineteenth century the patriarchal household was a centerpiece of elite discourse and a foundation of family law; however, social practice was considerably different. Households headed by females were almost as common as those headed by males. The Latin American family was not cast in a traditional patriarchal mold.[43]

As many believe that female subordination is reproduced primarily in the household, the discovery of high rates of female householders has led historians to suggest that women have been more autonomous in Latin America than previously perceived.[44] While this is an attractive proposition, one that many of us want to believe, it underscores the need for more research on gender and power, particularly in the public realm. My study of rural Nicaragua indicates that patriarchalism was a system which subordinated all women. While the forms of their oppression varied in kind and degree, no female escaped its field of force. Female heads of household may have felt less domination within the

113

home, but they were often more subordinated to patriarchal power in the overtly public areas of life.[45] Patriarchalism was institutionalized everywhere they went: in the government, in church, at fiestas, in the courts system, the fields, the markets, and the *haciendas*. We might consider whether the patriarchal household was a privileged family form to which most women aspired, but many found unattainable.

NOTES

My ideas for this chapter developed through discussions with Bradford Burns, Deniz Kandiyoti, Maxine Molyneux, John Weeks, and the University of Portsmouth (UK) Research Team on Gender and Development in Latin America (GENDLA). I particularly appreciate Brad Burns's encouragement to critically examine the conclusions of his work, and fine editing by Karen Judd and Ethan Young.

1. See Jean Franco, "The Gender Wars," *NACLA Report on the Americas* XXIX, no. 4 (January-February 1996): 6-9.
2. For a standard interpretation of classical patriarchy see Sylvia Walby, *Theorising Patriarchy* (Oxford: Blackwell, 1990), pp. 19-21. For critiques of this orthodoxy see Carole Pateman, *The Sexual Contract* (Cambridge: Polity Press, 1988). For an analytical discussion of the ethnographic literature on classical patriarchy in Africa and Asia, see Deniz Kandiyoti, "Bargaining with Patriarchy," *Gender & Society* 2, no. 3 (September 1988): 274-290.
3. Elizabeth Dore, "Property, Households and Public Regulation of Domestic Life: Diriomo, Nicaragua, 1840-1900," *Journal of Latin American Studies,* 1997 (forthcoming), and "El patriarcado público en la Nicaragua rural: Diriomo, 1830-1875," *Revista de Historia* (Costa Rica), forthcoming.
4. Mark D. Szuchman, *Order, Family and Community in Buenos Aires, 1810-1860* (Stanford: Stanford University Press, 1988), and E. Bradford Burns, *Patriarch and Folk: The Emergence of Nicaragua, 1789-1858* (Cambridge, MA: Harvard University Press, 1991).
5. Like class, gender is a category of political economy; but it is a different category. Class analysis explores how access to the means of production reproduces relations of power that sustain the social order. Gender analysis is about how material and ideological practices regarding sexual difference reproduce power relations.
6. See Jean Franco, "From the Margins to the Center: Recent Trends in Feminist Theory in the United States and Latin America" (this volume), and Judith Butler, *Gender Trouble: Feminism and the Subversion of Identity* (New York: Routledge, 1990); and *Bodies that Matter: On the Discursive Limits of "Sex"* (London: Routledge, 1993).
7. Elaine Showalter, *Sister's Choice: Traditions and Change in American Women's Writing* (Oxford: Clarendon Press, 1991); also, *Sexual Anarchy: Gender and Culture at the Fin de Siecle* (London: Virago, 1992). For a critique of the

public/private dichotomy, see Ben Fine, *Women's Employment and the Capitalist Family* (London and New York: Routledge, 1991).

8. Joan Scott, *Gender and the Politics of History* (New York: Columbia University Press, 1988), ch. 1.

9. For early articles that made women visible, see Asunción Lavrin, "In Search of the Colonial Women in Mexico: The Seventeenth and Eighteenth Centuries," and the other chapters in Lavrin, ed., *Latin American Women: Historical Perspectives* (Westport, CT: Greenwood Press, 1978). For an excellent analytical bibliography of Latin American women's history, see K. Lynn Stoner, "Directions in Latin American Women's History, 1977-1985," *Latin American Research Review* 22 no. 2 (1987): 101-134.

10. Joan Kelly, "Did Women Have a Renaissance?" in Joan Kelly, *Women, History and Theory: The Essays of Joan Kelly* (Chicago: University of Chicago Press, 1984), pp. 19-50.

11. Donna Guy, *Sex and Danger in Buenos Aires: Prostitution, Family and Nation in Argentina* (Lincoln: University of Nebraska Press, 1991), and "Women and Peonage in Argentina," *Latin American Research Review* 16, no. 3 (1981): 65-89; Sandra McGee Deutch, "Gender and Sociopolitical Change in Twentieth Century Latin America," *Hispanic American Historical Review* 71, no. 2 (1991): 259-306, and "The Catholic Church, Work and Womanhood in Argentina, 1890-1930," *Gender and History* 3, no. 3 (1991): 283-297; Carmen Diana Deere, *Household and Class Relations: Peasants and Landlords in Northern Peru* (Berkeley: University of California Press, 1990); and Eugenia Rodríguez, "From Brides to Wives: Changes and Continuities in the Ideals of and Attitudes Towards Marriage, Conjugal Relations and Gender Roles in the Central Valley of Costa Rica, 1750-1850," PhD diss., Indiana University, 1995.

12. For families' political and economic role, see Diana Balmori, Stuart F. Voss, and Miles Wortman, *Notable Family Networks in Latin America* (Chicago: University of Chicago Press, 1984). For gendered power relations within families, see John Tutino, "Power, Class and Family: Men and Women in the Mexican Elite, 1750-1810," *The Americas* 39, no. 3 (1983): 359-382.

13. For the classic model of the patriarchal family in pre-industrial Europe, see nineteenth-century French social scientist Pierre G. Frédéric LePlay, *L'Organisation de la Famille* (Paris: Bibliothécaires de l'Oeuvre Saint-Michel, 1871). A patriarch in the field is Peter Laslett of the Cambridge Group for Population Study. See Laslett with Richard Wall, *Household and Family in Past Time: Comparative Studies in the Size and Structures of the Domestic Group over the Last Three Centuries in England, France, Serbia, Japan and colonial North America, with further Materials from Western Europe* (London: Cambridge University Press, 1972). LePlay and Laslett disagree about whether the early modern family was extended or nuclear, but concur that the family was almost universally male-headed.

14. Martine Segalen, *Historical Anthropology of the Family* (Cambridge: Cambridge University Press, 1986).

15. Burns, *Patriarch and Folk,* p. 80. Szuchman makes a similar analysis *in Order, Family and Community*, pp. 225-36.

16. Burns, ibid.: in describing public outrage over a marriage that did not enjoy paternal consent, Burns mines the depth of the patriarchal belief system.

17. Ibid., p. 66-67.

18. For analysis of this uprising, see ibid., pp. 145-59; and Elizabeth Dore, "Land Privatization and the Differentiation of the Peasantry: Nicaragua's Coffee Revolution, 1850-1920," *Journal of Historical Sociology* 8, no. 3 (September 1995): 303-326.

19. I use the English term *patron* in its Spanish-language sense of "the boss," the person with political and economic power who maintains relationships of unequal reciprocity with those who are poorer and less powerful, as in *patron-client relations.*

20. Dore, "Property, Households and Public Regulation of Domestic Life."

21. Agustín Vijil, "Datos de Curia de la Ciudad de Granada durante el Año de 1846. Granada, enero 1, 1847," *Revista del Archivo General de la Nación* (Managua), January-March 1964, pp. 5-7, cited in Burns, *Patriarch and Folk,* pp. 77-78.

22. Charles Murray, a right-wing sociologist and philosopher, is renowned for relating social disintegration to the growing incidence of single-parent families. Peter Lilley, UK minister of social security, has drawn on Murray's ideas in targeting single-parent families.

23. Szuchman, *Order, Family and Community,* pp. 226-36.

24. This and much of the following analysis of patriarchal law in the early to mid-nineteenth century is drawn from Silvia M. Arrom, *The Women of Mexico City, 1790-1857* (Stanford: Stanford University Press, 1985), ch. 2, pp. 55-96; and Arrom, "Changes in Mexican Family Law in the Nineteenth Century: The Civil Codes of 1870 and 1884," *Journal of Family History* 10, no. 3 (Fall 1985): 376-391. See also Donna Guy, "Lower-Class Families, Women and the Law in Nineteenth Century Argentina," *Journal of Family History* 10, no. 3 (1985): 318-331.

25. For analysis of the colonial legal system, both civil and ecclesiastical, in particular how it was variably enforced see Patricia Seed, *To Love, Honor and Obey in Colonial Mexico* (Stanford: Stanford University Press, 1988).

26. Luis Zúñiga Osorio, "Patria Potestad," tesis para el doctor en derecho, Managua, pp. 32-38.

27. As Arrom points out, Hispanic property law discriminated against women less than property law in the Anglo-Saxon tradition. In the United States and England in the early nineteenth century, property usually was transmitted through the male line, and married women could not own property, enter into contracts, or make wills; see *Women of Mexico City,* p. 83.

28. Dore, "El patriarcado pública en la Nicaragua rural."

29. Zúñiga Osorio, "Patria Potestad," p. 47.

30. Arrom, "Cambios en la condición jurídica de la mujer mexicana en el siglo XIX," in *Memoria del II Congreso de Historia de Derecho Mexicano* (Mexico City, 1981), pp. 493-518, cited in Arrom, *Women of Mexico City,* footnote 122, p. 311.

31. In the words of one legal scholar, "when the husband kept a mistress (concubine)

discretely outside of his home, and conducted his affairs without public scandal, he suffered no castigation in the law"; Zúñiga Osorio, "Patria Potestad," p. 53.

32. We should not for a moment consider this a peculiarly Latin American or Nicaraguan custom, as the conjugal practices of French President Francois Mitterand suggest it was tolerated in France as well.

33. For Mexico City, see Arrom, *Women of Mexico City*. For Brazil, see Donald Ramos, "Single and Married Women in Vila Rica, Brazil, 1754-1838," and Elizabeth Anne Kuznesof, "Sexual Politics, Race, and Bastard-Bearing in Nineteenth Century Brazil: A Question of Culture or Power?", *Journal of Family History* 16, no. 3 (1991): 241-282.

34. Elizabeth Kuznesof and Robert Oppenheimer, "The Family and Society in Nineteenth Century Latin America: An Historiographic Introduction," *Journal of Family History* 10, no. 3 (Fall 1985): 224.

35. Arrom, *Women of Mexico City,* pp. 151-152.

36. Ramos, "Single and Married Women," and Kuznesof, "Sexual Politics, Race, and Bastard-Bearing." Alida Metcalf presents evidence that throws into question this commonly held view, arguing that matrifocality was no more a feature of slave society that of other strata in Brazil. See "Searching for the Slave Family in Colonial Brazil: A Reconstruction from São Paulo," *Journal of Family History* 16, no. 3 (1991): 283-298; and *Family and Frontier in Colonial Brazil* (Berkeley: University of California Press, 1992).

37. Robert E. McCaa, "Introduction," *Journal of Family History* 16, no. 3 (1991): 211.

38. "Female and Family in Nineteenth-Century Latin America," *Journal of Family History* 16, no. 3 (1991).

39. In the words of McCaa, "... the central issue for future studies of the Latin American family is no longer a matter of ascertaining the frequency of female householders ... but rather to interpret context, perception, and change." "Introduction," ibid.: 211.

40. Ibid.

41. Arrom, *Women of Mexico City,* pp. 149-50, and "Historia de la mujer," p. 399.

42. Dore, "El patriarcado público en Nicaragua rural"; Barbara Potthast-Jutkeit, "The Ass of a Mare and Other Scandals: Marriage and Extramarital Relations in Nineteenth Century Paraguay," *Journal of Family History* 16, no. 3 (1991): 215-240; Heather Fowler-Salamini, "Gender, Work and Coffee in Córdoba, Veracruz, 1850-1910," and Francie R. Chassen-López, " 'Cheaper than Machines': Women and Agriculture in Porfirian Oaxaca, 1880-1911," in Heather Fowler-Salamini and Mary Kay Vaughan, eds., *Women of the Mexican Countryside, 1850-1990* (Tucson: University of Arizona Press, 1994), pp. 27-73.

43. For an analytical literature review, see Elizabeth Anne Kuznesof, "The History of the Family in Latin America: A Critique of Recent Work," *Latin American Research Review* 24, no. 2 (1989): 168-186.

44. Kuznesof and Oppenheimer, "The Family and Society in Nineteenth Century Latin America": 224.

45. Elizabeth Dore, *Nicaragua: A Myth of Modernity: Property, Gender and Patronage in Rural Granada, 1840-1979* (forthcoming).

THE CHARM OF FAMILY PATTERNS: HISTORICAL AND CONTEMPORARY CHANGE IN LATIN AMERICA

RICARDO CICERCHIA

Recent scholarship has shown considerable interest in the family in relation to cultural history and political agendas. For the most part this discussion lacks engagement with the evidence that family forms as social organization contribute to social change. One of the consequences of the gradual abandonment of functionalism and its approach to the process of modernization has been the reorientation of the social sciences toward the dynamic of social change, multidirectional transformations, and social history.[1] Within this process, initiated approximately thirty-five years ago, the thematic field of the family is viewed with renewed enthusiasm. From sociological studies—the most fecund—to models of psychoanalytic interpretation, the family has emerged as a solid subject of study that is incontrovertibly interdisciplinary. This theoretical rupture was heightened by the evidence of drastic changes occurring in the family in Europe and the Americas, among which were the transformation of sexual values, an increase in the divorce rate to previously unthinkable levels, and, among women, the massive abandonment of their traditional spaces and open questioning of patriarchal power. This chapter analyzes heterogeneity of family forms and dynamic changes in the family. The argument is divided into two sections. The first presents a discussion of history and historiography, which clearly demonstrates the different ways in which tension between social reality and family models is solved. The second analyzes debates about present trends and policy directions in family matters.

It is clear that demographic, economic, legal, and cultural studies all focus on the family as a historical subject. This multidisciplinary diversity reflects the strategic position the history of the family occupies within the social sciences. A particular focus of historical analysis has been on the texture of intrafamiliar roles and the functionality of the relationship between the internal organization of the family and the structural needs of social change. The social history of the family has been enriched by diverse influences from sociology and demography. For example, Friedrich Engels tried to link family organization to industrialization, and his contemporary Pierre Le Play established the first typology of family structure, from the extended to the nuclear family.[2] An important marker in family history is the theory of the demographic transition. From preliminary observations, scholars concluded that a significant decline in birth and death rates led to transformations in family size and population patterns. Legal and institutional history had an important impact on studies of the family, particularly research into marriage customs and laws of inheritance. Later, anthropologists' preoccupation with kinship structures, taboos, and matrimonial endogamy and exogamy was adopted by historians. And finally, the women's movement introduced the theme of the domestic sphere and the family as a conflictive social space into scientific debate, compelling historians to critically reflect on gender as a central social relationship.

In Latin America, only with the end of the 1970s has the family been the subject of scientific study.[3] The first researchers adapted to the Latin American context the traditional hypothesis that control over economic and political resources moved from the family, kinship, and lineage groups to the new institutions which arose along with the emergence of the modern state. In a second stage, Latin American scholars emphasized the family as the central social actor in determining economic, political, and social conditions in the region. They looked particularly at the entrepreneurial role of the family and the relationship between family and politics in the period of the construction of nation-states. Other research themes were kinship and the organization of urban space, and intrafamiliar relations. Current work confirms the crucial importance of regional history.[4]

A study that strongly influenced the social sciences throughout the region was Gilberto Freire's analysis of the extended family with slaves and dependents on sugar plantations in Pernambuco in the northeast of Brazil during the sixteenth century.[5] Freire's model, only flimsily supported by historical sources and methodologically suspect, demonstrated that the Portuguese family had been the dominant social institution in Brazil. Freire's study stimulated a series of historical investigations into family patterns which focused on the relationships between public and private powers, and between domestic patriarchy and political patronage. These studies explored how the clan or lineage affected class relations, the role of race and gender in familial interactions, and the links between the domestic economy and family structure.[6]

Later, Woodrow Borah's analysis of the relationship between the decline of the indigenous population and the depression of the seventeenth century stimulated research on family history, including family patterns among the indigenous populations and household strategies developed in the context of "cross-culturization."[7] While Freire provided the skeletal model for élite families, Borah offered one for the popular classes.

Among the most significant historical discoveries, we find that some tendencies, usually perceived as contemporary phenomena, began to appear relatively clearly as early as the end of the eighteenth and beginning of the nineteenth century. These include the tendency toward a decline in the average size of the household and a significant increase in the number of female heads of households. Between 15 and 25 percent of the total family units (varying according to region) were headed by females, with percentages far higher than the 12 percent calculated for Europe during the same period. Finally, Latin American society was characterized by an extremely high percentage of consensual unions, around 30 percent of all conjugal unions.[8]

From another perspective, the studies have shown the permanent tension between legal and religious prescriptions and historically given social behaviors. Here, far from scholastic rigidity, the mechanism linking the hegemonic patriarchal discourse and marginal practices has been the pragmatism of the social actors themselves. It is important to note not only the enormous variety of family situations but also the degree of legitimacy and consensus some of these unusual family forms achieved.[9] The verification of this same diversity leads us, finally, to reemphasize that whenever family organization is being characterized, it is important to draw an analytic distinction between residential group (habitat), family (organization with a biological substratum), domestic unit (integration of related and unrelated individuals), reproductive unit (generational replacement), and economic unit (activities of production and daily consumption of food and other goods and services for subsistence). As an idea, the family—even though it has a biological substratum related to procreation—should be understood in its diverse forms as a social institution that transcends the normativity of sexuality and affiliation.

There are two ways of conceptualizing the family. One perspective, subscribed to here, is both scientific and realistic, while the other is ideological, and as such is an important component of the dominant official discourse. Within the first tendency, it seems imperative to replace *family* with the category *family patterns* in order to understand familial organization as a complex historical subject with a multiplicity of socially determining factors. This position has been ratified by the Proclamation of the International Year of the Family, in which the United Nations expressly mentions families that "assume diverse forms and functions ... that express a diversity of individual preferences and social conditions."

We are still suffering from the narrow limitations of a debate whose guidelines continue to be framed by the Catholic doctrine which, in general terms, supports an ahistorical view of family organization.[10] From a scholarly perspective, the legitimacy of any discourse should center on its capacity to exercise critical rigor, particularly concerning its own *corpus*, something that does not occur within Catholic doctrine. In fact, the Catholic church has made few, if any, changes in its positions. Such hermeticism makes discussion difficult and congeals it into an unproductive moral viewpoint. The result is doubly perverse. In terms of society, discriminatory criteria exclude any family arrangement contrary to the traditional model. The view of such families as "incomplete" is only one of the pernicious effects of such indoctrination. In terms of the domestic universe, a sacramental character is ascribed to matrimony. With matrimony seen as the inviolable foundation stone of family organization, the impossibility of any kind of intervention is reinforced. In this way, the phenomenon of domestic violence—one of the most frequent and least penalized types of crime—is concealed by a supposed natural harmony of the sacred family.[11] The conceptual rigidity that draws an absolute line between the public sphere and the "private" universe calls for a detailed examination of the relationship between family patterns and the state. A basic premise is that the state should defend the fundamental rights of its citizens. There is no exception to this responsibility, not even when these rights are violated in the "private" area of the domestic world.

121

THE LATIN AMERICAN FAMILY: HISTORICAL REALITY AND SOCIAL CHANGE

During the process of consolidation of nation-states in the second half of the nineteenth century, the family was an active agent in national and regional policy, influencing the formation of economic structures relating to finance, markets, and labor systems. There occurred an accelerated trend toward secularization of the means of social reproduction which placed limits on the church's jurisdiction over social matters, particularly those related to the family sphere. This involved an institutional transfer of exclusive authority over the mechanisms of order and social control from the church to the state. In this framework, family groups from diverse social classes participated in economic processes and in political decision-making in order to consolidate and utilize resources and influence in favor of their family interests. With the process of individuation barely begun, and the institutionalization of nation-states still embryonic, families, and particularly family networks, occupied a privileged position as social organizations. Families and domestic units were very flexible, informal groups with legal identities and common interests capable of creating what order characterized the region well into this century. It was not only elite families that were pivotal in these national formations; popular families also participated in the emerging states. As Tamara Hareven suggests, the family acted as a "crucial intermediary" between society, institutions, and social change.[12] It is important to be conscious of the various ways in which the conflict between social reality and family model is solved. The lesson of the past, if any, is *diversity*.

Analysis of contemporary social processes has centered on systems of production and generally halted at the questionable stigma of "private life" allotted to the domestic world. The creation of specialized production areas separated from the residence and the family is a relatively new historical phenomenon. With this, the degree of self-sufficiency of the domestic unit declined, and most daily needs came to be satisfied through market exchanges. Despite these changes, a group of fundamental activities remains, and not in isolation, within the family area: tasks of maintenance and reproduction closely linked to the public areas of power and social production. In other words, family space continues to be shaped interdependently with the public world of services, legislation, and social control. Therefore, its social nature is unquestionable. In the same sense, social images of the family are constructed through confrontation and resolution of considerable discursive variety: an official discourse holding up a model, versus dissenting voices that emerge from the same social reality.

A necessary phase in inaugurating a debate about official discourses versus social practices is to observe the varieties of family patterns in the region. Latin American and Caribbean countries share many of the world trends in family organization: a reduction in size, growing conjugal instability, a boom in single-parent homes, women as heads of households, increase in consensual unions, and changes in sexual morality.[13] Furthermore, in a more symbolic dimension, we witness the desacralization of marriage, the loss of family "order" directly proportional to the erosion of the power of the *pater*, and the dissociation between sex (pleasure) and reproduction (commandment-obligation). These phenomena can be viewed as a definitive crisis of the family as a basic social organization, since in principle these changes seem to imply profound modifications in family "common sense" in the majority of Latin American countries. Yet this reading is contradicted by two facts: (l) it is precisely other patterns, also pertaining to the family, that emerge from this altered scenario; and (2) many of the family practices that now seem novel have actually been in existence for some time but have remained invisible to the social sciences. In other words, the idea of a crisis in the Latin American family arises only if we hold to the traditional model, one coined definitively by the Catholic church in the middle of the sixteenth century, and still today the backbone of its doctrine on marriage and the family.

It is important to note the relevance of religious discourse in constructing images of the family, and this has a long history. As the key institution of the entire medieval social edifice, family organization was affected by both material and symbolic practices which maintained the structure of the system of domination that organized society. This included matrimony, the regulator of the transmission of property and sexual activity, which was definitively placed under the tutelage of the church, becoming a sacrament in the twelfth century. It is the only one of the seven sacraments not instituted by the Bible. Any other form of conjugal union implied a grave transgression of the Christian postulates dramatized by Catholicism. Ever since, and without many variations, the "matrimonial morality" conforms to three precepts: monogamy, exogamy, and the repression of pleasure, consecrated in a unique, heterosexual, and permanent act: the *legitimum matrimonium*. Given that this model has never represented the reality of the social family, it cannot be used as a parameter to define and/or measure the existence of a supposed crisis. The increased gap between this model and reality, however, suggests the existence of profound transformations, some of them potentially positive.

When we refer to the contemporary Latin American family we must be aware, to begin with, that the region is characterized by a very young population. In 1990, 36 percent of the total population of Latin America and the Caribbean was under fourteen years of age. That percentage is critical in determining social priorities. Almost 45 percent of the total population of the region lived in poverty, most of them in urban zones. Poverty influences the formation, structure, and the functions of the family. According to data from the Economic Commission for Latin America and the Caribbean (ECLAC), consensual unions and homes headed by women without partners were concentrated in the lower income strata. Between 1980 and 1990, the proportion of homes with children under fifteen years of age climbed from 14 to 19 percent, and from 21 to 26 percent in the lowest income strata. As a result of this trend, at the end of the 1980s, 20 percent of children under fifteen lived in nuclear homes headed by women without partners or organized in consensual unions, while this proportion reached 25 percent in the lower income strata.[14]

As noted above, consensual unions are increasingly frequent and are even more common in the lowest socioeconomic levels. Although there are no in-depth studies of these kinds of family arrangements, they tend to be less stable than formal marriages, and, perhaps, women in them have less negotiating power. It is possible that such circumstances alter the functions of diverse members of the family, bringing changes that do not correspond to a family proposal but to social forces beyond its control. A father's unemployment may necessitate migrations, interruption of children's schooling, or one of the spouses abandoning or fleeing the home (almost always the male). Also, the lack of adequate living quarters and overcrowding directly affects the nutrition and health of minors. Furthermore, in the past few years, governments of the region have cut back on public spending, which has had serious consequences for the provision of educational, health, and social security services.

NOTES ON THE FAMILY SITUATION OF LATIN AMERICAN WOMEN

Within this dramatic socioeconomic picture, the change in women's social role is the transformative center of contemporary family life. During the decade of the 1930s, very few women in the cities had any other prospect in life but shaping their identity to suit their family status: that is, the limited universe of domestic space and "private life."[15] In the 1960s, a great change began: the massive entrance of women into the labor market, accompanied by their greater visibility produced by statistical redefinitions. Although there were large regional variations, this included an increase not only in the participation of young single women but also of married women with children. The consequences were not confined to the impact on the labor market, but also affected the organization and experiences of daily life. The new models of women's entrance into the workforce and their access to the social and public arena determined a profound transformation of family life. Unemployment among male heads of household increased dramatically between the 1970s and 1990, and by more than 100 percent in Argentina, Colombia, Brazil, and Venezuela. This, combined with a deterioration in salaries, has catapulted other members of the family group into the world of work. In nonmetropolitan areas of Brazil the economic participation of women heads of households between 1979 and 1985 increased by 16 percent, while for the same period, the increase was more than 25 percent among females who were not heads of households. In other countries the same trend is observable. With the exception of Colombia, real salaries decreased substantially between 1980 and 1989 in every country in the region. For example, in Venezuela they suffered a reduction of 37 percent, in Argentina of 31 percent, in Mexico of 16 percent, and in Guatemala of 24 percent.[16] These processes altered the distribution of power in the bosom of the family. The traditional basis of legitimacy centered in the authority of the father-husband, based on the fulfilment of male responsibilities as the sole support of the family, as in the case of the single breadwinner system, began to be irreversibly eroded.

Yet regardless of their work situation, women continued to be responsible for domestic tasks and the care of children. Gender relations were still dominated by asymmetric forces that not only excluded women from decision-making opportunities but also, and even more importantly, generated inclusion mechanisms that condemned them to positions of subordination and high vulnerability. Taking into account the fact that women's rates of labor force participation have increased, particularly in the case of women between the ages of twenty and thirty, that is, those who currently have the greatest domestic burden, the combination of domestic and extradomestic work in this group results in a significantly heavy overload. Furthermore, the observation that women take on a greater role as protagonists in a crisis period is one of the hypotheses that could explain changes in the composition of domestic units, among them, the constant increase in the proportion of households headed by women, both through voluntary separation and male abandonment. For women in the popular classes, such situations almost invariably lead to extreme poverty.[17] Concomitantly, the weight of the cutbacks in public services during the 1980s also fell on women in charge of reproductive tasks.

On the other hand, the search for alternative solutions to unsatisfied basic needs has impelled women to go out into the "public" arena, organizing themselves and proclaiming their collective rights. All these experiences imply an important change in the way in which daily tasks of reproduction and maintenance are organized, as well as in the prevailing attitude toward public space. The continent has witnessed a multiplicity of collective actions that range from the *cacerolazos,* protests expressed by women banging on saucepans, to community initiatives in health care. In this sense it is important to note that while the absence of male heads of households increases the possibility of persistent poverty, it has the potential to produce more balanced consumption models. One aspect of males abandoning households may be that fewer resources are dedicated to the consumption of alcohol, tobacco, and non-nutritious foods in favor of education, health, and nourishment of the family group. In addition, their absence may generate more democratic power relations within the family.[18]

A CASE STUDY: FAMILY LIFE IN ARGENTINA

Although the great majority of Argentineans live in a family (85.5 percent of the total homes in 1989), the proportion of those who choose or find themselves in alternative types of residence is relatively high and growing.[19] These include people who live alone, especially mature widows, young exponents of personal autonomy, and separated people without children. Nevertheless, these phenomena are most common in the middle and high income brackets. The great majority of Argentineans are still linked to various types of families, the fundamental basis of organization for daily life. What are these households like?

Censuses taken between 1960 and 1991 reveal that the average size of households continued to decline. In 1991, the average number of members per residence was 3.2. Single-person homes went from 6.8 to 13.0 percent of the total from 1960 to 1991. Corresponding data demonstrate an increase in households with female heads, generally widows of advanced age, and on the other hand, a decrease in the birthrate, expressed in the growth of households composed of two persons. In relation to the types of families, the distribution reveals that in 1991, 75 percent of the total households were composed of a family nucleus (in its three variants: head with spouse and children, head with spouse without children, and head without spouse with children), and 25.1 percent were extended families.

Concerning the head of the household, by 1980 female heads of household had reached 19 percent of the total (9 percent widows, 4 percent married, 2 percent separated or divorced, and 4 percent single). The 1980 census showed major changes in marital status, however. While in 1960, 35.4 percent of the population over fourteen years of age was single, in 1980 that percentage

126

declined to 31.3 percent. The percentage of married people also declined from 54.1 to 52.9 percent in the same period. On the other hand, the population of people in consensual unions rose from 4.3 to 6.8 percent in 1980. This last figure reflects a kind of social legitimacy for unmarried couples, which while it represents a change from the recent past is not exclusive to this period.

Between 1970 and 1980, fertility rates progressively increased in all age groups except teenagers from fifteen to nineteen years of age. The older the group, the greater the increase. In 1980, the global fertility rate was 3.3 percent per thousand. As for what was traditionally called "legitimacy" during the years 1984 to 1987, approximately 35 percent of births were extramarital. However, even though teen pregnancy is a constant topic of debate, between 1980 and 1985 the adolescent fertility rate in Argentina decreased from 38.7 percent per thousand to 32.9 percent per thousand, with the lowest rate corresponding to the Federal District of Buenos Aires.

During the period from 1960 to 1980, despite a relative decrease in the general working population from 53.6 to 50.3 percent, women's participation in the workforce was characterized by an opposing trend, increasing from 23 to 27 percent, a percentage maintained in 1990. The increase in the participation of women between twenty-five and sixty-four years of age is especially notable. In relation to marital status, the figures show that 43 percent of single women, 20 percent of married woman, 23 percent of those in consensual unions, 12 percent of widows, and 60 percent of separated or divorced women were economically active; they worked for remuneration. According to some studies, the women in the poorest sectors of the population were transformed from "secondary" workers to primary breadwinners.[20]

Women's greater workforce participation also transferred the double stigma of "woman and poor" to the world of work, which confined women to low-paying, low-prestige jobs, generally lacking security. Social scientists thus began to investigate strategies for family survival. Abandoning models of the family that posited an almost mechanical and seamless transition from the traditional to the modern family, the new research examines the ways in which family segments reproduce old mechanisms in order to confront new problems arising from the reproduction of generational and daily life patterns, such as the continuity and recovery of family "customs": the reinforcement of ritual kinships, for example.[21]

In particular, new studies focus on households that are "abnormal" or deviant forms of the nuclear family. They examine the occasional status of some members of the family unit, the activities involved in production for consumption, and the extensive participation in the labor market of many household members. Their findings confirm the cultural, historical, and flexible nature of the family organization as well as family behavior involved in the so-called poverty strategies. In these actions and in the daily organization of the family lies the capacity to control always-limited resources, making it possible for the urban popular classes to survive within the models of sharply increasing poverty throughout the region.[22] Responses to the austerity policies of the decade of the 1980s varied according to the socioeconomic stratum of each family. The most vulnerable are those belonging to the universe of poor families, in which were found larger family groups, higher fertility rates, younger heads of households, higher rates of dependency, precarious employment, and overcrowded housing conditions.

The legal and policy debates about whether and to what extent the state has the right to penetrate a "private" area in the framework of a democratic system needs clarification in the context of contemporary Latin America. In particular, the relationship between state and family should be situated in terms of (1) the nature of those family conflicts that *authorize* state intervention and (2) social spending. In fact, much of family life is determined by public policies.[23] For example, respect for children's rights implies state responsibilities to guarantee them and to offer appropriate support so they can be fully exercised. Penalization and assistance in the face of domestic violence is another inescapable task of the state, as is guaranteeing the enjoyment of social rights involved in housing, labor, health, and cultural policies. Mere "policing" tends to penalize poverty, while effective state action ought to aim at ensuring the conditions for a life of dignity without any sort of discrimination.

In the case of Argentina, despite the fragmentary data available, it is clear that the state's provision of social resources was improving until the late 1950s. Since then, public social services have deteriorated markedly. National social spending as a percentage of the GNP stagnated from 1930 to 1970, then, beginning in 1977, declined brusquely.[24] Educational infrastructure, hospital care, and the construction of public housing lagged behind social demand. Moreover, the real value of family benefits for a typical family in 1970 had declined by 84 percent by 1982, constituting only 3.7 percent of the industrial salary at that time. More recently, in the framework of an economic crisis, the absence of state spending on social services—which redistributed income— and an increasingly regressive income tax system have had a negative impact on the popular classes.

CONCLUSION

In looking at the contemporary social map of family forms in a historical perspective, this chapter has reframed the concept of family in three ways: as an analytic category, as a social reality, and as the subject of public policies. The first conclusion is the need to adopt a flexible category *family patterns* rather than the ideological term *the family*. This implies viewing the family group as a social subject determined by, and determining, the global context. As such it is a complex historical subject, a receiver of a multiplicity of ethnic, class, gender, regional, and other determining factors. Family diversity should be legitimized by emphasizing the social, historical, and multicultural nature of family organization rather than the notion of a natural, sacralized, permanent, universal, rigid, and ideal unit, acceptance of which leads to discriminatory social policies that seek to reinforce the appearance of homogeneity and harmony that are essential components of official discourses.

More than 85 percent of the Latin American population is part of a family scenario. Women much more frequently head the family group, and their participation in the labor force is increasing, while consensual unions have been invigorated as a legitimate form of family arrangement. This, in broad strokes, is the family map of Argentina, and of Latin America in general. At the same time, the state has practically retired from the provision of social services. In this context, the contributions and strategies of the popular sectors are crucial. Since it is women who are the protagonists of family and collective strategies of survival, their gender revindications (explicit or not) are proposed as indispensable prerequisites to the respect and viability of human rights and social development. It is precisely the homes headed by women that demand greater attention from the state. What are needed are initiatives that would stimulate women's potential to definitively modify the patriarchal family structure that still governs our societies ideologically.

In conclusion, the relationship between family and state in Latin America, as in the United States and Europe, is characterized by unsatisfied social demands in the framework of an unprecedented crisis, with high vulnerability of poor families and a drastic reduction in social spending. This is occurring amidst a public debate biased in favor of a traditional perspective on the issue of the family. Official discourse *consecrates* the idea of family and legitimizes the lack of public intervention as a consequence of the inviolability of the "private" sphere. The result is an absence of mechanisms of conflict resolution for families. For example, the official response to domestic violence and the abuse of minors, in terms of shelters, emergency aid systems, or other types of intervention, is almost nonexistent.

The challenge is to introduce mechanisms of state intervention that would harmonize policies designed to generate dignified material conditions and the provision of excellent social services to reinforce family life with policies that promote a democratization of intrafamily relations. The indispensable premise for the realization of such policies is an extensive debate and a more honest and tolerant approach to social reality that would allow the actual protagonists to be heard. Despite the contradictory nature of some of the changes in the Latin American family, particularly among the popular classes, it is possible to detect the emergence of a democratizing process in the bosom of the family. The development of this renovative potentiality is unthinkable, however, without the active role of the state. It must be affirmed that the family, which is a predominant form of social organization, should continue to be subject to public policies. Within this universe, some households need particular attention, especially those headed by women and those founded on consensual unions with extramarital children. Any program of mother-infant nutrition, or of planning of services for families with mothers working outside the home, or of educational assistance, should center on this population. Only through an increase in social spending and an improvement in planning for it can a more just and efficient system of state intervention be implemented.

NOTES

1. The theory of functionalism asserted only one form of family "evolution," from traditional-extended-patriarchal to modern-nuclear-domestic. Critiques of the Talcott Parsons model have challenged his assertions about the isolation of the modern nuclear family and have documented models of interfamily assistance. See Bert Adams, *Kinship in an Urban Setting* (Chicago: Markham, 1968). In the field of historical demography, studies documenting the existence of the nuclear family model before the industrial revolution in Western Europe ultimately exposed the ideological nature of the structural-functionalist perspective. See Peter Laslett and Richard Wall, eds., *Household and Family in Past Time* (London: Cambridge University Press, 1972).

2. Friedrich Engels, *The Origin of the Family, Private Property and the State* (Moscow: Foreign Languages Publishing House, 1981); Pierre G.F. Le Play, *L'Organisation de la Famille* (Paris: Bibliothécaires de l'Oeuvre Saint-Michel, 1871).

3. See *Journal of Family History* 3, no. 4 (1978), a landmark special issue on Latin America.

4. All these issues are better represented in case studies of Mexico than those of any other Latin American region, and diverse reviews of the state of the question concur that the élite families have received preferential treatment. See Silvia Arrom, "Mexican Family History," paper presented at the American Historical Association, New York, 1990; Elizabeth Kuznesof, "The History of the Family in Latin America, a Critique of Recent Work," *Latin American Research Review* 16, no. 2 (1989): 168-186, and "Primary Trends and Interpretations in Brazilian Family

History," New York, 1990; and Mark Szuchman, "The Estate of Family History in Spanish South America," paper presented at the American Historical Association, New York, 1990.

5. Gilberto Freire, *The Master and the Slaves: A Study in the Development of Brazilian Civilization* (New York: Knopf, 1967).

6. Various studies have focused on the élite families as businesses, revealing common models of family organization as economic businesses that made it possible to mobilize credit, train personnel, expand and diversify commercial or producer activities, and guarantee areas of political power. The greatest contributions to this subject have been made by Susan Socolow, *The Merchants of Buenos Aires, 1778-1810. Family and Commerce* (Cambridge: Cambridge University Press, 1978); A. Twinam, "Enterprise and Elite in Eighteenth-Century Medellín," *Hispanic American Historical Review* 49, no. 3 (1979): 444-475; J. Kicza, *Empresarios coloniales. Familias y negocios en la ciudad de Mexico durante los Borbones* (Mexico: FCE, 1986); S. Ramírez, *Provincial Patriarchs, Land Tenure and the Economies of Power in Colonial Peru* (Albuquerque: University of New Mexico Press, 1986); R. Lindley, *Las haciendas y el desarrollo económico. Guadalajara, México, en la época de la independencia* (México: FCE, 1987); and L. Lommnitz and M. Perez Lizaur, *A Mexican Elite Family, 1820-1980: Kinship, Class and Culture* (Princeton: Princeton University Press, 1987).

7. Woodrow Borah, *New Spain's Century of Depression* (Berkeley and Los Angeles: University of California Press, 1951). There are notable studies by Claude Morin, *Santa Inés Zacatelco (1646-1812): Contribución a la demografía histórica del México Colonial* (Mexico: INAH, 1984); Cecilia Rabell, "El patrón de nupcialidad en una parroquia rural novohispana; San Luis de la Paz, Guanajuato, Siglo XVIII," in Consejo Nacional de Ciencia y Tecnología, ed., *Memorias de la reunión nacional sobre investigación demográfica en México* (México: 1978); Tomás Calvo, "Familles Mexicaines au XVIIe Siecle; une tentative de reconstitution," *Annales de Demographie Historique* (1984): 149-174; and Herbert Klein, "Familia y fertilidad en Amatenango, Chiapas, 1795-1816," *Historia Mexicana* 36, no. 2 (1986): 273-286.

8. The works on Mexico point to a dual interpretation: an early and "dangerous" process of mobilization of women counteracted by the reinforcement of patriarchal ideals promoted by the state, which materialized in the ratification of the Real Pragmática of 1776. See Sylvia Arrom, *The Women of Mexico City: 1790-1857* (Stanford: Stanford University Press, 1985): Introduction. The research on Brazil offers a much more dynamic impression of the social visibility of women. The different population policies and the advantages women obtain by their "victimization" (as a survival strategy) demonstrate the existence of less moralistic and more pragmatic scenarios. See Maria Costa da Silva, *Sistema de casamento no Brasil colonial* (São Paulo: USP, 1984); E. Kuznesof, *Household Economy and Urban Development: São Paulo, 1765 to 1836* (Boulder: Westview Press, 1986); K. Mattoso, *Familia e Sociedade na Bahia do Seculo XIX* (São Paulo: Corrupio, 1988); and Eni Samara, *As mulheres, o poder e a familia: São Paulo, Seculo XIX* (São Paulo: Editora Marco Zero, 1989).

9. For a case study of such diversity of family patterns and their degree of social

131

consensus, see Patricia Seed, *To Love, Honor and Obey in Colonial Mexico: Conflicts over Marriage Choice, 1574-1821* (Stanford: Stanford University Press, 1988); Verena Martinez Allier, *Marriage, Class and Colour in Nineteenth Century Cuba* (Cambridge: Cambridge University Press, 1974); and Ricardo Cicerchia, "Vida familiar y prácticas conyugales. Clases populares en una ciudad colonial, Buenos Aires, 1800-1810," *Boletín del Instituto de Historia Argentina y Americana "Dr. E. Ravignani,"* Third Series, No. 2, 1st semester (Buenos Aires: 1990), pp. 91-109.

10. The doctrine established in the Documento del Pontificio Consejo para la Familia (Document of the Papal Council on the Family), 1992, continues to define the family in terms not unlike those of the Council of Trento in 1564: as "the sanctuary of life," as a natural union founded on marriage that unites, in a permanent communion of life and love, one woman and one man. Just as it did 400 years ago, the church continues to condemn family planning as a transgression of divine commandments; sexual pleasure as a disorderly expression of venereal pleasure separated from the ends of procreation and union; and homosexuality as acts that contravene natural law. On the resolution of Trent, see "Doctrina sobre el Sacramento del Matrimonio" in *El Sacrosanto y Ecumenico Concilio de Trento*, translation by Ignacio López Ayala according to the authentic Rome edition published in 1564 (Paris: 1857).

11. There is very little reliable data on the phenomenon of domestic violence in Latin America. It is estimated that around 25 percent of all homicides are domestic murders in which the victim is a family member, and that between 70 and 80 percent of Latin American women have been victims of conjugal violence. See Roxana Carrillo, "La violencia contra la mujer: obstáculo para el desarrollo," in Virginia Guzmán, Patricia Portocarrero, and Virginia Lagos, eds., *Una nueva lectura: género en el desarrollo* (Lima: Ediciones Flora Tristán/Entre mujeres, 1991). Cultural violence is not peculiar to marginal groups, but derives from cultural attitudes learned as a "natural" way of resolving conflict. A study carried out by the Fundación Alicia Moreau de Justo of 500 cases of women victims of conjugal violence between 1989 and 1991 in Buenos Aires reveals that slightly more than 80 percent of men who abuse their spouses have middle or upper middle class incomes.

12. Tamara Hareven, *Family Time and Industrial Time* (Cambridge: Cambridge University Press, 1982), Introduction.

13. All data taken from *Familia y futuro. Un programa regional en América Latina y el Caribe* (ECLAC, 1994).

14. See documents of the Economic Commission for Latin America and the Caribbean (ECLAC), *Hacia un perfil de la familia actual en Latinoamérica y el Caribe* (LC/R. 1208, 1992); and *El perfil de la pobreza en América Latina a comienzos de los años 90* (LC/L. 716, 1992). In 1990, 34 percent of urban homes were classified as poor; see Mercedes González de la Rocha, "The Urban Family and Poverty in Latin America," *Latin American Perspectives* 22, no. 2, whole no. 85 (Spring 1995): 12-21.

15. The most recent study on the current situation of women in the region is Edna

Acosta-Belén and Christine E. Bose, eds., *Researching Women in Latin America and the Caribbean* (Boulder: Westview Press, 1993).

16. See ECLAC, *La equidad en el panorama social de América Latina durante los años ochenta* (LC/R. 1686, 1991).

17. The relationship between poverty and households headed by women and the tendency toward the *feminization of poverty* is well documented. See T. Merrick and M. Schmink, "Households Headed by Women and Urban Poverty in Brazil," in *Women and Poverty in the Third World* (Baltimore: Johns Hopkins University Press, 1983).

18. Sylvia Chant, "Mitos y realidades de la formación de familias encabezadas por mujeres: El caso de Querétaro, México," in L. Gabayet, P. García, M. González de la Rocha, S. Lailson, and A. Escobar, eds., *Mujeres y sociedad. Salario, hogar y acción social en la Occidente de México* (Guadalajara: El Colegio de Jalisco/CIESAS, 1988).

19. Some data of this section have been taken from Catalina Wainerman, ed., *Vivir en familia* (Buenos Aires: UNICEF/Losada, 1994), the first interdisciplinary work about family in Argentina.

20. Alberto Minujín, "From 'Secondary Workers' to Breadwinners: Poor and Non-poor Women Facing the Crisis," (Buenos Aires: mimeograph, 1990).

21. On this topic, see a critique of the positions of Gino Germani in María del Carmen Feijóo, *La pobreza latinoamericana en perspectiva*, Documento Cedes, no. 40 (Buenos Aires: 1990).

22. Lourdes Benería, "The Mexican Debt Crisis: Restructuring the Economy and the Household," in Lourdes Benería and Shelley Feldman, eds., *Economic Crises, Persistent Poverty, and Women's Work* (Boulder: Westview Press, 1992).

23. One of the pioneering works on this debate is Elizabeth Jelin, *Familia y unidad doméstica: mundo público y vida privada*, series Estudios CEDES (Buenos Aires: CEDES, 1984).

24. Data in this section are found in Susana Torrado, *Estructura social de la Argentina, 1945-1983* (Buenos Aires: Ediciones de la Flor, 1992).

SEX/GENDER ARRANGEMENTS AND THE REPRODUCTION OF CLASS IN THE LATIN AMERICAN PAST

MURIEL NAZZARI

This chapter examines several practices and ideologies in the sex/gender arrangements of colonial and nineteenth-century Latin America, which not only structured gender roles and reinforced patriarchy, but also served to reproduce class. In it, I have adopted the theoretical framework of Beth Anne Shelton and Ben Agger, who argue against a conceptual separation between two systems of oppression, capitalism and patriarchy, and for a theory that is not simply about class, but is also a theory of everything, including women. They argue that housework produces workers and therefore produces surplus value, so that sex/gender arrangements that apportion these tasks to women serve the interests of capitalism.[1]

I would amplify this argument to add that within the roles assigned to them by sex/gender arrangements, women have produced not only free wage workers,

134

but also slaves and the ruling class. Sex-gender arrangements therefore are and have been a vital part of the reproduction of caste and class society.[2] In fact, biological reproduction itself is, in the words of Mary O'Brien, the substructure (or deep structure) of history.[3]

Women have not only reproduced their class and ethnic groups physically, but through the socialization of children have reproduced the identities of these groups. Jill Vickers argues that these reproductive abilities give women power that those who do not share it (men) have had to control and regulate through the construction of sex/gender arrangements.[4] Such arrangements can be viewed as establishing modes of human reproduction. Sexual asymmetry results from the way the current mode or modes of human reproduction articulate with the current mode of production.[5]

The importance of women's reproductive roles as the main cause of sexual asymmetry is shown in one case in nineteenth-century Cuba, where because nobody expected women to reproduce, practically no sexual asymmetry existed. Female field-hand slaves on sugar plantations experienced no inequality with their male peers: they did not experience a sexual division of labor, for they were expected to perform the same work as males, side by side with males. They were never categorized as housewives, and probably never did housework, and they usually refused to become mothers, practicing abortion or infanticide instead. As workers, they suffered the same amount of exploitation that men did. They worked as hard and as long as men (twenty hours a day during the harvest, even during the ninth month of pregnancy), and they were punished as severely as men.[6] And there was no discrimination against women as workers.[7] Sexual discrimination started only after slaves were emancipated, when women and men began competing for wages.[8]

What made this state of "equality" possible was undoubtedly the fact that neither slaveowners nor slaves themselves wanted slave women to be mothers, so that there was no specific female role. This came about because slaveowners found it more economically efficient to replace slave losses by buying new slaves, rather than having to subsidize the bearing and raising of slave children. In the 1830s a Jamaican journal estimated that it cost 112 pounds to rear a slave to age fourteen. In Cuba at that time the purchasing price of a field hand was forty-five pounds.[9] The early-nineteenth-century Cuban historian Francisco de Arango y Parreño stated explicitly in 1811, "the black born on the estate has cost more, by the time he can work, than one of the same age bought in the public market."[10]

The result of these calculations was that in nineteenth-century Cuba no labor was expended on the raising of slave children, or, more accurately, little labor, for the few live babies that were born in a given plantation were entrusted to the minimum care of an old slave nurse, and did not usually survive infancy.[11] Thus the reproduction of that particular workforce took place externally, in the African continent, allowing (or condemning) the women in the slave workforce to experience "equality" with their male peers.

An interesting question is whether a slave-breeder mentality on the part of the slaveowner would have meant better or worse conditions for slave women. One suspects that it would have meant better conditions, at least for children and women of childbearing age, giving women, instead of men, a privilege. When the price of slave replacements rose above the opportunity cost of having women slaves care for children plus the cost of the means of subsistence necessary to raise them, the slaveowner could rationally decide he would not risk the success of his project by continuing the abysmal living and working conditions of slave mothers.

The example of female field slaves in Cuba suggests that when reproductive roles were eliminated, gender roles also disappeared. Most Latin American women, however, exercised their reproductive roles and lived within highly structured sex/gender arrangements. In colonial times and in the early nineteenth century, these arrangements included the system of family honor, which both prescribed gender roles and stratified society, thereby reproducing class.

The word "honor" had meanings at two different levels: status and virtue. The honorable status of a family of the colonial élite was gained through ascription if ascendants had belonged to the conquistadors or early settlers or if the crown had granted them privileges in return for services. It was also inherited through purity of blood, that is, genealogical proof that there was no mixture of Jewish, Moorish, Indian, or black blood in one's ancestry. The honorable status of these families was maintained with the circumspect behavior of their members and their refusal to participate in manual labor.

Honor as virtue also reflected on the entire family as a corporate group, but in contrast to honor as status, it had different definitions according to gender. The men of a family were honorable when they were manly, honest, and loyal, and exercised their authority over family and subordinates wisely. Women's honor was mostly related to their sexual conduct: they should retain their virginity until they married, and as wives they should be chaste and faithful. They should also be concerned with their reputation, and discreet in the presence of men. If women deviated from this code they were considered shameless, and this shamelessness dishonored the whole family.[12]

Yet colonial society had contradictory expectations. The honor system led men to protect the women in their own family from sexual assault, and thereby preserve the family honor, whereas contemporary views on masculinity led them to attempt to seduce women in other families, thereby dishonoring them. Men's sense of virility rose as a function of how many women they were able to conquer.

This contradiction meant the honor system would not work without the sexual laxity of some women. These tended to be lower-class women because they were less secluded and less protected than upper-class women. Many may also have made calculated choices between illicit relationships with an upper-class man and marriage with a man of their own class. Verena Martínez-Alier has shown that mulatto women in nineteenth-century Cuba, those with little honor, felt that "rather mistress of a white than wife of a negro."[13] In relations of concubinage they received a certain economic security while bearing lighter-skinned children who, because of their color, would have increased opportunities to achieve upward mobility. Women who made these realistic choices, however, did so at the price of their honor.

This sex/gender system of honor therefore functioned not only to differentiate women from men but also to divide persons by class. The colonial élite distinguished between people who had honor, *gente decente*, and people who did not, *gente baja.*[14] Thus when a woman chose or accepted a relationship of concubinage, she lost her honor and reinforced her lower-class status. Because of the double standard implicit in this gender system, upper-class men did not lose their honor if they had concubines of an inferior class or race, only if they married them.[15]

A marriage system based on endogamy was thus at the root of the gender system of honor, and endogamy was also a sex/gender arrangement that reproduced class. Men and women were expected to marry their equals, and were there any inequality in status or property between spouses, it was the wife who should be superior to her husband and not vice-versa. The mechanism used to enforce this system was the dowry.[16]

I have argued elsewhere that daughters were a more valuable resource than sons in seventeenth-century São Paulo because only men migrated from Portugal. The first men had married Indian women, leading to the formation of mixed-blood families that required the infusion of European blood to maintain their élite status. This could come about only through the marriage of their children to European immigrants, mostly men. Thus, because it was daughters and not sons who could whiten the lineage, parents favored daughters and gave them the largest amounts of property.[17] If we consider race as an approximation to class, we can see that the strategies used in interracial marriages and even concubinage all led to the conservation or enhancement of a family's class.

The colonial practice of endogamous marriage meant that any long-lasting sexual relationship with a woman who was of an inferior class or race or who had no dowry usually took place only within concubinage. I have found that it was not only secular society that accepted the prevalent discourse about equality and inequality of class, property, and/or race between marriage partners, but also the Catholic church.

In a study of the church's legal prosecution of cases of concubinage in colonial São Paulo, I found that, contrary to what would be expected, church officials did not require that single couples who had been living together marry. Though between 70 and 90 percent of the concubinage processes studied consisted of single partners, church officials usually tried only to separate them, not marry them. Studying the individual cases, I found that most of the couples were either racially unequal, usually a white male with a mestizo, mulatto, or black concubine, or unequal regarding class or property ownership.[18]

I concluded that church authorities subscribed to the current view on endogamous marriage, and thus found it difficult to oblige a man to marry a woman who was not his equal, proposing instead the separation of the sinning couple, or that the woman marry a third party. For instance, in the concubinage suit against José Rodrigues Padilla and Bernarda Lopes, the ecclesiastic sentence passed in the Diocese of São Paulo did include the possibility of marriage. The wording was "on condition that they prepare to marry *or* have his accomplice, Bernarda Lopes, marry outside this parish."[19] This sentence gave the male partner a choice: if his partner was too unequal to marry, he could find her a husband (which usually implied endowing her). Another woman, responding to her confessor's pressure, married a newcomer to São Paulo, who left for Rio de Janeiro and abandoned her after a few months. In later testimony, she declared that she married him only because she felt so pressured by her parish priest. It is significant that the priest, however, had not made her marry the man she was alleged to be living with, though he was a widower and therefore free to marry.[20]

The questions asked of prospective brides and grooms in colonial Brazil further demonstrate church concern with the equality of marriage partners. One of the routine questions was what inheritance each prospective spouse had received or expected to receive. (Because the Portuguese inheritance system did not allow the disinheritance of children, most children of property owners had an approximate idea of what they would inherit.) The question was asked of all, rich and poor alike, and every couple sought to prove their equality.[21] Furthermore, the Bishop of the Diocese of São Paulo passed a sentence in a betrothal suit in 1779 that made this church concern explicit when he stated that "since there is no inequality between the betrothed ..., the Reverend Vicar can continue with the publication of the banns."[22] His words confirm the church's adherence to the concept of endogamous marriage and help explain its obvious disinterest in pushing the marriage of couples sentenced for concubinage, most of whom consisted of a man of higher status with a woman of lower status.

The honor system and the requirement of endogamous marriage combined to successfully reproduce the colonial élite and consolidate its property while at the same time reproducing the insecurity and lower-class status of the rest of the population. In colonial countries such as Brazil, where there were great racial inequalities and disparities in civil status between free and slave, marriage itself remained mostly an institution for property owners. Donald Ramos, among others, has shown that households headed by a married man were a minority in late-eighteenth- and early-nineteenth-century Minas Gerais, and that they all tended to be property owners. Female (mostly single) heads of household were more numerous, and owned little property.[23]

In colonial Latin America, therefore, the gendered honor system and the requirement of endogamous marriage combined with class, race, and property ownership to determine the type of sexual role a woman fulfilled, whether wife or concubine. Moreover, the requirement of class-endogamous marriage may have worked to lessen the asymmetry between wife and husband. Insofar as women of the propertied class tended to marry men who had less property than they did, it is probable that they had more power within marriage than has previously been attributed to them in such patriarchal societies. The Portuguese newcomer who married a woman from a prominent family of São Paulo in the seventeenth or eighteenth century received access to the clan network and influence though his wife, and also received from his wife all the property the couple owned, making him beholden to her. Such wives undoubtedly gained power in this way, as illustrated by a case in which a husband explicitly deferred in public to his wife's judgment.[24] There were also instances in which it was mothers, rather than fathers, who decided what property, or how many and which slaves or cattle would integrate a daughter's dowry. Furthermore, the importance of mothers in the arrangement of their daughters' marriages is confirmed by the words of Governor Antônio Paes de Saude, who wrote in 1698 that the women of São Paulo were "industrious, and more inclined to marry their daughters to strangers who would raise their status, than to local men who were their equals."[25]

In addition, children's surnames in colonial São Paulo society reflected their mothers' importance within the family structure. Lineage was ambilineal, transmitted by both fathers and mothers, but there was great latitude in the choice of surnames, so that children of the same married couple frequently bore different mixtures of their father's, mother's, or grandparents' surnames. Coming from a society in which all legitimate children bear their father's name, a twentieth-century historian of seventeenth-century São Paulo is first struck by the many élite families in which all children carried their mother's surname, and not their father's, despite their father's presence, and despite being legitimate children. For example, there is the family of Manoel João Branco, a Portuguese merchant who married Maria Leme of a prominent São Paulo family in the early seventeenth century and none of whose children carried his surname. Their three children were Anna Leme, Izabel Paes (maternal grandmother's surname), and Franciso João Leme.[26]

The choice of their mother's surname or surnames for most or all children suggests that in these cases the wife's superior class and status overrode the usual gender asymmetries within the nuclear family. In fact, 40 percent of the children of mid-seventeenth-century São Paulo property owners did not carry their fathers' surnames at all, showing the importance of their mothers' lineage. But this situation was not to continue. By the nineteenth century, most children bore their fathers' names. Moreover, it was in that century that wives started to use their husbands' surnames.[27]

These nineteenth-century changes document a further subordination of the wife in marriage that took place as marriage was transformed from mostly a property relation between class equals to a marriage based on the personal relationship between the spouses, in which wives were usually economically dependent on their husbands. At the same time, the honor system was considerably weakened and tended to disappear, and the practice of arranged marriages and dowry declined.

These changes in the way classes were reproduced, specifically in the way the ruling class was reproduced, entailed a kind of marriage that was much more like concubinage than was the previous system, in which wives contributed substantially to the support of their new families with a dowry. They also represented the transformation from a system of patriarchalism, in which one male not only had authority over the females in his family but also over all younger males, including married sons and nephews, and sometimes even cousins, to a system of patriarchy restricted to the nuclear family, in which the male had power only over his wife, unmarried daughters, and minor sons.[28] The new patriarchy allowed individual men much more independence from their families of origin to choose a wife or pursue a career, leaving individual women freer to choose a husband, but without the support and protection of their

140

fathers, brothers, and families of origin, who could no longer exert patriarchal authority over their sons-in-law.

Marriage became a strictly personal matter. On one hand, women of the propertied class gained the freedom to choose their husbands, but lost the right to receive a dowry from their parents, that is, the wherewithal to contribute to the support of the new family, so they became instead their husbands' dependents. On the other hand, women with no property benefitted from the change, for it increased their chances of marrying. Demographic studies confirm that as the nineteenth century progressed, a greater percentage of the adult population married. Silvia Arrom showed that the proportion of those never married in Mexico City decreased from 19.5 percent of men and 16.6 percent of women over 40 in 1790 to 8.4 percent of men and 12.3 percent of women over 40 in 1848.[29] In 1872 in Rio de Janeiro, only 23 percent of the population of marriageable age was married, but the percentage increased to 31 percent by 1890 and to 40 percent by 1906.[30] Though marriage, an institution that regulated gender relations, no longer separated people by class as starkly as it had in the past, to this day there are more never-married persons in the lower classes than in the upper.

Latin American history demonstrates that gender roles within marriage also have varied according to class, thereby reproducing class. For instance, the gender norm that frowned on wives' work outside the home separated women by class, for lower-class women could rarely afford to conform to that norm. It was only when a family's income level increased and the family wage became a reality that it became possible for women to become solely "housewives." When industrialization came to parts of rural Mexico in the early twentieth century, for example, peasant families moved to town as the men became industrial workers. Their wives rose in the community's estimation, in part because family incomes and standard of living increased, leading to a decrease in infant mortality and greater education for children, and in part because wives no longer performed the hard agricultural work they had previously shared with their husbands. They were considered more "modern," yet asymmetry between the spouses had increased, and wives had lost power within the family.[31]

In fact, studying Latin American women in relation to work performed outside the home forces us to consider the evolving class character of work itself. During colonial times there remained an aristocratic aversion to manual labor. Of course, manual labor did not include productive investment and the administration of an estate or other property, so that within the upper classes, all men, and some women—especially widows, abbesses, and nuns—did carry out this kind of economic activity routinely throughout colonial history.[32] In

141

addition, though husbands were legally the administrators of the community property belonging to a married couple, wives, especially when there were no adult sons, took over such administration in their husband's absence, which in the case of wars or expeditions of exploration could last for years.[33]

The only wealthy men to labor long hours in colonial times were merchants, but their status suffered because of their occupation, so that they sought to become landed proprietors.[34] It was only with the proliferation of professions at the end of the eighteenth century and during the course of the nineteenth that the idea that work was denigrating changed, and the bourgeois work ethic became predominant.

During the period in which manual labor and work itself were not valued in society, large numbers of Latin American women had gainful occupations, but they were stigmatized by their work. In early nineteenth-century Mexico, for example, it was acceptable to sew for one's own family, but to "sew for a stranger" was shameful. Women supported themselves and their families by becoming domestic servants, small tradeswomen, or peddlers, or by running small neighborhood stores, or working in the tobacco factory, or as midwives or herbalists. Yet their jobs or dealings in petty commerce did not enhance their status; if anything, status was lowered by such engagement. Many women therefore found domesticity and a husband's or father's protection to be attractive options, suggesting that the sex/gender arrangement that decreed that wives should not "work" outside the home derived originally from the general upper-class contempt for most such work.[35]

Not only was work outside the home a question of class, but so was work within the home, housework. Historically, Latin American middle- and upper-class women have usually at least managed their homes. Moreover, to this day, most middle- and upper-class Latin American women usually do not perform the manual housework, making it easier for scholars to separate analytically the concept housework from the concepts wife and mother.

At the same time, the large proportion of domestic servants within the employed female population from the beginning of the nineteenth century to the present has stimulated numerous studies which have contributed to an understanding of the class-relatedness of housework itself.[36] As Latin America developed, there were decreasing opportunities for rural women, who then migrated to urban centers where the same development process increased the middle class that could afford to hire servants. Already in the early nineteenth century, one of three women in Mexico City worked outside the home, 57 percent as domestic workers.[37]

Within the families that supplied servants, female children substituted for their absent mothers, caring for their siblings and doing housework, that is, learning to be servants. Within the families who hired servants, children were learning not to do housework, but how to command. The patriarchal system by which the master had separate women performing separate subordinate roles— wife, mistress, and servant—was thereby reproduced.[38] We can conclude, therefore, that who does the housework is therefore not only a gender issue but also a class issue. The same is true of some functions of motherhood, for servants not only performed housework; they were also wet nurses, nannies, and tutors or governesses—that is, they exercised the maternal role.

The continued existence of domestic servants may have contributed to the fact that Latin American women entered traditionally male professions earlier than in the United States. For example, in the University of Buenos Aires in 1965, 50 percent of the graduating dentists were women, versus 0.7 percent in U.S. universities; also, 22 percent of graduating lawyers and 21 percent of doctors were women, compared to 3 percent and 7 percent respectively in the United States at the time.[39] Because of the availability of domestic servants, middle-class women were able to combine professions with marriage and motherhood, even with their husbands' approval, for there was no need to change male roles.[40] Several scholars have found a positive correlation between the existence of domestic servants and the rate of participation by women in other economic activities.[41] In this case, therefore, the class division of labor regarding housework (between mistresses and their domestic servants) permitted the blurring of the gender division of labor at the occupational or professional level (between women and their husbands, brothers, sons, and fathers).

CONCLUSION

An issue raised by some of the examples presented here is the question of the importance of class differences within sexual relationships. When élite mestizo women of seventeenth-century São Paulo married white men with much less property and status, their class superiority appears to have lessened the gender asymmetry within marriage. The opposite case is that of relations of concubinage in which the higher class or race of the male reinforced gender asymmetries. The question we could ask is to what degree gender inequality is class difference, and whether feminist movements are movements to erase these class differences.

However, women's role in biological and cultural reproduction, so important to the reproduction of class, still remains as a source of gender asymmetry. In the case of Cuban female slave field hands, we found a situation of complete equality between women and men. Yet this was equality at the bottom of a highly stratified society, equality of wretchedness, and, as we concluded above, due to the fact that these women were not expected to become mothers.

Sex/gender arrangements in Latin America, such as endogamous marriage, the honor system, or the precept that wives should not work outside the home, have historically reproduced class. The honor system, with its demand for wives' initial virginity and faithfulness within marriage, guaranteed that property would be transmitted to lawful heirs. Marriage as a relation between approximately equal property owners, with its utility in terms of consolidation of property, also served to reproduce the ruling class. The precept that wives should not work outside the home divided women by class, for lower-class women could not follow it. Within the upper- and middle-class home itself, there was a class division of female roles, the mistress of the house and the domestic servant, with the result that each in her own family reproduced her class. Sex/gender arrangements not only served to reinforce patriarchy, they also consolidated class divisions and reproduced class society.

NOTES

1. They call it "feminized Marxism." See Beth Anne Shelton and Ben Agger, "Shotgun Wedding, Unhappy Marriage, No-Fault Divorce? Rethinking the Feminism-Marxism Relationship," in Paula England, ed., *Theory On Gender/Feminism On Theory* (New York: Aldine de Gruyter, 1993), p. 36. The best exposition of the value of housework for capitalism in Latin America can be found in Isabel Larguía and John Dumoulin, "Aspects of the Condition of Women's Labor," in *NACLA Report on the Americas* 9, No. 6 (September, 1975): 2-13.

2. I have adopted the phrase "sex/gender arrangements" as used by Jill Vickers, "A Political Theory of Sex and Power," in H. Lorraine Radtke and Henderikus J. Stam, eds., *Power/Gender: Social Relations in Theory and Practice* (London: Sage Publications, 1994). See also Gayle Rubin, "The Traffic in Women: Notes on the 'Political Economy' of Sex," in Rayna R. Reiter, ed., *Toward an Anthropology of Women* (New York: Monthly Review Press, 1975).

3. Mary O'Brien, *The Politics of Reproduction* (London: Routledge and Kegan Paul, 1981), cited in Vickers, "A Political Theory," p. 181, note 2.

4. See Vickers, ibid.

5. See Annette Kuhn and AnnMarie Wolpe, "Feminism and Materialism," in Kuhn and Wolpe, eds., *Feminism and Materialism: Women and Modes of Production* (London: Routledge and Kegan Paul, 1978); Deborah Fahy Briceson and Ulla Vuorela, "Outside the Domestic Labor Debate: Towards a Theory of Modes of Human Reproduction," *Review of Radical Political Economics* 16, nos. 2/3 (1984): 137-166; Nancy Folbre, *Who Pays for the Kids: Gender and the Structures of Constraint* (London and New York: Routledge, 1994). See also Muriel Nazzari, "The 'Woman Question' in Cuba: An Analysis of Material Constraints on Its Resolution," in Sonia Kruks, Rayna Rapp, and Marilyn Young, eds., *Promissory Notes: Women in the Transition to Socialism* (New York: Monthly Review Press,

1989); and "The Significance of Present-day Changes in the Institution of Marriage," *Review of Radical Political Economics* 12, no. 2 (Summer, 1980): 63-75.

6. For the long hours, and the work of pregnant women, see Franklin Knight, *Slave Society in Cuba During the Nineteenth Century* (Madison: University of Wisconsin Press, 1970), p. 76; for the work and punishment of pregnant women, see Manuel Moreno Fraginals, *The Sugarmill: The Socioeconomic Complex of Sugar in Cuba, 1760-1860* (New York, London: Monthly Review Press, 1976), p. 143.

7. Moreno Fraginals traces the historical sequence by which planters first bought almost exclusively male slaves, believing that they would be more productive, but later, as prices of male slaves rose, started using females, reasoning that, "although they yielded less, they cost enough less to compensate" (see *The Sugarmill*, p. 142.) A troubling question from a theoretical feminist point of view is whether the initial preference for male over female slaves can be considered discrimination. In a mode of production in which workers have no freedom of choice and merely receive the minimum means of subsistence in return for their work, is it a privilege to be chosen?

8. Rhoda E. Reddock, "Women and Slavery in the Caribbean: A Feminist Perspective," *Latin American Perspectives* 12, no. 1 (Winter 1985). On the other side of the picture, historians have also found that women slaveowners could be and often were as cruel and sadistic with their slaves as men slaveowners. See, for example, Gilberto Freyre, *The Masters and the Slaves,* Samuel Putnam, trans. (Berkeley: University of California Press, 1986), pp. 350-51. And despite their subjection to husbands or fathers, women of the slaveowner class experienced a life of leisure and the same material advantages that their male counterparts did.

9. Reddock, ibid., pp. 67-68.

10. As quoted by Moreno Fraginals, *The Sugarmill*, p. 142.

11. Ibid., p. 143.

12. See Ramón A. Gutiérrez, "From Honor to Love: Transformation in the Meaning of Sexuality in Colonial New Mexico," in Raymond T. Smith, ed., *Kinship Ideology and Practice in Latin America* (Chapel Hill: University of North Carolina Press, 1984) and "Honor Ideology, Marriage Negotiation, and Class-Gender Domination in New Mexico, 1690-1846," *Latin American Perspectives* 12, no. 1 (Winter 1985), esp. p. 86. See also Verena Martínez-Alier, *Marriage, Class and Color in Nineteenth-Century Cuba: A Study of Racial Attitudes and Sexual Values in a Slave Society* (London: Cambridge University Press, 1974), especially ch. I; Patricia Seed, *To Love, Honor, and Obey in Colonial Mexico: Conflicts Over Marriage Choice, 1574-1821* (Stanford: Stanford University Press, 1988), p. 61.

13. Black men, rejected by most women, were therefore also at the bottom of the social scale. See Martínez-Alier, *Marriage, Class and Color,* p. 118.

14. See Ann Twinam, "Honor, Sexuality, and Illegitimacy in Colonial Spanish America," in Asunción Lavrin, ed., *Sexuality and Marriage in Colonial Latin America* (Lincoln and London: University of Nebraska Press, 1989), p. 123.

15. See Martínez-Alier, *Marriage, Class, and Color*, pp. 118-19.

16. For the requirement that marriage be endogamous, see ibid., esp. pp. 118-19. Also Gutiérrez, *When Jesus Came the Corn Mothers Went Away* (Stanford: Stanford

University Press, 1991), pp. xix, 255; Susan Socolow, "Acceptable Partners: Marriage Choice in Colonial Argentina, 1778-1810," in Lavrin, ed., *Sexuality and Marriage,* pp. 219-21. For questions of racial endogamy, see Robert McCaa, *"Calidad, Clase,* and Marriage in Colonial Mexico: the Case of Parral, 1788-90," *Hispanic American Historical Review* 64, no. 3 (August 1984): 481, 493, 496. For the requirement that the wife be superior in an unequal relationship, especially regarding property, see Muriel Nazzari, *Disappearance of the Dowry: Women, Families, and Social Change in São Paulo, Brazil, 1600-1900* (Stanford: Stanford University Press, 1991), especially pp. 36-39.

17. Nazzari, ibid., especially ch. 2 and pp. 30-34.

18. See Muriel Nazzari, "Concubinage in Colonial Brazil: The Inequalities of Race, Class, and Gender," *Journal of Family History* 21, no. 2 (April 1996): 107-124; also Eliana Maria Rea Goldschmidt, "Virtude e Pecado: Sexualidade em São Paulo Colonial," in Albertina de Oliveira Costa e Cristina Bruschini, eds., *Entre a Virtude e o Pecado* (Rio de Janeiro: Rosa dos Tempos; São Paulo: Fundação Carlos Chagas, 1992), p. 28; also Ronaldo Vainfas, *Trópico dos Pecados: Moral, Sexualidade e Inquisição no Brasil* (Rio de Janeiro: Campus, 1989), pp. 76-77. For similar conclusions in Venezuela, see Kathy Waldron, "The Sinners and the Bishop in Colonial Venezuela: The *Visita* of Bishop Mariano Martí, 1771-1784," p. 158, and for Mexico, Thomas Calvo, "The Warmth of the Hearth: Seventeenth-Century Guadalajara Families," especially p. 296, both in Lavrin, *Sexuality and Marriage.*

19. My emphasis. Arquivo da Cúria Metropolitana de São Paulo, hereafter called ACMSP, Processos Crime, Concubinato, 1779, Interior S.P., Mairiporá, Denunciados: José Roiz Padilla, Bernarda Lopes.

20. ACMSP, Processos Crime, Concubinato, 1748, cidade, Denunciados: Josefa Maria de Jesus Avila, Francisco Leite, viúvo, concubino da ré; citados: Francisco de Avila, Nataria, bastarda.

21. See Nazzari, "Concubinage in Colonial Brazil."

22. ACMSP, Processos Esponsáis, Auto de Justificação Entre Partes, São Paulo, 1780, Maria Gertrudes, Justificante, Joaquim Pereira Machado, Justificado.

23. Donald Ramos, "Marriage and the Family in Colonial Vila Rica," *Hispanic American Historical Review* 55, no. 2 (May 1975): 200-225; "City and Country: The Family in Minas Gerais, 1804-1838," *Journal of Family History* 3, no. 4 (Winter 1978): 361-375; and "Single and Married Women in Vila Rica, Brazil 1754-1838," *Journal of Family History* 16, no. 3 (1991): 261-282.

24. Nazzari, *Disappearance of the Dowry,* pp. 26-27.

25. Maria Odila da Silva Dias, *Quotidiano e poder em São Paulo no século XIX: Anna Gertrudes de Jesus* (São Paulo: Brasiliense, 1984), p. 75.

26. See Muriel Nazzari, "The Waxing and Waning of Matrilineality in São Paulo, Brazil: Historical Variations in an Ambilineal System, 1500-1900," in Mary Jo Maynes, Birgitte Soland, Ulrike Strasser, and Ann Waltner, eds., *Gender, Kinship, Power: A Comparative and Interdisciplinary History* (New York: Routledge, 1996).

27. See Nazzari, "The Waxing and Waning of Matrilineality"; and *Disappearance of the Dowry,* p. 141.

28. For an excellent analysis of patriarchalism in Latin America, see John Tutino, "Power, Class and Family: Men and Women in the Mexican Elite," *The Americas* 39, no. 3 (January 1983).

29. Silvia Arrom, *The Women of Mexico City, 1790-1857* (Stanford: Stanford University Press, 1985), p. 120.

30. Sandra Lauderdale Graham, *House and Street: The Domestic World of Servants and Masters in Nineteenth-Century Rio de Janeiro* (Cambridge: Cambridge University Press, 1988), p. 192.

31. Frances Rothstein, "Two Different Worlds: Gender and Industrialization in Rural Mexico," in Madeleine B. Leons and Frances Rothstein, eds., *New Directions in Political Economy: An Approach from Anthropology* (Westport, CT:Greenwood Press, 1979); and *Three Different Worlds: Women, Men and Children in an Industrializing Community* (Westport, CT: Greenwood Press, 1982).

32. Edith Couturier, "Women in a Noble Family: The Mexican Counts of Regla, 1750-1830," in Asunción Lavrin, ed., *Latin American Women: Historical Perspectives* (Westport, CT: Greenwood Press, 1978); Tutino, "Power, Class and Family"; Edith Couturier and Asunción Lavrin, "Dowries and Wills: A View of Women's Socio-economic Role in Colonial Guadalajara and Puebla," *Hispanic American Historical Review* 59 (May 1979); Asunción Lavrin, "Women and Convents: Their Economic and Social Role in Colonial Mexico," in Berenice Carroll, ed., *Liberating Women's History: Theoretical and Critical Essays* (Urbana: University of Illinois Press, 1976); Susan Soeiro, "The Social and Economic Role of the Convent: Women and Nuns in Colonial Bahia, 1677-1800," *Hispanic American Historical Review* 54, no. 2 (May 1974).

33. Nazzari, *Disappearance of the Dowry*, p. 7.

34. For the low esteem of merchants in colonial São Paulo, see Sergio Buarque de Holanda, *Monções* (São Paulo: Alpha-Omega, 1976), p. 115; for colonial Bahia, see Jean Dell Flory and David Grant Smith, "Bahian Merchants and Planters in the Seventeenth and Early Eighteenth Centuries," in *Hispanic American Historical Review* 58 (1978): 576. For colonial Mexico, see David Brading, *Miners and Merchants in Bourbon Mexico, 1763-1810* (Cambridge: Cambridge University Press, 1971).

35. Arrom, *The Women of Mexico City*, pp. 157-58, 201.

36. See, among others, Elizabeth Jelin, "Migration and Labor Force Participation of Latin American Women: the Domestic Servants in the Cities," in Wellesley Editorial Committee, *Women and National Development* (Chicago: University of Chicago Press, 1977); Elsa Chaney and Mary García Castro, *Muchachas No More: Household Workers in Latin America and the Caribbean* (Philadelphia: Temple University Press, 1989); J. Filet-Abreu de Souza, "Paid Domestic Service in Brazil," *Latin American Perspectives* 7, no. 1 (Winter 1980).

37. Arrom, *The Women of Mexico City*, pp. 157-58.

38. Anna Rubbo and Michael Taussig, "Up Off Their Knees: Servanthood in Southwest Colombia," *Latin American Perspectives* 10, no. 4 (Fall 1983).

39. Nora Scott Kinzer, "Professional Women in Buenos Aires," in Ann Pescatello, ed.,

Female and Male in Latin America: Essays (Pittsburgh: University of Pittsburgh Press, 1973), p. 184.

40. Kinzer, "Sociocultural Factors Mitigating Role Conflicts of Buenos Aires Professional Women," in Ruby Rohrlich-Leavitt, ed., *Women Cross-Culturally* (The Hague: Mouton, 1975).

41. Jelin, "Migrations and Labor Force Participation"; Heleieth Iara B. Saffioti, *Emprego Doméstico e Capitalismo* (Petrópolis: Vozes, 1978), pp. 161-62.

READING GENDER IN HISTORY

CARMEN RAMOS ESCANDON

Is there a history of women? If so, what is it? The questions were initially approached by attempting to situate women as historical subjects, that is, to assess their presence, importance, and significance in a society at a given time. Emphasis was placed on finding women in specific historical moments and in diverse social groups, subject to a series of limitations, and with specific interests and activities. This approach, dominant in the 1970s, has been labeled revindicative, starting from the premise that women needed to be reincorporated into history.[1] It did not take long to observe that from the perspective of women, the image of a given historical event or period could be seen differently from the way it was traditionally interpreted.[2] The enlargement and reversal of the historical lens has increasingly led research in the field of women's history to embrace a nontraditional point of view, posing a new set of questions. Reformulating questions also implies favoring a new type of information and posing new methodological problems. The historical task consists not only of compiling "facts" but of organizing and interpreting that information analytically, making it relevant as it refers to the question posed.

By "historical facts," historians typically have understood those that refer to political life, dominated by men. How would this compilation of facts and their analysis be different from another perspective? Is it possible that the significant questions for women are different from those for men? What, then, does a "feminine" historiography mean? Mary Nash has pointed out that recent work on women's history has gone beyond the traditional subjects, including notable women's biographies, and histories of suffrage and of women's education. Historical studies of gender now focus on two central problems: the elaboration of a conceptual framework linked to contemporary feminist theory and the elaboration of a new methodology based on the insights of postmodernism and poststructuralism.[3]

FROM A FEMININE PERSPECTIVE TO THE CATEGORY OF GENDER

If we admit the existence of a particular set of subjects and issues that is important to women, it becomes necessary to adopt a perspective that is consistent with this approach. The set of questions, the manner in which they are asked, the sources, all would develop out of this new perspective. This implies a nontraditional set of issues, problems, and historical subjects that differ from the conventional ones. In particular, we need to investigate the way in which the categories feminine and masculine have been socially constructed in different historical periods. Posing questions about historical events in this manner we are, in fact, engaged in two parallel and interrelated processes. One examines the category "women"; the other gives preference to subjects and problems relevant to women, regardless of ethnic, social, and economic differences among them.

The category "women," far from being universal, univocal, and unchanging, is changing continually. It thus reflects what was considered womanly at different times and places; "feminine" implies issues and subjects that might be significantly different for women than for men. In other words, the importance of the questions and the ways of questioning are transformed according to the interlocutor and the period about which they are posed. What is feminine can be further understood by posing yet another more encompassing question. The notions of women and men are not absolute value-free analytical concepts, but historically bounded ones. We need to know how the feminine is opposed to the nonfeminine, how social relations between men and women condition femininity and masculinity. Both are historical constructions determined by social relations that assign patterns of conduct to individuals with dichotomous boundaries that in turn build feminine/masculine paradigms. How do individuals conform or deviate from those paradigms and how does society sanction

150

those who deviate? This is the field of enquiry about processes of gender formation.

A gendered view of history recovers the presence of women in all aspects of social, economic, political, cultural, symbolic, and private life. It studies how women have been represented visually and linguistically, and analyzes gender relations as one of the ways in which power relations operate. A gendered approach to history examines how social relationships between men and women are shaped and to what extent social relationships shape the actors. This is a new way of conceptualizing history, for it implies an "expansion of the boundaries of history, it is both a supplement and a radical replacement."[4]

This perspective necessarily modifies the view of what has traditionally been understood as history: the exercise of public power. It also modifies the premises of the categories of historical analysis by making gender relations a privileged subject of inquiry. Relations between the sexes then is analyzed as a sociopolitical, an economic, and a cultural relation. What is considered feminine or masculine and validated as such is understood to be a social construction, not as a static, immutable relation conditioned on, and predetermined by, biology. The postulation of gender as a social category can be considered one of the most important contributions of women's historiography, especially in Great Britain, the United States, and increasingly in Latin America.

WOMEN AND HISTORY IN LATIN AMERICA

Social science research on women in Latin America has mushroomed during the last fifteen years, focusing primarily on the effects of economic change on women, women's political organizations, and changes in household composition.[5] Research on Latin American women's history is increasing rapidly, although gender is not yet widely used as an analytical tool.[6] Awareness of the need for an analysis of gender relations in Latin America has emerged only recently, as has feminist awareness about history's relevance to the women's movement.[7] This can be partially explained by the nature of historical discourse in the region, where history has been used as a tool to legitimize power. This practice has been particularly damaging for Latin American women, because it conceptualizes history as a mere chronicle of changes in political power, and formal politics is a sphere in which women have had a limited role. It is within this view of history that Latin American women are often presented. From Malintzin (the noblewoman of Tlaxcala who succumbed to Cortés) to Eva Perón, traditional history has focused on the "heroine" who is an adjunct to a famous man.[8]

Feminist historians have debated the specificity of women's history. According to Joan Scott there have been three major approaches within women's history. One sees patriarchy as the universal cause of women's oppression. A second, Marxist approach, explains women's oppression in terms of women's relationship to socialized production and generational reproduction. A third, the psychoanalytical school, examines unconscious adherence to gender roles.[9]

Inspired by work that looked at the origin and persistence of the oppression of women by men, feminism in the 1970s focused on the category of patriarchy, defined as the manifestation and institutionalization of male dominance over women and children in the family, and by extension male dominance over women in society in general.[10] Whether reproduction or sexuality is seen as the cause of patriarchy, however, it is problematic to explain the origin of women's subordination in terms of patriarchy, precisely because historical differences are not considered. Patriarchy often presupposes an ahistorical constant in the forms of feminine subordination. If in all social organizations women are subjected in the same ways on the basis of sexuality or reproduction, the historical specificity of different forms of feminine oppression is lost. Knowing that all women are oppressed does not explain the reasons for their oppression. Nor does it reveal how gender subordination modifies social structures and conditions nongendered social inequities. According to Scott, to explain the existence of patriarchy by starting from the male appropriation of children or from male sexual objectivization of women is to reduce gender subordination to physical difference alone. This presupposes a universal, immutable significance of the human body and disregards different cultural constructions of the body and of sexuality and has been widely refuted by feminist criticism, which sees changing representations of the female body as central to the symbolic production of Western culture.[11]

By contrast, Marxist approaches have analyzed women's oppression as rooted in relationships of production within the family and in wider society. This perspective has dominated Latin American women's studies in the social sciences, including the debate on the effects on women of the economic crisis of the 1980s and 1990s.

The theme of women and everyday life has received considerable attention in sociological studies of gender.[12] Because historical transformations in daily life are sometimes imperceptible they have been less chronicled. However, the tension between permanence and change in the relations of daily life is important to an understanding of the social construction of gender. While relationships of power within the family are important, it is more important to know how this domestic web is related to social processes in a broader sense and how the organization of the family contradicts or reflects society's structures. Moments in which alternative forms of family organization have represented a challenge to the prevailing social system are rare, and for that reason, of maximum interest. In particular, a major question is how they have propitiated change.

The area of family history has received considerable attention in Latin America and has proved very useful in understanding changing gender relations.[13] In the Brazilian case, Elizabeth Kuznesof challenges traditional interpretations about the nuclear family, Muriel Nazzari explains the relationship between class formation, property transmission, and female interests, illustrating the connections between women of different social classes; and Sandra Lauderdale Graham describes the everyday lives of élite women and their female servants and slaves in nineteenth century Rio de Janeiro.[14]

The third approach to gender and history outlined by Scott investigates the identity formation processes from the perspective of psychoanalysis. This approach stresses the subjects' experiences during the first stages of life; the relationship between rationality, mental health, and gender identity; and language as a vehicle of gender construction. In Latin America this is still a virtually unexplored area. Analysis of systems of rationality/irrationality and deviant/accepted sexuality extends to how these relate to other economic, social, and power systems. Conceived in this way, "power" is not only political power but also the capacity for articulation and representation. In this sense, it is important to analyze cultural systems insofar as they reflect not only a gendered division of roles but also how the concept of culture itself is tinted by gender differences.

A number of feminist theorists have fashioned the category "feminine culture" as the space in which femininity is generated. "Feminine culture" appears to perpetuate the opposition feminine/masculine and the system of values this represents. A serious consequence of this is that "feminine culture" is based on the category "woman" as immutable and ahistorical. Contemporary feminist criticism is aligned against this essentialist notion and proposes a deconstruction of absolute categories which negate temporal variations. Historians, in particular, analyze the changing forms of oppression and their specificity in a given time and space. To explain what gender is, then, historians stress transformations in the mechanics of femininity and masculinity. Studies of this type go beyond the unconscious sense of gender construction and make it conscious, make it an object of historical analysis, and integrate it into historical analysis. This approach is new to Latin American women's history.[15]

The importance of looking at gender in a historical perspective questions the immutability of a world organized according to biological differences. It reveals how sex has been wielded as a legitimizing element of social relations in the economic and political realms. Historical analysis can describe how "male" and "female" are concepts related to norms of the social order, the exercise of power, and the distribution of wealth. If to the category of "sex" we oppose that of gender, as a process of social construction, gender becomes an element for understanding forms of human interaction. In this methodology differences between men and women are not based on biological differences, but on differences that are historically created. Put another way, biological difference of individuals are recognized, but the values and implications resulting from these differences are seen as the result of culture and the social relations between groups and individuals.[16] The way in which societies organize relationships between the sexes constitutes the gender construction process. Clearly, this approach generates the need for a new reading of historical development. A gendered re-reading of Latin American history opens up major questions about social and political processes. What follows is a broad overview of Mexican history since the conquest from a gender perspective.

A GENDERED READING OF MEXICAN HISTORY

If one form of periodization involves the selection of events that signal fundamental change in economic, social, and political organization, a gendered periodization selects key events which prove relevant to social relations among the sexes. This leads us to revise the traditional periodization of Mexican history. We have to ask, for instance, what the conquest meant for gender dynamics. How were the relationships between men and women modified by this process? Magnus Morner states that in a certain sense the conquest of America was the conquest of women: women were considered part of the spoils of war and Spaniards obtained indigenous women both by force and by peaceful means.[17] For Morner the enslavement of women was one element in the general process of subjugation of the indigenous population by the Spanish in the sixteenth century. In a reading of this phenomenon from the perspective of gender, the conquest represented a new type of subjection for indigenous women, both as women and as Indians. The presence of white men altered relationships between indigenous men and women, and later the presence of indigenous men and women altered gender relations between white men and women in Latin America.[18]

The conquest represented an important change in the lives of women and men insofar as it brought ethnic differentiation to gendered relationships. Over time, the Spanish crown and the Catholic church issued a multitude of legal regulations specifying what was properly feminine and masculine among the different social/ethnic groups. Thus gendered identity, in addition to sexuality, was socially regulated: it was not a private but a social matter. Serge Gruzinski has pointed out, for example, how concepts of sexuality, marriage, and family represented Western conceptions that were projected onto pre-Hispanic realities.[19] The history of sexuality explores these processes.[20] From the perspective of gender, however, these studies need to take into account the connections between individual relationships and systems of power. In other words, analysis would concentrate on the relationships between biological differences, and specific social, political and ideological constructions of gender.

In another study of the colonial period, Patricia Seed analyzes the relationship between the gender formation process and broader social structures by focusing on the policies and practices of marriage choice. She examines the process of the consolidation of patriarchal authority over children, as freedom of choice in marriage partners was progressively restricted in the seventeenth and eighteenth centuries.[21] Seed's work provides a good example of the interrelationship between processes of public and private life. In colonial Mexico social edicts made explicit the class-gender system. However, practices of sexuality differed from the prescriptions that sought to regulate it. Many authors have analyzed colonial discourses on sexuality, highlighting contradictions in indigenous and Spanish ideologies and practices. They describe how women were represented in discourse, in iconography, and in culture, and how relationships between the sexes revealed aspects of social organization. Now it is important to broaden the central question to explore the relationship between gender and power.[22]

Adapting Fredric Jameson's idea of the master narrative and applying it to colonial society, Jean Franco argues that the master narrative of colonial society did not provide a space for women. For this reason women appropriated a cultural space of their own, the convent. Since women were deprived of the power to speak and the power of representation, the convent was the only space available for feminine discourse.[23] Asunción Lavrin's study provides evidence of the importance of convent culture as a feminine space. She shows that the power of the convents was not only religious but also economic and social.[24] Nonetheless, despite the undeniable importance of convents in the social life of New Spain, it was not the only space for women. The economic and political power of women who were not cloistered, especially those of the lower social classes, needs to be researched.[25]

From the point of view of gender formation, the nineteenth century presents the consolidation of the national state and of the nuclear family.[26] Social control

155

of female behavior was exercised through various institutions: the family, the law, the education system, and the workplace. While we know that Victorian morals were adopted in Mexico, the strong indigenous component of society affected standards of education and female conduct in most classes, even when the mores of the Europeanizing oligarchy were held up as the universal norm for all women.[27]

While the nineteenth-century family has not been studied as closely as the colonial household, it is clear that in this period the state sought to prevail over the church in controlling civil society, with consequences for the domestic lives of men and women and the relations between them. A new ordering of family relations prompted new family legislation during the last third of the century.[28] While we know that civil marriage emerged only in the 1850s, and took a long time to become a common practice, the relation between legal prescriptions and forms of conduct in different regions of the country and different social groups still needs to be studied. For the era preceding the Mexican Revolution in 1910, it is necessary to explore the relationship between the positivist idea of women aloof from politics, in the home, and the beginnings of a Mexican feminism, seen in the emergence of figures such as Laureana Wright de Kleinmans, Dolores Jimeno y Muro, or Juana Belén Gutiérrez de Mendoza. The presence of women in political activities, when the social system was clearly repressive, points to alternative forms of political life.[29]

Perhaps a new type of periodization could be used for analyzing the whole of the nineteenth century from a gender perspective. For instance, the creation of civil marriage in 1856, or the implementation of the new Civil Code in 1870 could be substituted for the traditional political chronology. A gendered reading of Mexico's nineteenth-century history might substantially modify our perception of the period.

The revolutionary process that engulfed Mexico at the beginning of the twentieth century transformed lives, attitudes, and institutions. In the case of women this change was profound.[30] From a political perspective, a central characteristic of the twentieth century has been the consolidation of a strong government apparatus and of an enormous bureaucracy. Historians have studied how women were integrated into this process.[31] But the presence of women in the bureaucratic sector did not necessarily represent access to power. A study on women and power shows that women are found less frequently the higher one looks in the bureaucratic apparatus.[32] The percentage of women office workers is high, but that of high-level women officials and governors is low. Women's access to power in Mexico continues to be primarily through family networks.[33] This is one approach to developing a new periodization of Mexican history, one that places gender at the center of the analysis. But in fact, this periodization may be too orthodox in nature—as it retained the standard moments of conquest, liberal reforms, and revolution as the major historical turning points. It may be that further research on gender in Mexican history will reveal that other periods were more critical in shaping and changing relations than the big political cataclysms.

NOTES

1. A pioneer work in this regard is Mary Beard, *Women as a Force in History: A Study of Traditions and Realities* (New York: Macmillan, 1946). A more recent study is Sheila Rowbotham, *Hidden from History: 300 Years of Women's Oppression and the Fight Against It* (London: Pluto Press, 1973).
2. See Joan Kelly Gayol, "Did Women Have a Renaissance?" in Renate Bridenthal and Claudia Koonz, eds., *Becoming Visible* (Boston: Houghton Mifflin, 1976), and *Women, History and Theory* (Chicago: University of Chicago Press, 1984), pp. 19-50.
3. See Mary Nash, "Nuevas dimensiones en la historia de la mujer," in *Presencia y protagonismo: aspectos de la historia de la mujer* (Barcelona: Ediciones del Serbal, 1984), p. 24.
4. Joan Scott, "Women's History," in Peter Burke, ed., *New Perspectives on Historical Writing* (University Park: Pennsylvania State University Press, 1993), pp. 49-50.
5. Examples would include Edna Acosta-Belén and Christine E. Bose, *Researching Women in Latin America and the Caribbean* (Boulder: Westview Press, 1993); Carmen Ramos Escandón, "Perspectivas femeninas en ciencias sociales en América Latina, una visión retrospectiva," *Revista Interamericana de Bibliografía* XLIII, no. 3 (1993): 439-449; Elizabeth Jelin, *Family, Household and Gender Relations in Latin America* (London: Kegan Paul International, 1991); and K. Lynn Stoner, ed., *Latinas of the Americas: A Source Book* (New York: Garland, 1989).
6. See K. Lynn Stoner, "Directions in Latin American Women's History 1975-1985," *Latin American Research Review* 22, no. 2; and Edna Acosta-Belén, *Researching Women in Latin America and the Caribbean* (Boulder: Westview Press, 1990), p. 14.
7. See Edna Acosta-Belén, *Opening New Paths: Research on Women in Latin America and the Caribbean* (Washington: The Latin American Program: Woodrow Wilson International Centre for Scholars), Paper Series 204, 1994; Silvia Arrom, *New Research in Latin American Women's Studies* (Bloomington, Indiana: Women's Studies Program, Indiana University Press, 1991); and Ramos Escandón, "Women in Latin American History: trends for future research," in *Retrieving Women's History* (Paris: UNESCO, 1989) pp. 303-319, among many others.
8. June Hanher, *Women in Latin American History: Their Lives and Views* (Los Angeles: UCLA, 1980); Gertrude M. Yaeger, ed., *Confronting Change, Challeng-*

GENDER POLITICS IN LATIN AMERICA

ing Tradition: Women in Latin American History (Willington: D.E. Scholarly Resources, 1994).

9. Joan Scott, "Women's History," in Burke, ed., *New Perspectives on Historical Writing,* pp. 49-50.

10. Gerder Lerner, *The Creation of Patriarchy* (New York: Oxford University Press, 1986). Although the word *patriarchy* has been in constant use, its definitions have varied. The *Diccionario de la Real Academia Española* (Madrid, 1984) defines it as a "Primitive social organization in which authority is exercised by a male, the head of each family, extending this power even to distant relatives of the same lineage." *Webster's Third New International Dictionary* (1981) defines it as "A social organization marked by the supremacy of the father in the clan or family in both domestic and religious functions, the legal dependence of wife or wives and children, and the reckoning of descent and inheritance in the male line; a society so organized."

11. See Susan Rubin Suleiman, *The Female Body in Western Culture: Contemporary Perspectives* (Cambridge: Harvard University Press, 1985); Edward Shorter, *A History of Women's Bodies* (London: Penguin, 1984). Analysis of the representation of Caribbean women's bodies in the minds of Europeans has proven extremely fruitful: see Barbara Bush, *Slave Women in Caribbean Society 1650-1838* (Bloomington: Indiana University Press, 1990); and Vera Kutzinski, *Sugar's Secrets: Race and the Erotics of Cuban Nationalism* (Charlottesville: Virginia University Press, 1993).

12. See Orlandina de Oliveira, *Trabajo, poder y sexualidad* (México: El Colegio de México, 1989); and Teresita Barbieri, *Mujeres y vida cotidiana* (México: Sept. FCE, 1984). For a synthesis of the various theoretical positions on the effects of development crisis on women in Latin America, see Susan Tiano, "Women and Industrial Development in Latin America," *Latin American Research Review* 21, no. 3 (1986): 158.

13. See Sylvia Arrom, "Perspectivas sobre la historia de la familia en México," in Pilar Gonzalbo Aizpuru, ed., *Familias Novohispanas* (México: El Colegio de México, 1991).

14. See Elizabeth Kuznesof, "A familia na sociedade brasileira: parentesco, clientelismo e estrutura social. São Paulo 1700-1980," *Revista Brasileira de Historia* ANPUH 9, no. 17 (September 1988-February 1989): 37-63; *Household Economy and Urban Development: São Paulo, 1765 to 1836* (Boulder: Westview Press, 1986); and "Household and Family Studies," in Stoner, ed., *Latinas of the Americas,* pp. 237-304. See also Muriel Nazzari, *The Disappearance of the Dowry: Women, Family and Social Change in São Paulo, 1600-1900* (Stanford: Stanford University Press, 1991); and Sandra Lauderdale Graham, *House and Street: The Domestic World of Servants and Masters in XIX Century Rio* (Cambridge: Cambridge University Press, 1990).

15. Jean Franco, *Plotting Women: Gender and Representation in Mexico* (New York: Columbia University Press, 1990). On feminine irrationality and its connections with social repression systems, see María Cristina Sacristán, *Locura y*

Disidencia en el México Ilustrado 1760-1810 (México: Instituto Mora, Colegio de Michoacán, 1994).

16. Lerner, *The Creation of Patriarchy,* p. 6.
17. Magnus Morner, *Race Mixture in the History of Latin America* (Boston: Little Brown and Co., 1967), p. 22.
18. June Nash, "Aztec Women: Transition from Status to Class in Empire and Colony," in Etienne and Eleanor Leacock, eds., *Women and Colonization* (New York: Praeger, 1980), pp. 134-48.
19. Serge Gruzinski, "Matrimonio y sexualidad en México y Texcoco en los albores de la conquista o la pluralidad de los discursos," in Solange Alberro, ed., *Seis ensayos sobre el discurso colonial relativo a la comunidad doméstica* (México: INAH Departamento de Investigaciones Históricas, 1980), Cuaderno de Trabajo No. 35, p. 19.
20. See Alberro, ed., *Seis ensayos.*
21. Patricia Seed, *To Love, to Honor and Obey in Colonial Mexico: Conflicts over Marriage Choice, 1574-1821* (Stanford: Stanford University Press, 1988).
22. See, for example, Sergio Ortega Noriega, ed., *De la santidad a la perversion o de por qué no se cumplía la ley de Dios en la Sociedad Novohispana* (México: Grijalbo, 1985); Ortega Noriega, *El placer de pecar y el afán de normar* (México: Planeta, 1988); and Solange Alberro, *Inquisition et societe au Mexique 1571-1700* (Mexico: Centre D'etudes Mexicaines et centroamericaines, 1988).
23. Franco, *Plotting Women.* For a review of Franco's work, see Carmen Ramos Escandón, "Plotting Women," *Feminist Review* no. 42 (Autumn 1992): 104-108.
24. See Asunción Lavrin, "The Role of Nunneries in New Spain in the Eighteenth Century," *The Americas* 22 (October 1965): 182-203.
25. See David Sweet and Gary Nash, eds., *The Struggle for Survival in Colonial America* (Berkeley: University of California Press, 1984).
26. Sylvia Arrom, *The Women of Mexico City 1790-1857* (Stanford: Stanford University Press, 1985).
27. Mary Kay Vaughan, "Women, Class, and Education in Mexico 1880-1928," *Latin American Perspectives* 4, nos. 1/2 (1977): 135-152.
28. Sylvia Arrom, "Cambios en la condición jurídica de la mujer mexicana en el siglo XIX," in *Memoria del segundo congreso de historia del Derecho Mexicano* (México: Instituto de Investigaciones Jurídicas, 1981), pp. 492-518.
29. For an initial analysis of the effects of new legislation on women's roles, see Carmen Ramos Escandón and Ana Lau, *Mujeres y Revolución* (México: INHERM, 1993).
30. See, for example, Clementina Basols Batalla, *La mujer en la Revolución Mexicana* (México: 1960). Although some facts are known about the presence of the *adelitas* (camp followers) in the revolutionary armies, information on women's role in actual combat, in supporting the armies, attending the wounded, or in substituting for men on the battlefield remains anecdotal. See Elizabeth Salas, *Soldaderas in the Mexican Military: Myth and History* (Austin: University of Texas Press, 1990); and Ana Macías, *Against All Odds: The Feminist Movement in Mexico to 1940* (Westport, CT: Greenwood Press, 1982).

31. For example, Enriqueta Tuñón traces the efforts of women to get the vote during the 1920s and 1930s, concentrating on the Frente Unico Pro Derechos de la Mujer (Front for the Rights of Women); Tuñón, *Mujeres que se organizan* (México: Editorial Porrúa, 1992). For the period after the 1930s, see Tuñón, "La lucha política de la mujer mexicana por el derecho al sufragio y sus repercusiones," in Ramos Escandón, ed., *Presencia y Transparencia,* pp. 181-88.

32. Luz de Lourdes De Silva, "Las mujeres en la élite política de México, 1954-1984," in Orlandina de Oliveira, ed., *Trabajo, poder y sexualidad* (1989), pp. 269-308.

33. Among the few studies on the political participation of women in a historical context are: Ramos Escandón, "Women's Movements, Feminism and Mexican Politics," in Jane Jaquette, ed., *The Women's Movement in Latin America* (Boulder: Westview Press, 1994), pp. 199-222; William Blough, "Political Attitudes of Mexican Women," *Journal of Inter-American Studies and World Affairs* 14, no. 2 (1972); Benita Galena, *Benita, autobiografía* (Mexico: Imprenta Rústica, 1940); Lynn Stephen, "Women in Mexico's Popular Movements: Survival Strategies Against Ecological and Economic Impoverishment," *Latin American Perspectives* 19, no. 1 (Winter 1992): 73-96; Lau Jaiven, Ana, *Nueva ola del feminismo en México* (México: Planeta, 1987).

PROBLEMS OF DEFINITION IN THEORIZING LATIN AMERICAN WOMEN'S WRITING

DEBORAH SHAW

The growing body of fictional writing and critical studies by Latin American women since the 1980s has prompted critics to provide all-inclusive theories to define and categorize this new "boom femenino." The predominant debate over the past decade focuses on whether there is such a thing as "women's writing" which is fundamentally different from men's. The debate has become increasingly polarized: on one side, those who tend to conceive of "masculine" and "feminine" literature as occupying two distinct spaces, two mutually oppositional blocs; on the other, those who believe that to enclose literature within gender categories is to ghettoize and marginalize work by women. The latter argue for an androgynous position, claiming that art has no sex.[1]

This chapter looks first at some of the problems which have arisen from the desire to make generalizations about the nature of women's writing which are intended to be applicable to all Latin American women who write fiction, and from the denial that gender has any bearing on a writer's work. It argues that any attempt to identify defining characteristics of something as heteroge-neous as women's writing in Latin America is bound to be essentialist; but equally, a denial that gender has any bearing on literature is untenable, and attempts to take this position result in a series of contradictions. The chapter then analyzes some more sophisticated approaches to theory: it suggests that critics who view gender as a complex cultural construct which cannot exist independently of factors such as race, ethnicity, nationality, and class, can tell us more about "women's writing" than can those whose theories are blind to differences among women, due to an overreliance on traditional notions of the masculine/feminine dichotomy.

A tendency among those who favor the notion of *escritura femenina* is to set out a prescriptive list of adjectives to define and enclose. These adjectives are often negative, and rank low in the hierarchy of artistic standards. A key exponent of this is the Argentinian writer Marta Traba. In her essay *Hipótesis sobre una escritura diferente* ("A Hypothesis on a Different Way of Writing"), Traba claims that women write from a space where abstraction and the use of metaphor and symbols are less common, where explanation and facts replace interpretation, where there is less invention than memory, and where a focus on small details and an inner world replaces a concern for greater things. Abstraction, explanation, interpretation, invention, and a concern with the world are, then, associated with men's writing, leaving them as the writers of the "great works of literature."[2]

Women, Traba believes, are writing from a counterculture, and the power of women's writing comes from an acceptance of their marginal positions. Women should, she writes: *"accept their particularities,* without trying to reverse the domination process [my italics]."[3] Here she suggests that a marginal position is a natural position, women should accept their "particularities," that is, what is intrinsic to their gender, and accept that they can never reach the cerebral heights of male literature. This is clearly to ascribe to women a set of "qualities" which art and literature have traditionally accepted as being femi-nine, and to deny their potential to tackle metaphysical, philosophical, or intellectual themes.

Traba is not alone in this belief; Mexican novelist and critic Sara Sefchovich has written that women's literature "(has) little complexity, less problemization, a flat and even linear structure, a less rich language, less formal innovation, less experimentation, and less metaphor."[4] Traba's and Sefchovich's definitions of feminine writing would assume that all women are writing in a literal, realist mode, a generalization which is not only untenable, but which also belongs to a long tradition of misogynistic conceptualizations

162

of women, as Josefina Ludmer explains in the introduction to her well known essay "Tretas del débil":

> It is well known that in the distribution of emotions, functions and faculties (transformed into mythology and fixed in language) women were given pain and passion in opposition to reason, the concrete in opposition to the abstract, the inner in opposition to the outer words, reproduction in opposition to production. To read these attributes in women's language and literature is simply to read what has been and continues to be inscribed in their social space.[5]

In the light of such definitions, it is little wonder that a number of writers have expressed concern with the very concept of a "women's writing."[6]

In her readings of Latin American women's writing, however, Bell Gale Chevigny has come to precisely the contrary conclusion to Traba, talking of "a greater tendency toward literary experimentation toward the South" in her comparison of North American and Latin American women writers, citing Rosario Ferré, Ana Lydia Vega, Luisa Valenzuela, and Julieta Campos in support of her argument.[7] Susan Bassnett, in her introduction to *Knives and Angels,* also talks of the strong influence of surrealism on Latin American women writers, while Cristina Peri Rossi confesses to feeling confused by a commonly held view that women are not given to abstraction.[8] Does this mean, Rossi asks, that her own writing, with its heavy use of symbolism, is masculine?

Other critics and writers—such as Claribel Alegría, Elena Poniatowska, and Sara Castro-Klarén—prefer to find the "true nature" of women's writing in its social and political content, claiming that women as an oppressed group are almost exclusively concerned with those who suffer from various forms of marginalization, whether political repression, social discrimination such as that suffered by indigenous groups, or economic misery.[9] While there clearly are women writers who are predominantly concerned with these themes, there are others who are not. Many male Latin American writers are also concerned with political and economic oppression, without needing the stimulus of gender oppression.

It would appear from these contradictory definitions of "a body of writing" that critics can manipulate their choice of texts to fit a particular perspective of how they conceive Latin American women's writing to be. This highlights the dangers of formulating a neat, prescriptive theory to apply to all writers of the same sex in an entire continent. No critic would dare to do the same for all Latin American male authors, as even a limited knowledge of the range of these writers would show this to be impossible.

It is interesting that those who are most against the concept of a gendered

163

writing are women writers themselves, mainly because they do not want to be separated from their male contemporaries and judged by different artistic standards. Just as they resist the traditionally misogynistic treatment of women writers by male critics, they want no special favors from overenthusiastic feminists, as, I suspect, they feel this means they have not quite made it in universalist (male) terms. Denial also corresponds to legitimate fears of potentially reductive elements of feminist criticism, which could approach a writer's work purely in terms of her gender concerns, ignoring other aspects. All this is part of a larger concern that if they are seen (only) as women they will be relegated to forming a subgroup rather than constituting an integral part of literature. As Jean Franco notes: "We have to understand this denial (of the existence of women's writing) as a rejection of labelling, remembering the histories of literature which placed women in a separate paragraph at the end of the chapter."[10]

While we can understand what lies behind the rejection of the label "woman writer," it has proved to be difficult to deny the influence of gender on literary production. By examining the declarations of two important Latin American writers, Isabel Allende and Rosario Ferré, I intend to show that any attempt to refute something as important in the makeup of identity as gender results in a series of contradictions.

Isabel Allende is a writer who underplays notions of gender as a strategy to be taken seriously. She has shown a certain internalization of prejudice against what has been considered feminine. In an interview with Magdalena García Pinto, Allende reacts particularly defensively when asked if she has chosen a diary technique in *La casa de los espíritus* (*The House of Spirits*), as it is a novel about women; she replies: "No, and had I known it were a feminine technique, I would not have used it"—suggesting that she would be prepared to change her technique if it meant not being judged as a woman.[11] She attempts to the deny the influence of gender on literary production, saying: "I do not think that literature has a gender, and one should not set out to write like a woman because it is a form of self-segregation which I find forced. I believe that one should write as well as possible as an open, tolerant and well educated human being."[12]

Allende confuses several points in her defense of a sexless literature; she confuses the notion of setting out to write like a woman with a literature which is informed by gender, and she confuses independence of gender with quality. What exactly does writing like a person, like a human being, mean? Does writing from the perspective of a Chilean woman of the wealthy classes mean that she cannot write like a person? Each writer is coming from somewhere, and to attempt to claim freedom from important factors informing identity is dishonest. She suggests that anyone reading *La casa de los espíritus* would not know if it were written by a man or a woman if the author was anonymous, although in a later comment she contradicts herself and reveals her reasons for such statements. She concedes, after some pressure from García Pinto, that "it is possible that my female characters are stronger, or that I have a female perspective," but she resents the label of "woman writer," and, as we have seen, is even willing to distort a judgment of her own work if she can escape its application. Her subsequent comments are revealing: "I want the language, the structure, the final product, the book, to be primarily accepted for its intrinsic value, for its literary quality. I'm not asking for any special favors as a woman, nor do I accept superfluous demands for being a woman."[13]

Allende's tone is insistent and above all defensive—she wants to be judged with male writers and accepted on their level; hence her denial of the gendered nature of her own writing, and her insistence, in the above quotation, on the separation of stylistics and thematics. Her response is a symptom of the marginalization women writers have faced; it is a cry of anger at not being taken seriously. Despite the fact that *La casa de los espíritus* is an international bestseller, she is frequently judged in the shadow of Gabriel García Márquez, and seen as a sort of lightweight female version of the Colombian novelist. Her response has actually very little to do with whether she believes that men and women have different approaches to literature, and everything to do with her own position in the field of Latin American literature.

Rosario Ferré is another author who has expressed views on the question of gendered writing, and who falls into contradictions in an attempt to both deny and accept the notion. She begins her famous essay, "The Writer's Kitchen," like Allende, by making a distinction between form and content in order to assert that women can write as well as men. She chooses the example of the sonnet to illustrate her point; a sonnet has fourteen lines and its own conventions of rhyme and meter, and execution of this art form is free of gender implications.[14] Again, this is a defensive response to historical discrimination against women writers. Form and content cannot be neatly split in two; a perfectly constructed sonnet could be composed of words which, when placed together, made no sense at all. A work of literature is the sum of its contents, of the way it is written and the themes it deals with. A desire to separate the two seems to be a way of saying, "Yes, I know the protagonist is a woman, and I am looking at issues that are important to her/me, but please consider my book as a work of art."

Where women's literature does exist as different from men's, for Ferré, is

165

"in the themes that obsess women," and this is at first attributed to "biological fate." After denying that there is a female style as there is no "immutable female nature," this attempt to connect theme with biology seems contradictory. She argues that women, as mothers and nurturers of children, have a special relationship with their bodies. This "biological fate" creates problems for professional needs, "but it also puts us in contact with the mysterious generative forces of life" and it is this, for Ferré, that determines the question of women's writing: "That is why women's literature has, much more so than men's literature, concerned itself with interior experiences, experiences that have little to do with the historical, the social or the political."[15]

Ferré confuses the cultural and biological acts of motherhood, and holds biology responsible for women's exclusion from the "public" worlds of history, society, and politics, choosing to interpret these categories in a way that denies women's involvement in them. She assumes all women are mothers and primary caretakers of their children, implies that mothering is a nonpolitical, nonsocial event, and then argues that women writers can only write from this position of motherhood. She then adds to the confusion by suggesting that women's "experience ... may change becoming richer and broader."[16] It is not clear how this would be possible if we are writing from within a biological determinism, as she initially proposes.

After highlighting the commonality of all women's writing thematically, Ferré concludes by reiterating the view that the craft of writing has nothing to do with gender, revealingly using a cooking metaphor to make her point. She writes, a little earlier, "I often confuse writing and cooking," and goes on to insist on cooking as a specifically woman-centered activity, defining it as a task passed down from mother to daughter, before concluding: "The secret of writing, like the secret of good cooking, has nothing to do with gender. It has to do with the skill with which we mix the ingredients over the fire."[17] Here she provides a fine example of the inseparability of style and gender, as the metaphor she uses comes from her own experience as a housewife, of which cooking is an integral part. In denying gender, she uses a gender-loaded language.

In examining these attempts at definitions, we see that each excludes the other; women's writing cannot at once be rooted in a realist mode and be surrealist and experimental; neither can it be exclusively concerned with the small details of private everyday lives and be interested primarily in the socioeconomic condition of oppressed groups. Likewise, form and content cannot be neatly divided in two to allow writers to speak of a style which has nothing to do with their social formation as women. These contradictory positions are due to an overambitious attempt to place all women within the same parameters, and to a preference for generalizations over theory. One of the main reasons for the contradictions and generalizations in pronouncements on the essential nature of women's writing can be found in the need to define and categorize that which can neither be defined or categorized; there is simply no single essential nature to women's writing.

Critics have spent much of their energies on a question which, as Jean Franco writes, is "mal planteada"—poorly posed—in order to justify their exclusive focus on women writers.[18] Women writers deserve to receive critical attention because they produce literature which is worthy of study, because past works of women writers have been largely ignored by the critical establishment, and because we are currently witnessing a genuine "boom femenino." Following a similar line of argument, Catherine Boyle identifies the weaknesses resulting from the emphases of much theory on women's writing:

> The parameters of the debate are artificially set, they are based on difference, on lack, on justification. On all that is negative. Women's writing in Latin America should be brought into the spotlight and studied because it has been ignored, and because there are writers who have contributed a huge amount to the cultural and literary wealth of Latin America who also happen to be women.[19]

We should not need to artificially organize works into one thematic or stylistic bloc in order to justify the exclusive study of women writers; there has, after all, rarely been any attempt to provide gender specific definitions of men's writing, despite numerous critical works which have only male writers as their objects of study. Of course gender has a bearing on literary production, but so too do factors such as social class, political consciousness, ethnic and religious identities, national and social political realities, and dominant literary and intellectual movements.

Reductionism or essentialism, so evident in the views of the writers studied in this chapter, has been the main focus of attack of recent feminist writings in a range of disciplines. For feminists influenced by a postmodern and poststructuralist approach, the subject is seen as constructed from multiple sites; race, ethnicity, class, sexual orientation are all considered as important as gender in the makeup of subjects, as are specific contexts of history and culture.[20] Recognition of these factors which divide women renders impossible the concept of a global sisterhood, and allows the very notion of a (universal, single) gender identity to be seen as an essentialist category, in its reductive dismissal of all other categories.[21]

I feel that I should incorporate a brief disclaimer at this point. Although I have deliberately drawn attention to limitations in Latin American writers' and critics' pronouncements on women's writing, this is not part of a project to denigrate these critics and writers in order to simply compare them unfavorably with the "more sophisticated" first world theorists. The tendency to perceive women's writing in universal terms is equally apparent in early attempts to theorize Anglo-American literature, and recent criticism from both Latin America and North America has become much more wary of easy generalizations.[22]

For these theorists, differences between women is an important notion that needs to be seen as liberating rather than divisive. That thinking in terms of difference can be empowering is clearly seen by women of color in the United States, who have adopted this as a key concept in their struggle to combat racism, classism, and homophobia in feminist literary criticism.[23] Notions of the 'same' are seen as products of racist and sexist stereotyping which only serve to make invisible those who do not fit into defining categories. An emphasis on difference does not mean, however, that alliances between women are no longer possible, as some feminists fear. Audre Lorde writes that "to recognize ... unity does not require that we be identical to each other. Black women are not one great vat of homogenized chocolate milk. We have many different faces, and we do not have to become each other in order to work together."[24] The same point (with the necessary changes in metaphors) is valid for any group of women for whom one totalizing label is used, be it third world, African, Indian, white middle-class or Latin American.

Barbara Christian is another critic who develops the concept of difference in the specific case of African-American women's writing. She criticizes the very notion of a black feminist literary theory as it presupposes a sameness in writers and in reading practices: "Instead (of inventing a monolithic theory), I think we need to read the works of our writers in our various ways and remain open to the intricacies of the intersection of language, class, race and gender in the literature."[25]

Critics who insist on a black women's writing are in danger of assuming that "there is only one way to be black." The only way to avoid falling into monolithic notions of African-American women, argues Christian, is to focus on variety and multiplicity.[26] What Christian seems to be proposing are theories that are born from the literary works themselves, not from theoretical dogma: "I have no set method since for me every work suggests a new approach."[27] Her call is echoed by the Chicana writer Gloria Anzaldúa, who stresses the need for *"mestizaje* theories" which allow for the creation of new spaces so that the critic can hear voices to which we have been deaf:

168

> Necesitamos teorías [we need theories] that will rewrite history using race, class, gender and ethnicity as categories of analysis, theories that cross borders, that blur boundaries—new kinds of theories with new theorizing methods. We need theories that will point out ways to maneuver between our particular experiences and the necessity of forming our own categories and theoretical models for the patterns we uncover.[28]

These critics are advocating theories and categories that originate from the texts themselves, not from any predefinitions of "woman," or even of "black woman," "Chicana woman," or "Latin American woman." Only in this way can spaces be opened up without the identities of texts and writers being subsumed into universalizing categories.

These new approaches to theory pioneered by women of color in the United States are particularly relevant to studies of writing by Latin American women. Women of color are attempting to open up the categories of gender in order to exist within a feminist literary theory which has had a white, middle-class, heterosexual, and Eurocentric focus, a focus which has little relevance to their writings or to the writings of Latin American women. Amy Kaminsky is one critic who has, not surprisingly, seen a natural ally for Latin American feminists in black and Latina feminism:

> Among North American varieties of feminism, Latin American feminism undoubtedly comes closest to black and Latina feminism in its political and economic urgency, its multiple allegiances, and its questioning of the effects of universalizing the notion of woman when the universalizing occurs from a dominant position.[29]

Latin Americanists have, indeed, found these recent theoretical tendencies useful in their analyses of women's writing. Since the late 1980s a number of highly sophisticated studies have taken debates on women's writing to a new level.[30] There are fewer overambitious projects that produce the contradictory positions critics were finding themselves forced into as a result of rather static notions of gender. Francine Masiello is one critic who has used a feminism enriched by poststructuralism to arrive at a deeper understanding of women's literary culture in the particular context of Argentina. In the introduction to her book, she rejects the view that there is "a basic unity among women, who speak in unison to a singular and generalized masculine opposition."[31] She goes on to explain her position thus:

> Literature should not be read as the unmediated experience of the female writer, oppressed or silenced by a relentlessly powerful group of men. This study is devoted rather to the constant traffic of representations by and about

169

women which are mediated by language and the effects of ideology on writing. The readings in the following chapters, in tracing the mutations of cultural texts, respond to changing literary values and conflicts in the nation and also to the intestitial contradictions among women writers themselves.[32]

An approach such as this allows a critic to analyze gender within texts without being forced to apply a fixed meaning to gender. Close readings of texts which are situated within specific historical periods and ideological tendencies permit the shifting meanings writers ascribe to gender to be recognized, and allow the reader to go beyond archetypal male/female paradigms. There are clear common points here with what Nancy Fraser and Linda Nicholson describe as a postmodernist feminist position: "explicitly historical, attuned to cultural specificity of different societies and periods and to that of different groups within societies and periods."[33]

Debra Castillo also finds recent theoretical discourses useful in avoiding the pitfalls awaiting the critic who hopes to provide the definitive list of categories within which to place all writers. Her tone is necessarily self-conscious: "I hope to offer a continually self-questioning theorizing, anchored in specific texts" as opposed to "an overarching theory." Her use of the term "theorizing" suggests that she is involved in an incomplete ongoing process. Castillo recognizes that Latin American women's writing is "multiple voiced and tends to operate within a field of sinuous and shifting positionalities rather than from a single, fixed position."[34] Thus, theories should, she argues, also eschew a single, fixed position and be prepared to engage with a range of theories where appropriate, whether they be Anglo-American, Latin American(ist) or French, while avoiding the wholesale blanket adoption of any one position.[35]

Multivocality is a useful theoretical concept as it allows for dissonance and for harmonies. Patterns may emerge as writers are engaging with specific social and historical realities from a variety of subject positions; however, the critic has to search for these patterns, rather than taking them as givens, and must be prepared to accept the existence of awkward texts which refuse enclosure within preexisting categories. What is most apparent from these recent attempts at theorizing women's writing is the need for an awareness of specifics. Theories of women's writing will thus be more honest, as they will originate from the texts and contexts rather than depending on lists of feminine essentials which have limited and distorted critics' readings of women's literary production.[36]

Notions of multiplicity, diversity, and *mestizaje* are crucial if we are to avoid the overgeneralized pronouncements on the literary production of the mythical Latin American woman. There can be no honest piece of theoretical writing on Latin American women's writing which is not sensitive to differences in the makeup of identities. It has thus become clear that gender cannot stand on its own as a single category, but is rather a relational term which needs to be studied in the context of particular historical and geographical locations, and in its relationship with other important categories which inform identity, if it is to have any meaning. One only has to compare poor Guatemalan Maya-Quiché woman (Rigoberta Menchú) with white wealthy Argentinian woman (Victoria Ocampo) with middle-class Mexican lesbian woman (Rosamaría Roffiel) with middle-class Jewish Mexican heterosexual woman (Margo Glantz) with privileged Nicaraguan revolutionary woman (Gioconda Belli)—all Latin American women who have produced books; and the lists of combinations of categories could go on. What the categories "woman" and "man" mean for each writer depend on how s/he locates him/herself within the gender systems of his/her society. Moreover, to further complicate matters with concepts from reader response theories, it must also be recognized that the meanings the reader gives to "woman" and "man" in the text will in turn depend on how s/he locates him/herself within the gender systems of his/her society.

At its best, feminism should be confident enough in its existence to be able to accommodate differences among women and common points among men and women. Specificity is not denial: a focus on gender which incorporates culture, class, and economic and political conditions of country of origin facilitates theory, rather than making it redundant. Specificity should, however, also be able to accommodate transcultural common points: ideals of how women should be, and the roles they should take, have many shared elements from culture to culture and class to class. This point is particularly pertinent when one is studying the writings of a continent, which has shared factors in its historical, linguistic, religious, political, and economic makeup. Gender constructs vary as they travel from country to country and within countries, and writers, particularly women writers (as it is they who have been most restricted by their gender), will react to them. Difference, as this chapter has argued, is a useful concept but it does not have to exclude commonalities. Societies still organize themselves, in many respects, around gendered divisions. It is, for example, still true to say that in most societies women are expected to spend more time than men on domestic chores and child care, while they are excluded, in the main, from the higher echelons of institutions of power. Gender is a key organizing principle in the division of roles and labor, despite important exceptions. Thus, as Silvia Walby has argued, "The signifiers of 'woman' and 'man' have sufficient historical and cross-cultural continuity, despite some variations, to warrant using such terms."[37]

It is in responses to the particular constructs available to women writers that one element of their work can be found. What they are reacting to takes a limited number of forms, as their gendered identities have been written for them, and their engagement with prescribed roles can come from only a limited number of standpoints. These standpoints can either take the form of acceptance and conformity, with writers accepting what they see as their femininity; of rejection, with writers denouncing the roles to which women have been ascribed; and/or of recreation, with writers exploring the possibilities of new roles for women. Moreover, it is strategically useful, at present, to maintain the gendered distinctions in "men's writing" and "women's writing." A rather static notion of "woman" as a category has been useful and somewhat necessary in that it has acted as an organizing principle to allow for the creation of publishing outlets, bookshops, conferences, anthologies, and collections of critical essays to discuss and promote texts by underrepresented women writers.

The fact that a number of critics have chosen to focus on such traditionally feminine themes as domesticity, motherhood, and inner spaces cannot simply be reduced to a question of essentialism. A large number of Latin American women writers do address these themes (Isabel Allende, Clarice Lispector, Rosario Castellanos, Laura Esquivel, to name but a few). However, not all women writers are concerned with these feminine spaces and those who are rarely limit themselves to these themes. Therefore, even if we use pluralist notions of writers' positionality in relation to their gender to categorize their work, we can only provide restricted readings of women's literary production, for while gender informs writing it never entirely determines its totality. Fortunately, women's writing will always be as rich, varied, multifaceted, and as difficult to define and categorize as men's.

NOTES

1. My criticisms in my references to novelists are limited purely to their pronouncements on the above questions. I do not intend here to examine or to apply gender theory to their literary production.
2. See Marta Traba, "Hipótesis sobre una escritura diferente," in Norma Klahn and Wilfredo Corral, eds., *Los novelistas como críticos* (México D.F.: Fondo de Cultura Económico, 1991), pp. 212-16.
3. Ibid., p. 215.
4. Sara Sefchovich, *Mujeres en espejo,* 2 vols. (México: Folios, 1983), p. 17.
5. See Josefina Ludmer, "Tretas del débil," in Patricia Elena González and Eliana Ortega, eds., *La sartén por el mango* (Río Piedras, Puerto Rico: Huracán, 1985),

pp. 47-54. Ludmer writes that the best way to break this binary notion of masculine/feminine difference is "postular una inversión: leer en el discurso femenino el pensamiento abstracto, la ciencia y la política tal como se filtran en los resquicios de lo conocido" (p. 46). She employs this strategy in her analysis of "La Respuesta (the response)," a poem written by Sor Juana Inés de la Cruz to Sor Filotea.

6. See Liliana Heker, "Alguna cosa llamada literatura femenina"; and Vlady Kociancich, "Un asombro angustioso," both in Mempo Giardinelli, ed., *Mujeres y escritura* (Buenos Aires: Ediciones Puro Cuento, 1989).

7. Bell Gale Chevigny and Gari Laguardia, eds., *Reinventing the Americas: Comparative Studies of Literature of the United States and Spanish America* (London: Cambridge University Press, 1986), p. 152.

8. Susan Bassnett, ed., *Knives and Angels: Women Writers in Latin America* (London: Zed Books, 1990), p. 5; also Cristina Peri Rossi, "Literatura y mujer," in Klahn and Corral, *Los Novelistas como críticos*, p. 530.

9. See Claribel Alegría, "The Writer's Commitment," in Doris Meyer, *Lives on the Line: The Testimony of Contemporary Latin American Authors* (Berkeley: University of California Press, 1988). See also the works of Elena Poniatowska and Sara Castro-Klarén.

10. Jean Franco, "Apuntes sobre la crítica feminista y la literatura hispanoamericana," *Hispamérica* 45 (1986): 41.

11. Margarita García Pinto, *Historias Latinas. Conversaciones con diez escritoras latinoamericanas* (Hanover: Ediciones del Norte, 1988), p. 12. Also, Margarita García Pinto, "Entrevista con Isabel Allende en Nueva York," April 1985.

12. García Pinto, *Historias Latinas*, p. 13.

13. Ibid., p. 15.

14. Rosario Ferré, "The Writer's Kitchen," translated by Diana Vélez, in Doris Meyer, *Lives on the Line*, p. 226.

15. Ibid., pp. 226-27.

16. Ibid., p. 227.

17. Ibid., pp. 226-27.

18. For Franco an analysis of power relations is a better point of departure in Latin American feminist criticism; see "Apuntes sobre la crítica feminista": 41.

19. Catherine Boyle, "The Creative Force in Marginality—Women in Latin American Writing: Through the Body and the Word into the Centre," p. 108.

20. See Chris Weedon, *Feminist Practice and Poststructuralist Theory* (New York: Basil Blackwell, 1987); Susan Hekman, *Gender and Knowledge: Elements of a Postmodern Feminism* (Cambridge: Polity Press, 1990); and Linda Nicholson, ed., *Feminism/Postmodernism* (London: Routledge, 1990).

21. Nancy Fraser and Linda Nicholson, "Social Criticism Without Philosophy: An Encounter between Feminism and Postmodernism," in Nicholson, ibid., pp. 19-38.

22. See Elaine Showalter, "A Criticism of Our Own: Autonomy and Assimilation in Afro-American and Feminist Literary Theory," in Robyn Warhol and Diane Price Herald, eds., *Feminisms: An Anthology of Literary Theory and Criticism* (New

Brunswick, NJ: Rutgers, 1989), pp. 168-88; Gayle Greene and Coppélia Khan, "Feminist Scholarship and the Social Construction of Women," in Greene and Khan, eds., *Making a Difference: Feminist Literary Criticism* (London: Methuen, 1985), pp. 24-27.

23. See the excellent anthology edited by Gloria Anzaldúa, *Making Face, Making Soul, Haciendo Caras: Creative and Critical Perspectives by Feminists of Color* (San Francisco: Aunt Lute Books, 1990) for a large selection of writers who take this position.

24. Audre Lorde, "I Am Your Sister: Black Women Organizing Across Sexualities," in ibid., p. 321.

25. Barbara Christian, "The Race for Theory," in ibid., p. 337.

26. Ibid., p. 341.

27. Ibid., p. 344.

28. Anzaldúa, ibid., p. xxv.

29. Amy Kaminsky, *Reading the Body Politic: Feminist Criticism and Latin American Women Writers* (Minneapolis: University of Minnesota Press, 1993), p. 26.

30. See Debra Castillo, *Talking Back: Towards A Latin American Feminist Criticism* (Ithaca: Cornell University Press, 1992); Kaminsky, *Reading the Body Politic;* Franco, "Apuntes sobre la crítica feminista," and Paul J. Smith, *Representing the Other: Race, Text and Gender in Spanish and Spanish American Narrative* (Oxford: Clarendon Press, 1992).

31. Francine Masiello, *Between Civilization and Barbarism: Women, Nation and Literary Culture in Modern Argentina* (Lincoln and London: University of Nebraska Press, 1992), p. 8.

32. Ibid.

33. Fraser and Nicholson, "Social Criticism Without Philosophy," p. 34.

34. Castillo, *Talking Back,* pp. xxi-xxii.

35. Ibid., pp. 2-3.

36. Elizabeth Ordóñez is another critic who finds the concept of multivocality useful. For Ordóñez a critic has to be sensitive to the different voices a range of texts produces: "...[A reading which is] attentive to 'difference' in each text and differences among all, draws out readings that may otherwise remain ignored. Each text is perceived in terms of its relationship to the prevailing discourses of its time. However, within their corresponding field, women insert themselves and respond through a variety of voices." Elizabeth Ordóñez, *Voices of Their Own: Contemporary Spanish Narrative by Women* (London: Associated University Press, 1991), p. 27.

37. Sylvia Walby, *Theorising Patriarchy* (Oxford: Basil Blackwell, 1990), p. 36.

THE SUBVERSIVE LANGUAGES OF CARMEN OLLÉ: IRONY AND IMAGINATION

WILLIAM ROWE

The past fifteen years have witnessed a huge increase in the amount of poetry written by women published in Peru. A book of interviews with Peruvian women poets by Roland Forgues stands as an index of this new phenomenon— in the masculinist ways Forgues attempts to construe this writing, and in the refusals of a number of the poets to go along with these characterizations. The book's title itself, *Las poetas se desnudan* ("Women Poets Bare Themselves"), indicates a paradigm that relegates women's poetry to the erotic and to intimate confession: no place here for the public sphere, for ideas, or, crucially, for the invention of poetic forms. Only the themes matter, and these—as the questions reveal—are preconceived as the confession of what was previously hidden. As the introduction claims:

> A real aesthetic revolution would begin only in the 1970s and 1980s, with the rise of young women poets who, breaking all the taboos, especially the sexual

ones, would not hesitate to bare themselves to reveal their most intimate, hidden places.[1]

In response to the question, "Don't you think, for instance, that to claim your rights as a feminine poet is a way of claiming your rights as a woman?" Magdalena Chocano answers: "No, because I think that if you want to fight for our rights as a woman, then you don't do it through poetry. Its not the most effective way...." She adds that she is in total agreement with the struggle for "equality, liberty, democracy in this country, a country that is very authoritarian and repressive even in its daily dealings." The exchange shows the difficulty of refusing definition as a "poeta femenina" through a particular thematic agenda—namely, the difficulty of claiming artistic autonomy—without being condemned as reactionary.[2]

Carmen Ollé, similarly, refuses the prevalent labeling of women poets. One of the questions she is asked goes as follows: "How do you explain exactly that in your first book, *Noches de Adrenalina,* the erotic has so much importance, and the erotic is treated, I would say in an almost clinical way?...."

Here "clinical" has to be interpreted as meaning not a seductive confession of intimacy. Ollé answers by turning the question around and placing the erotic as part of larger concerns which include the understanding of the self as a process that moves beyond the private: "The erotic is part of a process and analysis of infancy, of youth, of facing up to life, of lamentation about culture...."[3] She is also critical of the term "poesía femenina":

To speak of feminine poetry could lead us to mistake what this process is. Certainly we women writing now, who have come out into the open since 1980, talk about women. But our experience is as women, because we are not men. But I don't think there's such a great difference between poetry written by women and poetry written by men. Perhaps it seems different because up to now women's poetry hasn't received much attention. That's why it seems striking that many women are writing now, and writing about themselves.[4]

This stance might suggest that Ollé is somehow the exception among women poets in Peru, but, on the contrary, she is seen very much as the spokesperson of her generation. She is especially unhappy with the imposition of a particular agenda upon women poets by critics: "That seems to me terribly castrating: for a reader to seek out a text because it says certain things, and not because s/he likes it. That's a way of destroying the reader's ability to approach the text with innocence, without criteria."[5] This innocence is already compromised by the social formation of the reader as interlocutor, a point I will amplify below. What needs saying at this stage is that the conversations with Forgues reveal difficulties of reception that arise as limits within the larger field of social communication, limits that are also a necessary starting point if that innocence is to be reached which will allow readers to be open to seeing and hearing what previously has been made invisible and inaudible.

Ollé's distance from a particular view of women's poetry does not mean that she is not concerned with what Elizabeth Vargas calls "individuación femenina."[6] She states that the most important aim of her poetry is "Perhaps the attempt to give form to the consciousness of a feminine personality who is a complex, conflictive, real human being [tal vez la tentativa de plasmar la conciencia de un personaje femenino que sea un ser humano complejo, conflictivo, real]."[7] *Noches de adrenalina* (Adrenaline Nights), through an architectural sense of language as public space, participates in the reformulation of private and public that Peruvian feminist authors underline as really taking off in the late 1970s.[8] Virginia Vargas traces the evolution of thinking in a particular generation of women: after participating in the left-wing political parties in the early 1970s, a situation which meant they had to suppress their particular experience as women, they then turned to the theory of patriarchy, which made it possible to discover "not only the richness and complexity of the private world, of personal relationships, but also the distortions of the political world [no sólo la riqueza y complejidad del mundo privado, de las relaciones personales, sino también las deformaciones del mundo político]."[9] Underlying this change was a new historical situation that had taken shape over the past two decades: "The transformation of the 'housewife' into a social subject implies, among other things, developing oneself as an integrated individual, in command of one's present, responsible for one's past and builder of one's future [La transformación del 'ama de casa' en sujeto social implica, entre otras cosas, formarse como individuo integral; dueño de su presente, responsable de su pasado y constructor de su futuro]."[10]

Although she has never been a member of a political party, Ollé belongs to that generation of women and has been through a similar radicalization. While the shift in power among women shantytown dwellers was more dramatic, in that pauperization from the mid 1970s meant that in order to fulfill their traditional domestic roles women had to enter public struggle and build new social movements,[11] middle class women like Ollé were also affected by the discovery that there was a broader experience of women that cut across class divisions. Ollé was also, if briefly, a member of the *Hora Zero* group of poets, who located poetry within experiences of urban marginalization, away from the traditional language of the well-off classes. But her work also moves decisively from language as a sign of social membership to language as material

177

for creative invention. This concern with language as form and not just as representation makes the discussion of her work particularly challenging, given the need to separate writing by women from the types of justificatory paradigm that Ollé condemns and that tend to affect even the most interesting debates.

In *Women, Culture and Politics in Latin America*, the editors write: "the overall corpus of research on women in Latin America shows little focus on woman's intellectual, literary, political, and pedagogical activity."[12] Nevertheless, when they come to discuss the contribution made by their book to correcting this situation, the emphasis is on "the issues of women's rights, especially with respect to civil status, family, and participation in literary life," and on women writers "as cultural innovators" in conflict with "the inadequacies of the traditional space from which they were allowed to speak and act."[13] Although these issues are crucial for any serious research on women's intellectual and artistic work in Latin America, the introductory proposals in the book, and to an important extent the various chapters, exclude consideration of inventiveness in language and form as key cultural actions. The problem is not specific to gender studies: it extends more broadly to current practice in literary and cultural studies. But it seems to me that it has a particular force in the study of women writers. If the prime emphasis is on women representing themselves differently from men, or vice versa, the danger is that not enough attention is given to transformations of artistic form, which—because they are alterations of the possible—are key cultural actions.

The most influential proposal of gender as basis of differences in form— not just in representations—is that of *écriture fémenine*. But the extension of gender categories into form—and equally into language—is problematic, since the result is not only, as many have noted, to essentialize the feminine, but also to disconnect writing from the sociocultural element which traverses it. Put quite simply, *écriture féminine* is not equivalent to writing by actual social and historical women[14] and—the paradox is only apparent—it can prevent a proper investigation of forms as engagements with social and cultural experience. One of the most interesting and useful aspects of *Women, Culture and Politics in Latin America* is, as Catherine Boyle writes, that "the book takes us into [...] an area where gender studies meets cultural studies."[15] The rarefying effect of *écriture féminine,* at least in the hands of some of its adherents, ghettoizes the excitement and unpredictability of artistic discovery inside knowing academic jargon.

A further concern of my presentation of Ollé's work is with how formulations of gender difference are extremely useful entries into her poetic use of language but that they exist alongside another type of action that moves into nongendered zones. These are not easy to name and the term I have preferred is "the productive body." The area is similar to Julia Kristeva's use of the term "chora," which she takes to be previous to the differentiation of male and female.[16] Kristeva asserts that the "chora is no more than the place where the subject is both generated and negated, the place where his unity succumbs before the process of charges and stases that produce him":[17] that is the body as productive rather than symbolized, categorized.[18]

Finally, the above are not justifications of my approach by lining up authorities but simply ways of making more explicit some of the implications of the discussion that follows. This must stand or fall according to the conviction it produces.

REPRESENTATION AND IMAGINATION

When representations are spoken of, a number of questions arise, such as who by, from where, to whom and in what medium. The questions have to be asked of critics as well as of writers.

In academic discussions, the referential and representational aspects of language are often taken to be its prime or only function. But reference and representation can only occur as effects thanks to the dialogical working of language. This is because meaning arises in verbal interchange, in conversation. Knowledge cannot be separated from the actual sensuous and persuasive occurrence of language between speakers and hearers. Therefore we need to be concerned with "the poetic and rhetorical, the social and historical, the pluralistic, as well as the responsive and sensuous aspects of language use."[19] If social knowledge passes through the poetic dimensions of language, then poetics in a more literary sense are concerned with the interventions of language in the social construction of reality.[20] If you accept this, then literature is no longer out on a limb, as somehow secondary to the social sciences.

There is a particular issue about representation in Carmen Ollé's poetry. She names sexual organs and practices in forbidden ways, ways that are particularly forbidden to women in Peru. But there is a question here about motivation. To take these simply as counter-representations would be to isolate representation from its bases in speaking and hearing and the positions from which these can be done. To dare to refer, to represent in specifically forbidden ways is to challenge the rules that govern what women are allowed to say. But is this the only motivation? By using that kind of language, is Ollé also doing something else? Does the process go further? This is a question I will be returning to.

The way I will approach Ollé's work is as follows. Firstly, I will give an account of her materials—broadly, the cultural/historical context her work engages with—and then I will go on to look more closely at the varieties of language that she uses and the possibilities they open up for a reader. One of the problems with this approach is that the materials depend on the languages in which they are handled and should not be separated from them. On the other hand, to make a partial and temporary separation does help in order to focus subsequently on the language.

First, though, some brief points to situate Ollé. She belongs, loosely, to what came to be known as the generation of 1970 in Peruvian poetry, although she was not included in the most important anthology of those poets' work, *Estos 13*.[21] She was born in Lima, and lives there now. In the 1970s she lived for several years in Paris with her husband, Enrique Verástegui, a prominent poet of that generation, and her baby daughter. After returning to Lima, she and Verástegui separated. Her first book, *Noches de adrenalina* (Adrenalin Nights), was published in Lima in 1981. Her second book, *Todo orgullo humea la noche* (Every Pride Pervades Night With Smoke), came out in 1988. Her third and most recent book, *¿Por qué hacen tanto ruido?* (Why Do They Make So Much Noise?), dates from 1992. *Noches de adrenalina* was recently published in translation in New York with an introduction by Jean Franco. Ollé is currently working on a novel and a book of essays on poetry in Peru.

Noches de adrenalina is particularly concerned with location in time and space, in terms of an autobiographical investigation of different times (adolescence and adulthood), places (Lima and Paris) and languages (Spanish and French). A quotation from Gaston Bachelard is used to help bring the complexities of time and place into focus:

> Dónde está el peso mayor del estar allí,
> en el estar o en el allí?
> En el allí —que sería preferible llamar
> un aquí— ¿debo buscar primeramente mi ser?
>
> [Where is the main stress in being there
> on being, or on there?
> In there—which it would be better to call
> here—shall I first look for my being?][22]

The processes of memory and perception are therefore both inward and outward, specific to a sense of self or selves and specific to its location in time and space.

In my presentation, in order to give a clear sense of the components of the book, I will separate out the different times and places that become interwoven in the text. The book starts with the sentence: "To be 30 changes nothing save one's proximity to a heart attack or uterine extraction [Tener 30 años no cambia nada salvo aproximarse al ataque cardíaco o al vaciado uterino]."[23] The sense of thirty years as a threshold is amplified in various statements of the body ageing, especially as the result of giving birth, which include an ironic sense of the female body as highly constructed, paradigmatic object: "Mona Lisa's smile shows the course of aging/stalled by creams [La sonrisa de la Monalisa indica el camino del envejecimiento/detenido por las cremas]."[24]

The geographical and spatial locations are given by Paris and Lima. The first is defined less as a cultural inheritance (in the sense of high culture) than by the Champs Elysées or the Mona Lisa becoming "the ménage/delegated to young third-world maids [el ménage/delegado a las jóvenes muchachas del tercer mundo],"[25] i.e., a Brechtian juxtaposition between cultural monuments and the women—from places like Peru—who do the cleaning. An aspect of life in Paris that gets mentioned frequently is looking after a small child, in particular changing diapers. To be a woman—more precisely a married woman—and an artist is an issue that is given considerable attention near the beginning of the book, where the Parisian scenario is being set out. But when it comes to the question which artists' work affects perception, the list is not Parisian: someone called Evelyne[26] (possibly the same Dutch woman painter mentioned later), Sylvia Plath, Diane di Prima, Burroughs, Cezanne, Van Gogh, Warhol.

Lima—in memory—is three friends from University days, associated with the world of political militancy, Avenida Venezuela (a working class area), cheap hotels (including one associated with lost virginity), books read (e.g., David Cooper's *Death of the Family),* and the molding of bodies into desirable and acceptable shapes: "I remember my shyness/in Lima beauty is a steel corset [recuerdo mi timidez/en Lima la belleza es un corsé de acero]."[27] One section consists of a dramatized conversation between several figures in a park in a working class district. One of the main topics is physical appearance: "a physical deformation makes us explosive [una deformación física nos hace pólvora]," says the Dama del chiclet. And a little later: "The impression of being tumbled, spilled into a plastic maquette [La impresión de ser tumbada derramada en una maqueta de plástico]."[28] Here Lima is no longer a frame of memory and becomes instead a grotesque spoken drama.

Lines of spatial and cultural tensions intersect with the axis of personal time. The main example would be the tracing of the characteristics of adult sexual pleasure ("cariños masoquistas," masochistic endearments) through mother's blush, puberty as exacerbated tensions between purity and dirtiness seen and scenified by the gaze of mother and doctors, with any move toward nostalgia prevented by irony: "after masturbating I wanted to cry with fear and shame/crossing myself became a nervous tic/masses for the dead were the chorus needed/for my adolescent misery [después de masturbarme quería llorar de miedo y de verguenza/tenía el tic de la señal de la cruz/las misas de difuntos eran el coro que necesitaba/la miseria de mi adolescencia]."[29]

These are some of Ollé's materials, with some unavoidable pointing to the form of expression. The book is perhaps as much a dramatization of languages as of locations. Take, for example, one of the main topics, the question of watching oneself/being seen. In language terms the question of who is see-ing/who is being seen becomes who is the speaker/interlocutor when this is being spoken of and what are their positions. On the back cover of the book there is a handwritten statement signed by Ollé which includes the following: "I want to be able to look at myself and abolish complexes and shame, in the permanent belief in the value of women [quiero llegar a mirarme y abolir complejos y verguenzas, en la creencia permanente en el valor de las mujeres]." The necessity of seeing oneself, as against the gaze of the other (mother, doctor, male lover are the main agents) is dramatized a number of times, with the mirror as central to the action. One of its most complex treatments opens with a meditation on living under a roof as key initiation of all restricted spaces. But after the initial declaration "Hay que huir de los techos [Must flee the roofs]," the poem proceeds to counterpose actions of escape with the other necessity of being seen or constructed within (the dominant forces of) the social; thus "poseer un cuerpo completo [to possess a complete body]" is "una suerte de arquitectura [a kind of architecture]"[30]—the body recognized as complete becoming socialized space, house, and, insofar as the architecture becomes exemplary representation, the spectacle has an "epic glow [epicidad]." Com-pleteness or incompleteness of body is distinguished from the effects of makeup: "no makeup artist could manage such effects [ningún maquillador lograría tales efectos]"; this is something more fundamental—to do with becoming substantial, as in the phrases "polvo abstracto [abstract dust]," "polvo incontenible [uncontainable dust]"—but something that is opposed by the body as that which makes and produces: "I should have made it home before nightfall but/I dallied in a hotel to make love./Beautiful word *to make* = poiesis/one makes a poem love and caca by a sort of/natural play/this making doen't require a patent [Debí volver a casa antes de anochecer pero/me detuve en un hotel para hacer el amor./Bella palabra *hacer* = poiesis/se hace un verso el amor y la caca por algo de juego/natural/este hacer no necesita patente]." Creative invention, imagination—not as in Lacan's Imaginary but as in Blake, Kant or Lezama

182

Lima (to cite a Latin American theory)—as alternative to being seen/recognized, is a very important concern of the book and I will come back to it later.

The incomplete body becomes, un-epically, in the final part of the poem, the lack of a tooth: "The nurse quotes me the price of teeth/teeth have gone up—she informs me firmly/[...] Now it would cost me an arm and a leg to restore my beauty. I will try not laughing as hard as I can [La enfermera me da los precios de los dientes/los dientes han subido- me avisa con firmeza/[...] Ahora me costaría un ojo de la cara recomponer mi belleza./Trataré de no reír lo más que pueda]."[31] But the speaker is already laughing, silently, ironically. This is not, however, ironical self-dramatization in the style of certain British poets (e.g., Philip Larkin and his admirers) where irony is used to keep ego in safe enclosure. It is an irony that arises in the choice of self-containment as the only way to survive and be heard in a given society—the cost of living under a roof. Because to be heard or read means adjusting to an interlocutor who has been trained by that same society to expect that women contain themselves. As Ollé writes in an essay on women poets in Peru:

> The need for composure, not to lose your cool among the upper middle classes of the 1960s becomes clear.... The boundary is strict, unalterable, it will not tolerate a lack of moderation in women. And it wounds, because it allows no space for desperation and there is a fear of crying out, or what is even more risky: there is a fear that in poetic language this crying out might be cheap, affected, a parody of crying. So the woman poet becomes ironic and is implacable with her own weaknesses: anguish, the void.

> The passionate pursuit of non-desperation manifests itself through black humor, scepticism. The wound remains, but not one that excludes suffering, which is rich, dialectical.[32]

That is, the body is lacerated not because it is an imperfect fulfillment of the social stereotype of the acceptable but because it is cut into/wounded by the impossibility of releasing despair. Referring to a text by the Peruvian poet Blanca Varela, Ollé writes: "Very seldom can one see a text as lacerating as "Of the Order of Things," lacerating in a sense opposite to passion, if it's possible to feel passion when we stop believing in desperation."[33] The body that's lacerated is the productive body, not the represented one. Productive in the sense that being cut into/open is also a capability of energy and feeling (I take it this is what Ollé means by calling the wound "dialectical"). As the U.S. poet H.D. writes, "The center of consciousness is either the brain or the love-region of the body." The latter can be visualized as "placed like a fetus in the body"; whereas consciousness centered on the "realm of the intellect or

183

brain" is something she became aware of "before the birth of my child."[34] But if passion is a source of creative invention, it occurs within specific limitations of language. If the wound as creative is one movement, the other, simultaneous one is the (socially and historically) specific interlocutor as cause of containment and laceration.

The subtitle of the essay is "¿Es lacerante la ironía? [Is irony lacerating?]" and it would be possible to suggest that the ability to receive that type of irony is a characteristic of a feminine reading. Ollé, however, chooses not to genderize reading in this case and states instead that "como lectores no alcanzamos la madurez [as readers we have not reached maturity]."[35] Her own poetry places its interlocutors/readers in the double position of being agents of the containment of women and of suffering it; that is, readers are not gendered but invited to discover the construction of gender as passing through them as both agents and sufferers.

The demand that women be moulded, malleable, is not one that comes from a particular place in the society. In the essay, Ollé mentions the upper middle class, but in *Noches* there is no such particularity—witness the voice of the dental nurse, whose legitimacy comes from its place in a total social rationality—*techos* (roofs), not from one social sector, and which is made to sound grotesque not in being contrasted with other sociolects but because of the counteractive irony: being complete is unaffordable.

In the scene in the park in Lima, Ollé experiments with a different method. The method here is to use an avant-garde style of grotesque drama, with working class areas of Lima as scenario, in order to try out a language capable of expressing desperation—that of women in Lima. The main dramatic event is the shooting of a lover by a woman; the speakers are women intellectuals, readers of Simone de Beauvoir for example. Their language is hard, violent, without vulnerability, except where a kind of litany interrupts, recounting the moment when mothers show menstrual blood to their first daughter as initiation into being "mujeres de carne y hueso tan íntegras para hacer el amor [women of flesh and blood, so integral for lovemaking]"—except that all the syllables are interrupted by and inseparable from childspeak: "WOMEN OF FLESH AND BLOOD" becomes "MUpuJEpeREpeS DEpe CAparRNEpe Ypi HUEpeSOpo [... etc.]." "Los pa-pe-pi's o po's" go on sounding in the memory of one of the speakers, and cannot be prised apart from the content of the utterance, the infantilization inexpungeable.[36]

To say languages in the plural can mean several different things. Analytically speaking they can be set out as follows.

1. Different sociolects.

2. The differential placing of speakers and interlocutors.

3. Different poetic options such as narrative, dramatic, lyrical and intellectual modes.

I have referred to 1. and 2. and will return to 2. shortly. The third set of possibilities is not my main concern in this chapter but needs brief comment. A significant proportion of the book consists in autobiographical narrative. As a way of writing poetry this was first explored in Peru by the generation of 1960 and further developed by Ollé's own generation (1970). Her use of dramatic form goes back to the avant garde of the 1930s (for example César Moro and César Vallejo in Peru), a connection which is also evident in Ollé's lyrical (in the sense of condensed, non-narrative) passages (e.g., p. 30). The fourth mode, the intellectual, is unusual. I refer not only to the inclusion of materials from Bachelard and Georges Bataille in direct quotation, but also to an ongoing elaboration of abstract and analytic statements—e.g., "en cariños masoquistas el sufrimiento es el yugo [in masochistic caresses suffering is the yoke],"[37]— which act as a diagnostic of the conditions explored and as a body of thought, a place to be. There is one point, however, when this intellectual component shows its limits. In a passage which looks ironically at the effect of racial and social models in eroticism, there are the following four lines:

> disponerse en el viaje a ser asaetada por el viento
> como por la pasión
> todo el que goza es verdadero y sus consecuentes
> silogismos

> [To be prepared on the journey to be pierced by the wind's arrows
> as by passion
> everyone who experiences pleasure is true and its consequent
> syllogisms][38]

Here the move from passion as epic (*saeta* = arrow) to passion as irony takes the energy out of merely intellectual consciousness and shows its tendency to move along pre-given tracks (*silogismos*).

To return to the question of speaking and hearing, as performed by the written text, you might well expect that the restrictive expectations placed upon women would be characterized as coming from a particular type of voice, belonging to a particular sector of society—which would make it possible to present a counter-voice (of the marginalized, the oppressed). But, as I began to indicate earlier, this is not what happens. The expectation that women should be contained—the main reason for irony—is not a particular voice of authority but an expectation that is inside the language as a whole. It is inside the language

185

not as a set of representations—you could change the vocabulary but the forcing of women into restrictive containment would still occur—but as orders given, orders whose prime example is: *Stay in your place.* The orders take effect without having to assume the form of commands in the grammatical sense. Consequently, neither the demand for containment nor its exposure are placed by Ollé as sociolects or confined to any one of the poetic forms of expression (e.g., the narrative or the intellectual).

Ollé responds to the restrictive effect of the language in two main ways. The first is irony, which I have already discussed. The second is by saying "cosas sucias [dirty things]"—what must not be said because it is dirty, impure, dangerous.[39] Here, as I mentioned at the beginning, the references are to female genitals, menstruation, and sexual practices, including particularly tabooed ones. Clearly, an important motive is a defiance of the ban on speaking, and a reclamation of what's denied. But the lacerating irony also comes in here, bringing into play the limits of possible reclamation. This means that Ollé's position is rather different from that of Luisa Valenzuela, who gives to the use of "la mala palabra [bad language]" by women writers a cathartic and transgressive function, as if the domination implicit in the prohibition of such words were reversible through saying them.[40] Take, as a contrast, Ollé's uses of the word "partes [parts]":

> ¿Nuestras partes se cercenan por falta de belleza
> o de carácter?
> ....
> Como antes aún sigo en estado de alerta ante cualquier
> extraño ante cualquier contacto presintiendo que debo
> relucir o impresionar con mis lecciones de piano como
> ahora con mis partes.
>
> [Are our parts less for lack of beauty
> or of character?
> ....
> Now as then I am in a state of alert with any
> stranger with any contact sensing that I must
> excel or impress with my piano lessons as
> now with my parts.][41]

In the first case it's *partes íntimas* (intimate/private parts) or *pudendas*, but in the second there's an ambiguity: *partes* as euphemism for genitals or *partes* as qualities, accomplishments? The equivalence is ironical, and speaks of being placed in an impossible (desperate) situation.

186

But there is also *suciedad* (dirtiness) as a condition of desire. The curves and folds of a naked body: "What are these if not the slug? [¿Qué son sino el caracol?]"—which in other circumstances ("on a leaf of lettuce [en una hoja de hortaliza]") "disgusts us [nos asquea]."[42] The technique of inquiry into inner experience is similar to that of Bataille, whose writing is explored at some length in another section.[43] Later, dirty diapers are included in the sights and smells that can cause repulsion, but this repulsion is placed as belonging to the mind ("mente"). And the mind is capable of transforming *lo sucio* into *lo limpio* (the dirty into the clean) through a certain type of memory.[44] Such mental processing takes us away from *suciedad* as a shape of desire.

Thus the concern with the unclean is not limited to social definitions of the clean or its genderization. *La suciedad* is different from being not perfect, the wrong shape; it breaks the certainty/passivity of the viewer of *estampas eróticas* (erotic prints).[45] Does it offer a possible way of breaking other moulds? Certainly it is not the certainties of social representation that are the source of this sense of the unclean, but the other, productive, inventive body—the body of imagination—that is involved when "in this mystique of telling dirty things I am alone/and feverish [en esta mística de relatar cosas sucias estoy sola/y afiebrada]."[46] Does this go beyond irony, or is there an uncertainty, a possible irony in the phrase "esta mística de relatar cosas sucias"?

BETWEEN SOUND AND SILENCE

If *Noches de adrenalina* was concerned with how to move from being seen to seeing oneself, *¿Por qué hacen tanto ruido?*[47] works with the difficulties of hearing and being heard, and the whole book is an invitation into ways of listening that go against the grain—of the Spanish language in Peru as the majority have been trained to hear it, of Peruvian poetry in the ways it is usually read.

The difficulty of being heard, which arises from all the noises that interpose themselves, includes the difficulty of hearing one's own inner life. If the voices of mother and other authorities, and of a lover who is a poet, plus the sounds of neighbors and the general social noise, are constantly interfering, then the movements of inner life become distorted or blotted out. The following passage responds to that situation not just as an existential problem but as a question of poetics:

I decipher. My spirit in these circumstances: It is empty. Empty means full of nothing. There is nothing in nature which resembles my spirit, neither the cold of the mist, nor a tree without leaves, for they are landscape. My spirit has no landscape, there nothing can grow nor does it die. There is an attempt to establish order there, cleanliness, the discipline of things that do not exist, for in all that exists there is a beautiful disorder, a cherished dirtiness, a smell of something. My image neither smells nor makes a noise.[48]

There is not just a refusal of pastoral or Romantic organicism but also a sense of there being no resonance with the world of external things. To be without that disorder of things that exist for the senses may involve an emptying or even death of the imagination but not the end of writing, "ya que no hay un punto cero que no sea también nodal, esa es la imposibilidad del silencio [because there is no zero point which is not also nodal, that is the impossibility of silence]."[49] "Nodal" in physics signifies an intersection of astronomic movements or of sound vibrations. Thus emptiness in Ollé's sense is also always the becoming of something. And to fail to resolve the existential is not artistic failure; on the contrary, not to achieve silence (that would be "terapia [therapy]" but instead "sólo el ruido [only the noise]" is the condition of "la gran maña [the great trick]" of art. Noise thus becomes a complex social and spiritual condition of art. And emptying the inner life can become a process of ascesis, the better to hear—and not just that, since change in any one of the senses involves the others.

The process, and the style, recall César Vallejo's poem, "Voy a hablar de la esperanza [I'm going to talk of hope]," and a key feature of the similarities is a dismantling of the language of symbolism, both in the specialized literary sense and as an influence within the wider language as ordinarily spoken. This is something I will return to.

The difficulty of hearing and being heard occurs not just because of the noise of the society, as in the lover's complaint that he is being attacked because of his poetry,[50] but also because both the inherited poetic language and the wider language are suffused with a particular imagery of desire that controls not so much what can be desirable (the object) as the inner life of the person desiring. These issues are worked out through a double journey, on the one hand existential and on the other artistic. Both are haunted by despair and the danger of remaining trapped in the past. The existential involves the painful break-up of a relationship, where a key difficulty is that of love based on an idealized image nurtured in childhood and adolescence, an image that induces passivity; a sense of emptiness following the break-up, troubled by dreams and memories; an emergence of new desires, those of maturity; and a decision deliberately to close the door, which is where, thematically, the book closes. The poetic journey passes through symbolism, a formative influence in childhood reading, as expression and containment of solitude and the inner life, to a sense of emptiness on the one hand and of the everyday material world on the other, the world which symbolism and Platonism exclude. The final stage is to articulate the values of a new poetics, which, embodied as form, are what make the writing of the book possible; to deploy artistic invention against despair and stasis.

Ollé abandons the method used in *Noches:* to delineate in *la suciedad* the body of love, freeing it from the idealizing representations that restrictively confine it, and that for women growing up in Lima in the 1950s and 1960s meant a material and linguistic *corsé de acero* (steel corset). To invent possible forms of expression of a woman's desire involves a contrastive delineation of Ignacio, the poet-lover. His confidence in poetry and in a particular form of expression of his desire go together: at one point he compares himself with Holderlin,[51] and at one of the most tense moments of the breakdown of the relationship declares: "quiero y quise y siempre querré que seas como la Nora de Joyce: mi puta [I want, I wanted, and I shall always want you to be like Joyce's Nora: my whore]."[52] Ignacio represents that other attitude where the relationship between desire and its expression is not problematic but confident, seamless. Two ways of writing, which are also ways of hearing and reading, emerge: in the first there is an unbroken road from desire to beauty, the pulsations of the body becoming, in language, cosmic. "Desde el sur me enviaba cartas quejándose de su soledad, amándome como sólo él sabía, como Dante a Beatriz, como Petrarca a Laura [He sent me letters from the south complaining of his solitude, loving me as only he knew how, as Dante loved Beatrice, as Petrarch loved Laura]."[53] Ollé does not resort to easy dismissal, and more than once speaks of Ignacio's beauty, but, as in her essay on Peruvian poetry written by women, finds in irony a way of making audible the restriction of what is permitted to women and its enactment in the language. The second way of writing involves making perceptible the obligatory *"compostura* [composure]" that women writing in Peru have to assume, the lack of any place for *"deses-peración* [desperation]," since it will be heard as *"huachafo* [tacky]" and *"panfletario* [propagandist]," and the diminution of poetry written by women to erotic and of the erotic to the sexual.[54]

There is, consequently, no question of a prestigious literary tradition to be inherited as there is for Ignacio (Dante, Petrarch, etc.). The situation for Ollé is quite the opposite: that dominant tradition gets in the way of being heard, and the need is to find ways of breaking with it. Once again life and writing are in close connection: "Lo irracional en mí radicaba en que lo poético sólo servía para que me dominaran [The irrational in me centered on the fact that the poetic only helped others to dominate me]." Whereas Ignacio, who makes himself represent "the poetic," turns it into an exclusive action: "Lo irracional en

189

Ignacio era no poder soportar la racionalidad de los otros [The irrational in Ignaco meant not being able to bear others being rational.]"[55]

César Vallejo enters here as ally for a reformulation of poetics. Ollé's title, *¿Por qué hacen tanto ruido?* can be heard as a reminder of "¿Quién hace tanta bulla? [Who's making such a racket?]," the first line of the first poem of Vallejo's *Trilce,* famous, at least to critics, because of their renewed attempts to find an interpretative key to it. Vallejo's poem links noise, formally, with an excess of meanings that cannot be controlled, making a parodic counter-luxury to Baudelaire's *"luxe, calme et volupté."* Thematically, Vallejo defines noise in terms of guano, excrement, money and lack of respect, enumerating some of the factors that foul up the sense of cosmic correspondences which symbolist poetics rely upon. The result is that the paths of interpretation multiply and become clogged—witness the unilluminating deluge of critical essays on "Trilce 1."

Symbolism has had considerable effect on twentieth-century Peruvian poetry. The language of poetry, from Eguren to Sologuren, to name the major line of transmission, has to an important extent been symbolist. Ollé's decision to break with that tradition can be compared with Vallejo's, but her method is different. In terms of semantic field, Vallejo's *bulla* is merely noise, whereas Ollé's *ruido* includes sound as well as noise: its ambiguities force an entry between dualisms of sound and silence. Ollé's writing opts for quietness, a zone in between sound and silence, where the usual frontiers between what can and cannot be heard become changed. The idea of eluding symbolism is most explicit when in response to a windy night that "se parece a un poema de Nerval, exquisitamente romántico [It resembles a Nerval poem, exquisitely romantic]," she delineates a contrasting imaginary poem: "un poema como una oreja que se corta sin hacer ruido, un simple cartílago que cae a tierra, que no es ningún símbolo sino un simple corte delicado. [A poem like an ear which is cut off with no noise, a simple cartilage which falls to earth, not any kind of symbol but a simple delicate cut.]"[56] This is clearly meant to be an antidote to the attraction to "los poemas misteriosos de todos los simbolistas [The mysterious poems of all the Symbolists],"[57] acquired in childhood.

But the method itself is less willed than that imaginary poem. It relies on an emptying of the space of writing so that resonance and echo between one thing and another, or between "mi espíritu [my spirit]" and the world, are minimized. Against the luxury of Baudelaire or Nerval, ascesis and discipline of the imagination are deployed. But the issue is not just literary: there is also the question of the on-going intensities inherited from a Catholic childhood and what, as a poet, to do with them. One option is the therapeutic action of

190

"limpieza [cleaning]" explored by Rodolfo Hinostroza—Ollé takes the word from the title of his book, *Aprendizaje de limpieza* (The Art of Cleaning)—also a prose work by a poet.[58] Its disadvantage is that, by systematically emptying the symbolic, through psychoanalysis, it risks, to use Ollé's phrase, the death of the imagination.

Another side to Ollé's method is the decision to let in to her writing the ordinary and the practical, the unresolved difficulties of everyday life and work which are excluded by Ignacio's purity: she reads Ignacio's letters, from his "exile" in the south, as moving toward "un encuentro definitivo con Dios (a definitive encounter with God)."[59] But inclusion of the "nonpoetic" does not of itself mean change. One of the shortcomings of the critical discourses which began to proliferate in Peru and elsewhere in the late sixties and early seventies was the idea that poetry had to be anti-élitist by embracing everyday life: the equivalent in poetics of populism in politics. What this does not answer is the need for the invention of new forms.

In a crucial passage, Ollé writes:

Culture suffocates me, the vitality hidden within this concoction, it's like taking shelter in a landscape where I am unable to take nourishment from the sun, or throw myself softly into the grass. Or as if my plump nudity is not artistic but hesitant before the mirror.

I'm suffocating by the fact that nothing is happening today and then writing that experience, that nothing is happening today. To see how something exists in this scrap of time in which nothing is happening unless I observe it in a rear-view mirror. I'm living through what I read.

I feel the anguish of approaching the sheet in the typewriter and surprising the image which does not emerge. Fantasy can do anything, but my imagination is like a blunt knife, it bites into fragments of reality because something pushes it from its blockage.

It is impossible to keep silent. He is watching me, he sits by my side and sees how I am only able to string together short sentences.[60]

A number of difficulties combine: writer's block, Ignacio's gaze, and the weight of inherited language and forms of perception. "Beber no es ningún símbolo [There is no symbolism in drinking]," as she writes one night after Ignacio has left.[61] But Ollé's way does require the interrogation of childhood idealizations and their artistic consequences. Of these she repeatedly uses the word Platonism. The diagnosis includes a list of men capable of eliciting "mi capacidad de entregarme a una imagen [...] cuando era adolescente [my capacity to give myself up to an image [...] as an adolescent]," among them not just "el

191

cura alemán (the German priest)," but also, with some irony, "el pintor de la casa, el albañil de al lado [the painter who did the house, the bricklayer from next door]." This interference of the "alter ego" in love has become, in the relationship with Ignacio, "un rabioso masoquismo platónico por la imagen que él proyectaba en mi fantasía [An angry platonic masochism provoked by the image that he projected in my fantasy]." In opposition to the transcendentalizing of desire in idealized figures, in exclusive synthetic images, Ollé exposes "mi puterío platónico [my platonic whoring]"—a phrase with plenty of irony in it, given the usual, puritanical, meaning of "platonic love."[62]

But Platonism is not just an autobiographical matter, it is also a burden of symbolist poetry. As James Higgins writes in his essay on Martín Adán, a key figure in the Peruvian symbolist tradition, "to live exiled in the world," fate of the soul in the neo-Platonic tradition, becomes in Adán's poems a condition of the poet in Peru.[63] However, Adán was not a neo-Platonist in any simple, unproblematic way; his writing enacts a struggle between the ideal world of neo-Platonism and the actual environment of twentieth-century Peru, between "perfección ideal [ideal perfection]" and "dimensión sensible [sensitive dimension]," as Edmundo Bendezú notes. Ollé's book is not, either, a simple junking of Platonic capacities, but a decision to turn them away from stasis and submission to a tradition.[64] One of the most powerful (moving) moments is when a surge of desire to make love with Ignacio opens the senses to the beauty of the material world of a Lima street: "Anything would excite my senses. The vitality of the school kids with their socks around their ankles, showing off multicolored plastic rings on their fingers... [Cualquier cosa alentaba mis sentidos. La lozanía de los escolares con sus medias remangadas, luciendo en sus dedos sortijas de plástico multicolores]." Renunciation of "ese sueño [this dream]"—because Ignacio has left—does not destroy the capacity of aliveness to the real or turn it to nostalgia. What is gained is understanding of the process—which makes this book utterly different from a confessional autobiography—and as a result Platonism goes through a "descomposición": "I thought of his beauty which also exalted that of the material world [pensaba en su belleza que exaltaba también la del mundo material]."[65]

Those beauties become the beauty of understanding, a resource against the seductiveness of Platonism—the danger of drowning in "Plato's honey head," to use Melville's phrase.[66] This understanding is brought to bear upon reading Yeats's "Byzantium," which is taken as exemplary of symbolism and the struggle with Platonism. Ollé makes particular mention of Yeats's first line, in which "unpurged images" make their passage into night to become changeless artefacts. If Yeats traces the distance between the Platonic and "human complexities," and moves within that tension, Ollé finds that understanding Yeats's poem, finding the form of her own experience, and preserving the capacity to move (figured as a game of chess) converge: "para comprender 'Bizancio.' para contenerme en lo que amo y no amo y desaparece [To understand 'Byzantium,' to limit myself to what I love and what I do not love and disappears]," a route ("una ruta") has to be found, one which is also adequate to handling the enemy queen, the most energetic piece.

The aesthetic decisions of *¿Por qué?* (Why?) consist in a choice of moves. The route is toward *"lo desconocido* [the new, the unknown],"[67] but depends on staying with the experience as opposed to willed resolution, which would include the Platonic or the therapeutic. There is a choice of restraint, as opposed to confession or self-legitimation, with an extraordinary absence of ego as its result. There is a choice of slowness, as opposed to lyrical speed, and of quietness, allowing the actual turns of inner feeling to be heard. There is a choice of movement, as opposed to a luxury of sensuality folded upon itself; the "lozanía" of the schoolchildren, though semantically close to lujo, is not luxury but aliveness. The writing moves without laying down a line of logic that signals or excludes deviations from itself. This is its openness, its nonexclusiveness. The transition from one topic to another is not a sequence in time. Ollé herself calls its genre hybrid.[68] The long sentences are achievements of responsibility for an existential/artistic process, and in that sense quite different from Octavio Paz's transcendent "instante poético [poetic instant]"; as Ollé writes, with some irony, "I read Octavio Paz: 'Piedra del [sic] sol.' I intentionally read an excerpt about lovers. How I wish I still could be that woman."[69]

NOTES

1. Roland Forgues, *Las poetas se desnudan* (Lima: Editorial el Quijote, 1991), p. 14. All translations from *Noches de Adrenalina* by Anne Archer; all other translations by Jane Freeland and Deborah Shaw.
2. Ibid., p. 252.
3. Ibid., p. 147-48.
4. Ibid., p. 150.
5. Ibid., p. 158.
6. Elizabeth Vargas, *Identidad femenina: cuestionando y construyendo estereotipos* (Lima: Desco, 1991), p. 20.
7. Forgues, p. 158.
8. Virginia Vargas, *El aporte de la rebeldía de las mujeres* (Lima: Editorial Flora Tristán, 1989), pp. 19-20.
9. Ibid., p. 21.
10. E. Vargas, *Identidad femenina,* p. 21.

11. V. Vargas, *El aporte*, pp. 12-19.
12. University of California, Stanford Seminar on Feminism and Culture in Latin America (eds.), *Women, Culture and Politics in Latin America* (Berkeley: University of California Press, 1992), p. vii.
13. Ibid., pp. 1-2.
14. Toril Moi, *Sexual/Textual Politics* (London: Routledge, 1985), p. 108.
15. Catherine Boyle, "Review of Women Culture and Politics in Latin America," *Bulletin of Latin American Research* 13, no. 2 (1994): 235.
16. Moi, pp. 161-65.
17. Toril Moi (ed.), *The Kristeva Reader* (Oxford: Basil Blackwell, 1986) p. 95.
18. Other work that could be cited on this issue includes Giles Deleuze and Felix Guattari, *A Thousand Plateaus* (London: Athlone, 1988) especially ch. 6; H.D.'s notion of "jelly-fish consciousness" in H.D., *Notes on Thought and Vision* (London: Peter Owen, 1982), pp. 18-20; also G. Bataille, *Inner Experience* (New York: State University of New York, 1988), especially pp. 7-14; or the work of the Peruvian poets César Vallejo and Emilio Adolfo Westphalen (particularly *Poemas en prosa* and *Las ínsulas extrañas*).
19. J. Shotter, *Conversational Realities: Constructing Life through Language* (London: Sage, 1993), p. 7.
20. P. Berger and T. Luckman, *The Social Construction of Reality* (Harmondsworth: Penguin, 1991 [1966]), pp. 26-28.
21. Oviedo, J., *Estos 13* (Lima: Mosca Azul, 1973).
22. Carmen Ollé, *Noches de Adrenalina* (Lima: Cuadernos del Hipocampo, 1981) p. 11.
23. Ibid., p. 9.
24. Ibid., p. 20.
25. Ibid., p. 12.
26. Ibid., p. 13.
27. Ibid., p. 21.
28. Ibid., p. 31.
29. Ibid., pp. 44-46.
30. Ibid., p. 18.
31. Ibid., pp. 18-20.
32. Carmen Ollé, "Poesía peruana escrita por mujeres: ¿Es lacerante la ironía?" Unpublished ms., 1994, recently published as "Las poetas del 80 seducidas por el mal" in *Todas las artes* (Lima) no. 1, (July 1994).
33. Ibid.
34. H.D., *Notes on Thought and Vision*, pp. 20 and 21.
35. Ollé, "Poesía peruana."
36. Ollé, *Noches*, p. 34-35.
37. Ibid., p. 44.
38. Ibid., p. 23.
39. Ibid., p. 17.

40. Luisa Valenzuela, "La mala palabra," *Revista Iberoamericana* LI. 132-133 (1985): 489-491.
41. Ollé, *Noches,* p. 23.
42. Ibid., p. 36.
43. Ibid., p. 16-17.
44. Ibid., p. 40-41.
45. Ibid., p. 49.
46. Ibid., p. 17.
47. Carmen Ollé, *¿Por qué hacen tanto ruido?* (Lima: Ediciones Flora Tristán, 1992).
48. Ibid., p. 13.
49. Ibid.
50. Ibid., p. 31.
51. Ibid., p. 22.
52. Ibid., p. 78.
53. Ibid., p. 65.
54. Ollé, "Poesía peruana," pp. 1, 2, 4.
55. Ollé, *¿Por qué...?,* p. 22.
56. Ibid., p. 29.
57. Ibid., p. 34; see also p. 71.
58. Rudolfo Hinostroza, *Aprendizaje de limpieza* (Lima: Mosca Azul, 1978).
59. Ollé, *¿Por qué...?,* p. 87.
60. Ibid., p. 37.
61. Ibid., p. 84.
62. Ibid., p. 78.
63. James Higgins, *The Poet in Peru* (Liverpool: Francis Cairns, 1982), p. 149; see also p. 1, p. 147.
64. Edmundo Bendezú, *La poética de Martin Adán* (Lima: Villanueva, 1969), p. 140; see also pp. 133-41.
65. Ollé, *¿Por qué...?,* p. 69.
66. Herman Melville, *Moby-Dick* (New York: W.W. Norton, 1967), p. 290.
67. Ollé, *¿Por qué...?,* p. 85.
68. Ibid., p. 51.
69. Ibid., p. 34.

FROM THE MARGINS TO THE CENTER: RECENT TRENDS IN FEMINIST THEORY IN THE UNITED STATES AND LATIN AMERICA

JEAN FRANCO

A Chilean friend of mine visited New York City a few years ago, bringing photographs of several of his performances in Santiago de Chile. He belongs to a performance duo, "Las Yeguas del Apocalipsis," who have staged a number of activities in drag or naked on the streets of Santiago, often combining performance with installation and using public events—for instance the Communist Party congress—for their staging.[1] They were photographed on one occasion as "The Two Fridas," both posing as the Mexican painter Frida Kahlo, who has become both a cult and kitsch figure in the United States. Her portrait appears on altars by Chicana feminists, but also on broaches, masks, posters, and book covers. In this self-portrait, she doubles herself, showing a Frida dressed in Victorian dress with surgical scissors in her hand, cutting the arteries of her heart and another Frida wearing a Mexican dress and holding a miniature portrait of her husband, Diego Rivera. In the United States the painting has become an icon, inspiring interpretations around themes of suffering woman-hood, the pain of divorce from Diego, the aesthetics of self-representation and self-fashioning, and so on.[2] Her personal story has also inspired a Mexican publishing boom, not only in Kahlo biographies but in biographies of other suffering women—for example, Elena Poniatowska's *Tinísima* and Adriana Malvido's *Nahuiolín. La mujer del sol*.[3] These books are titillating portraits of women whose political militancy gets upstaged by their suffering and who are usually depicted as abject.

The Chilean performance artists, in contrast, represented Kahlo's painting as a pastiche, a living copy transported into a different cultural environment and "performed" by two gay men. Bare to the waist, the two wear long Mexican and Victorian skirts like the Kahlo self portraits but they are clothed only from the waist down. Instead of the same person in different guises, there are two different faces, both of them dark mestizo faces.

There are, of course, many ways to read the Chilean performance, but in the "plague years," the years of AIDS, it suggests the fate of gay affect brutalized not by infidelity but by the threat of AIDS. At the same time, the pose of the artists, rather than abject, brings out the proud and defiant in Kahlo's portrait. One of the performers, Pedro Lemebel, who writes "chronicles of the city" for Santiago newspapers, said of the AIDS crisis, "It would seem that societies need these pandemics in order to stratify the borders that subvert them: the procedure gets rid of several birds with a single shot of the syringe. It reduces the demographic explosion, regulates contagion, punishes minorities, and turns the erotic into a sepia postcard of family life."[4]

The dual portrait-performance lifts individual suffering onto the political plane defined by the pandemia. The name the performers gave themselves, "Las Yeguas (the mares) del Apocalipsis," employs a slang term for gay men: *yeguas* is an alternative to the more common *locas* (madwomen). By crossdressing, the gay males lay claim to (feminine) affect. The portrait can thus be understood in terms of Judith Butler's theory about "queerness," which she sees as "a specific reworking of abjection into political agency." "The public assertion of 'queerness,' " she writes, "enacts performativity as citationality for the purposes of resignifying the abjection of homosexuality into defiance and legitimacy."[5]

The use of the body, the foregrounding of the precariousness of gender identity, the emphasis on performance is very much part of contemporary sensibility. In the United States queer theory has moved into the avant-garde of feminist theory. Thus Teresa de Laurentis refers critically to "the seductions of lesbianism and of its metaphorization in feminist thought and writing."[6] Gloria Anzaldúa in her well-known book, *Borderlands/Fronteras,* makes both the ethnically "other" and the homosexual bearers of a new sensibility:

> Being the supreme crossers of cultures, homosexuals have strong bonds with the queer white, Black, Asian, Native American, Latino and with the queer in Italy, Australia and the rest of the planet. We come from all colors, all classes, all races, all time periods. Our role is to link people with each other—the Blacks with Jews with Indians with Asians with whites with extraterrestrials. It is to transfer ideas and information from one culture to another. Colored homosexuals have more knowledge of other cultures; have always been at the forefront (although sometimes in the closet) of all liberation struggles in this country; have suffered more injustices and have survived them despite all odds. Chicanos need to acknowledge the political and artistic contributions of their queer.[7]

Anzaldúa's own experience as a Chicana lesbian, who as a Chicana suffered the racism of Anglo society and as a lesbian could not fall back on any idealized notion of the Mexican family, led her to privilege a third space, the space of the in-between, of those who did not fit into Anglo society—the *atravesados* (half-breeds).

Although they have gone different ways, she and Cherrié Moraga, co-editors of *A Bridge Called My Back,* introduced into what was then a predominantly Anglo feminism the disruptive voice of minorities struggling from a position of marginality within their own communities. The importance of this intervention has recently been recognized in Mexico, where a special issue of *Debate feminista* on "Fronteras, limites, negociaciones" included an interview with Anzaldúa. In it, Anzaldúa explicitly privileges lesbian Chicanas as an avant-garde who are developing new ideas, in alliance with those heterosexual women "que están escribiendo *the latest cutting-edge theory in the United States among art chicanas.'*[8] Moraga's recent work in theater has become the focus of important theoretical discussions on lesbian sexuality.[9]

Especially to those critics with a stake in psychoanalysis, lesbianism and transvestism constitute disruptions of the Oedipal story. It is easy to see why this should be so, since Freud from the very first categorized lesbianism as perverse. Transvestism, on the other hand, seems to highlight the masquerading which Joan Rivière described in the 1920s as the ruse of the oppressed female.[10] The transvestite performance, in this case, fakes an identity that is already a fake. This is underscored by the Spanish *travesti,* which also translates the English word *travesty:* a patently clumsy copy of an original. Thus the performance of the Kahlo painting is a travesty, a patent staging of an original which is already staged. Performance, pose, masquerade—all refer to this slippage in which the precarious nature of gender identity is exposed by a performance, whether a performance in keeping with society's norms or a deliberately exaggerated performance, a parody or pastiche. Of course there is nothing new in this. Marjorie Garber's influential *Vested Interests,* which studied transvestism over a long historical period, demonstrated how cross-dressing has continually surfaced on the margins of society.[11] But in recent times, the politicization of both U.S. and Latin American gay culture during the AIDS crisis has given new meaning to public performance and parody, since one way that gay men and women acquire visibility in the public sphere is by enacting stereotypical identities.

Transvestism and lesbianism have also been crucial to recent developments in feminist theory. Transvestism undermines the idea of socially constructed gender constituted on the basis of "natural" sexual difference. It thus questions a separation of sex from gender that is at the heart of much feminist thinking. The notion of sex as natural and gender as socially constructed was a key distinction in the arguments between "essentialists" and "constructionists." While essentialists tended to attribute male and female roles to biological differences, constructionists posited sexual difference as prior to social constructions of gender categories. While this move liberated "woman" from "nature," it all too often led to a functionalist account of women's oppression that ignored the nonheterosexual.

In her brief account of the history of the term *gender* in feminist theory, Donna Haraway notes that "the tactical usefulness of the sex/gender distinction in life and social sciences has had dire consequences for much feminist theory, tying it to a liberal and functionalist paradigm despite repeated efforts to transcend those limits in a fully politicized and historical concept of gender."[12]

According to Judith Butler, in her influential *Gender Trouble,* compulsory heterosexuality "requires that certain kinds of identities cannot exist—that is, those in which gender does not follow from sex and those in which practices of desire do not follow from either sex or gender."[13] In a second book, *Bodies that Matter,* Butler elaborates on this argument: sex is a materialization of regulatory norms that are in part those of heterosexual hegemony. These norms are secured through citation and repetition and "the limits of constructivism are exposed at those boundaries of bodily life where abjected or delegitimated bodies fail to count as 'bodies.' " I want to stress this point because clearly it

199

moves the marginalized transvestite and gay woman to the very center of both agency and theory.

What is striking in Butler's argument is that it often sounds like a transposition into gender of Marxist class consciousness, except that it is performance rather than praxis that does the trick. By performance, Butler means not only staging but also the performative in speech act theory. "A performative is that discursive practice that enacts or produces that which it names."[14] The hegemonic speech act can be delegitimized through parody, while the public staging of the abjected is intended to bring about a paradigm shift which affects conceptions of identity. This transformation of staging into agency is crucial to Butler's argument and is achieved by sliding from performance to performativity. The critique of the hegemonic constitution of gender comes about "through the contentious practices of "queerness" as a "specific reworking of abjection into political agency.... It is the politicization of abjection in an effort to rewrite the history of the term, and to force it into a demanding resignification."[15]

Butler's emphasis on performance and parody explains why transvestism plays such a crucial role in her arguments, since the transvestite is always a performer whose identity is always fashioned. In *Bodies that Matter*, she pays particular attention to the film "Paris Is Burning," directed by white, Jewish, lesbian Jenny Levingstone, which filmed black transvestites performing identities to which they could not realistically aspire—the corporate yuppie, mother and child, and so on. For bell hooks, the film reproduces the white ethnographic gaze by turning the camera on black voguing; for Butler, it opens the possibility of a resignification of terms which have always excluded gays, for instance, "mother" and "home."[16]

What Butler finally seems to be arguing for is a broadening of "cultural intelligibility" and active citizenship for the "queer." In this sense, her books respond to the politics of identity as practiced in the United States, where as George Yudice has pointed out:

> Identity became a practice, a performance, a deployment across the institutionalized terrain of the social formation because performing identity was the means to appropriate by reaccentuating or reconfiguring the genres available for social participation, forms for negotiating all aspects of life from health, education, and housing to consumption, aesthetics and sexuality. Moreover not only identity but the very understanding of "needs" and "satisfactions" are open to interpretability and performativity. Such an authoring process goes beyond the limits of the term constructionism, which emphasizes the pressures

on institutions and economy; the new or reinvented identity groups author and perform their identities contingently.[17]

Because globalization has speeded up the circulation of symbols and cultural repertoires, including feminism and gay culture, it is not surprising that the formerly taboo areas of sexuality are in Latin America increasingly the focus of discussion that is often triggered by events or discussions in the global North. In Nicaragua, for instance, the death of Rock Hudson from AIDS opened up public discussion of the disease and a debate on homosexuality followed in the press.[18] Even in Cuba, homosexuality is now discussed rather than merely stigmatized. Television talk shows such as "Cristina," based in Miami but telecast in Latin America, are public confessions of what had formerly been hidden or private, with a strong emphasis on sexuality. They are rapidly shifting the limits of the permissible. Everywhere, there is apparently greater pluralism, a liberalization of morals, more permissiveness. Yet abortion is still illegal and takes many lives in almost every country. Women's bodies are still defined according to Catholic morality even while everyday life is marked by the stresses of consumer culture, which implies large-scale exclusion of people from that culture.

This preoccupation with the sexual and the social has been translated into theory both in Latin America and among Latin Americanists in the United States. At recent Modern Language Association and Latin American Studies Association conferences, it was the gay panels—not the feminist or "political" panels—that drew crowds, and there is a growing interest in gay Latin American writing.[19] While much of this intellectual activity is focused on the retrieval of gay writing or the re-reading of texts not hitherto described as gay, what interests me, in the present instance, is the way in which both the gay and the transvestite have become metaphors for marginalization and for the political unconscious.

It is important, however, to stress the historical and regional differences which give these terms a different inflection in Latin America, where a tradition of paternalism secured by male bonding and expulsion of the feminine is only recently being transformed by modernization. One of the best accounts of this tradition is Roger Lancaster's *Life Is Hard,* in which he argues that there is a certain class of passive homosexuals in Nicaragua, known as *cochones,* who affirm rather than contest machismo. In a chapter entitled "Subject Honor. Object Shame," Lancaster argues that the *cochón* is essential to the self-definition of the macho in a society where homosexuality is identified with anal penetration. For Lancaster the *cochón* exemplifies the cultural difference between North and South.

Nicaraguan cochones are *ontologically* (my italics) different from Anglo-American homosexuals. Both are clearly stigmatized, but they are stigmatized in different ways, according to different rules…. An altogether different word (than homophobia) is necessary to identify the praxis implicit in machismo whereby men may simultaneously desire to use, fear being used by, and stigmatize other men.[20]

Although I prefer to think the difference between U.S. gay rights and the Nicaraguan *cochones* has more to do with the political matrix than with any ontological difference, the argument that homosexuality under certain circumstances reinforces the existing power structure is valid. What interests me, however, is the transformation now taking place between this traditional situation and the new situation of democratic pluralism. Nowhere is this change more apparent than in Chile, where first repression and then the "economic miracle" transformed society.

Some particularly interesting recent discussion in Chile links the feminine and the transvestite to broader theories of marginality. The mechanisms of the older regime (which were similar to those described by Roger Lancaster) were brilliantly exposed in José Donoso's *El lugar sin límites*.[21] The protagonist of this novel, Manuela, represents the forbidden and yet seductive limits of the paternalistic order, offering an apparent transgression of gender boundaries by dressing and performing as a flamenco dancer. Homoeroticism is permissible in this society, however, as long as it is disguised, marginalized in the brothel, and controlled. At the same time male pleasure seems to derive from the very ambiguity of the transvestite performance, since the macho can treat the performer as a woman and therefore as abject. When, as a crude joke, Manuela is forced by his patron to act like a man and to make love to the brothel owner, La Japonesa, apparently fathering a daughter, the "travesty" becomes quite blatant. A not-quite-man acts as a man while wanting to masquerade as a not-quite-woman. This has particular salience in a society where the social attributes of masculinity and femininity are rigidly governed by a hierarchy of power defined as masculine, and where woman possesses only the power of seduction and masquerade.

Donoso's novel links the transvestite to a society in which virility, together with economic and political power, sustain hierarchical relations—which are also actualized in the class and power differences between the macho and the passive homosexual. Set in a historical period of transition and modernization, *El lugar sin límites* is the tragedy of anachronism, both the anachronism of a town doomed to death and decay, having been bypassed by the railroad, and the anachronism of Manuela herself, whose devotion to her "art" allows the men to indulge in the fantasy of homoeroticism without appearing to succumb to it. The brothel acts as a kind of *heterotopia*—an alternative space within the system. However, it proves to be a fragile space. Modernization brings about the end of patriarchal protectionism and the male fantasies it encouraged. The aging Manuela can no longer sustain the illusion. Beaten, left to the dogs, she is redundant in modern society.

The marginalization of prostitutes and transvestites in brothels was essential to the patriarchal landowning order in which power was secured through filiation and male bonding, usually in opposition to the abject. In Chile, this relative tolerance came to an end (though without any essential change of the social structure) with the military regime of General Pinochet, which violently disciplined society to make way for economic transformation. It was not only communists and socialists who were stigmatized as subversive, but also gay men and transvestites. The Chilean case was not unlike that of Nazi Germany, in which the homosexual tendencies in the army were violently exterminated. In both societies the idea of discipline was paramount and the fear of sexual disorder correspondingly intense.[22]

This moment of increased repression is caught in *La manzana de Adán,* a collaborative photoessay by photographer Paz Errazuriz and writer Claudia Donoso, which can be read as a postscript to *El lugar sin límites.* The two authors lived with the transvestites in a brothel called, appropriately, "La Jaula (The Cage)," whose inhabitants were as secluded from society as if they were in a convent. Although the book was published after redemocratization, the material was gathered during the military regime, at the beginning of which transvestites were taken to a ship anchored offshore where they were tortured and sometimes killed. Those who survived risked imprisonment and persecution. Yet they took the risk, not for political reasons—indeed, some of them are quite right-wing—but rather because of love and their carefully nourished illusions of being "artists" and performers. Like Manuela, it is the ability to perform the illusion of womanhood that is important to them. "My show was so convincing that they all thought I was a woman," one of them says. "But at the end of the show I used to remove my wig so they could see I was a travesti."[23]

What made it impossible for the military government to tolerate this was the fear of ceding to the "pacifist, cowardly, immoral, lowly, base and demoralizing."[24] The "originality" of Chile, if it can be so described, is that the employment of shock tactics and the destruction of these undisciplined or insubordinate elements ushered in the "free market," which in turn brought about "deterritorialization," the abstraction of affect, and the opening up of new possibilities of desiring production. Once the military embraced the marketplace, it was impossible to stop the flow of "undisciplined" rock music across borders, or of television programs portraying permissive life styles. Redemocratization—with its staging of electoral democracy, free choice, and pluralism—was not so much a consequence of this, as a solution to the tension between control and commodification. The policing of the shopping malls and the ghettoization of the poor have ensured that the marginalized remain relatively invisible.

Whereas social scientists tend pragmatically to work within the limits of this situation and engage in struggles over violence against women, citizenship, and rights, a number of artists, writers, and cultural critics have become concerned with exposing the unfreedom of capitalist freedom, a project which, for them, includes theorizing feminism and transvestism as figures for marginalization.

Under the military regime, this group developed new forms of political art, designed both to overcome the "forgetting" of the past and to cross the rigid disciplinary lines, including those of gender, established by the government. Rather than defining themselves in terms of left or right, this group, whose work has been documented by Nelly Richard, focused on questions of exclusion, marginality, and the abject.[25] As Julia Kristeva has pointed out, "it is not lack of cleanliness or health that causes abjection but what disturbs identity, system, order. What does not respect borders, positions, rules. The in-between, the ambiguous, the composite."[26]

With the ending of the military regime, this political art has taken a new turn, demonstrating how deeply the social imaginary is still implicated in gender stereotypes. This was powerfully illustrated by a recent incident in Venezuela where the Chilean artist Juan Dávila exhibited a postcard depicting a berouged Simon Bolívar with female genitalia. The postcard was initially shown at the Hayward gallery in the "Unbound" exhibition, where it apparently caused no surprise, whereas in the subsequent exhibition in Venezuela it was taken as a national affront. In Dávila's work, Bolívar, the "father" of independence, is strangely transmogrified. Although on horseback in a traditional virile and martial pose, he wears a halter top that reveals women's breasts, and his trousers are open to show both a vagina and testicles. He also wears an earring and lipstick. Dávila's "Bolívar" thus interrogates the past in a particularly disturbing way by exposing the hero not only as public man but also as public woman. As Michael Taussig has shown, America has traditionally been figured by a woman and Bolívar is shown in one of his portraits embracing a diminutive female allegory of the continent.[27] When Bolívar's sex is radically altered, however, the male gendered heroic version of the emancipation narrative is disarticulated and the complicity between official history and the marginalization of the feminine becomes evident. But if heroism is a stereotype constituted as male, the feminine side of Bolívar seems to suggest prostitution and degeneracy. The two stereotypes coexist like twins in the postcard, which makes it all the more disturbing. The precarious and never sutured separation of gender and identity is, however, also the place of fantasy and the utopian, and this in turn is what permits a new *madre/patria* to be imagined. What distinguished the so-called *avanzada* (vanguard) from the traditional left during and after the military regime was precisely its focusing on the need to disrupt the gender categories that supported both the old authoritarianism and the new.

Starting from a position similar to that of French feminism, in which the feminine is essentially that which is dispersed, marginal, incoherent, the main theorist of the *avanzada,* Nelly Richard, makes the peripheral and the feminine the privileged site of insubordination. In a collection of essays, *Masculino/femenino,* she argues that the feminine (but not necessarily woman) is always on the side of destabilization. Yet it seems to be the transvestite whose parody most effectively highlights the precarious nature of gender and the insubordination at the periphery. Richard writes:

> the hyperallegorization of identity as mask which the painted transvestite enacts unmasks the Latin American practice of *"retoque"* (touching up, enhancing). Seen from the center the peripheral copy is the degenerate (*rebajado*) double, the devalued imitation of an original which has acquired surplus value because it has originated in the metropolis. But seen from its own point of view, that copy is also a postcolonial satire of the way that first world fetishism projects as its Latin American image false representations of originality and authenticity (primitivist nostalgia for a virgin continent) that Latin America then falsifies in a caricature of itself as Other in order to satisfy the demand of the other.... The feminized overacting, posing as what was is not (neither feminine nor original) resignifies both the copy and its mechanisms of doubling and simulation as a criticism from the periphery of the Eurocentric (paternal) dogma of the sacredness of the founding, single and true model, i.e. metropolitan signification.[28]

It is significant that in an essay entitled "Femenismo y postmodernismo," the issue is as much one of Latin American cultural autonomy as of feminism as such.

Diamela Eltit, who like Nelly Richard and Juan Dávila has been associated with the *avanzada,* has published an extraordinary series of novels in which the feminine, the marginalized, and the mad figure as the stigmatized *sudaca* (a derogatory term used in Spain for South Americans) and in similar fashion implicates gender and the aesthetic in the project of reconfiguring nation and America within globalization. Her novels, *Lumpérica* (1983), *Por la patria* (1986), *La vaca sagrada* (1991), *El cuarto mundo* (1988), her early performance of self-mutilation, her testimonial recording of a schizophrenic, her collaboration on a photo essay on love among the lunatics of Putaendo, obsessively hold up the distorting mirror of the marginal to reflect the monstrous image of the classical center.[29]

In order to draw together the threads of my argument, I shall briefly consider the novel *El cuarto mundo,* which figures a fourth world of virtuality out of the fragmented versions of family romance displaced from the center onto the peripheral third world. As Julio Ortega rightly points out, "The third world, facing greater rejection than ever as a result of violence at every level, is, in this text, transformed into a virtual 'fourth world'; unsocialized, apocalyptic and scandalous, capable of rejecting Western foundations of knowledge and action at their root. This violent parable answers ostracism with strength, and a transparent sedition."[30]

Eltit's novel begins in the period of repression following the victory of the "most powerful nation in the world," by which she may mean transnational capital. However, to represent the novel as an allegory of Pinochet's economic miracle would be a misrepresentation. Rather, the effects of discipline, repression, shame, and marginalization constitute bodies and subjects that are wounded, emaciated, "beautiful," suffering, feverish, and marked by plague and violence. A fragmented underclass with no stable identity engages in an intense play of affects dominated by desire, rejection, jealousy, loss, guilt. These *sudaca* bodies and subjects imperfectly live a version of the family romance that never conforms properly to the Oedipal paradigm. Indeed the very fact that the novel is narrated first by a twin brother who seeks his identity in difference from his sister, and then by the sister, indicates the wound (of gender difference) that the novel seeks to heal. The father acts as the surrogate of the state. The mother is by turns libidinous, faithless, a masquerader, abject. But masculine and feminine characteristics are not necessarily distributed along traditional gender lines. A younger sister is "more like the father"; the twin brother is feminized. The novel begins in the womb, and is narrated in the first person, first by a boy twin and then by a girl. However, the boy is secretly told by his mother that he is like María Chipia and later in the girl's account he will be given this feminine name. The novel begins with the conception and the birth of the twins within a family in which the mother enacts the *insensatez* of the woman. It ends with another birth, the birth of a daughter conceived by the twins which is also the child of the "diamela eltit," a child born into the marginalized world of the *sudaca,* who will go on sale (in other words, the novel itself as it enters into the circuit of exchange).

The novel closes with a birth that defies the incest taboo and foundational heterosexuality and endogamy. The "fourth world" of the novel is the accumulation of fragmented identities and affects of those who constitute the "carrion" of "the most powerful nation in the world"; their weapon against marginalization and eventual extinction is the utopian fantasy of a *"sudaca* fraternity" that sutures gender division. The novel can thus be described as a "travesty" of the Oedipal story as well as the story of the "privatization" of the periphery which has no public sphere and no history. Eltit speaks of the "virtuality" of fiction, making it a space where impossible can be imagined.

In the admittedly limited examples I have discussed, the reconfigurations of sexuality and gender respond to difficult questions of agency and transgression in a world where political issues have become increasingly blurred. My concern in this chapter has been less with practical politics, however, and more with the contrasting figuration of performance as agency in the United States and of marginality as transformative space in Chile, both of which correspond to quite different evaluations of the public sphere. What has fascinated me in both cultures is the way that new articulations of the utopian have been made possible by moving to the center of theory those bodies which were formerly marginalized as perverse.

NOTES

1. Since writing this paper, "Las Yeguas" have split up. Both men are writers. Pedro Lemebel publishes "crónicas de la ciudad" in newspapers. These have been published as *La esquina es mí corazón* (Santiago: Cuarto Propio, 1995). Francisco Casas is a poet.
2. The tacit rules of art criticism which excise biographical reference are almost always overlooked in discussions of Kahlo's paintings. See Jean Franco, "Manhattan Will Be More Exotic This Fall: The Iconization of Frida Kahlo," in *Woman: A Cultural Review* 2, no. 3 (Winter 1991).
3. Nahuiolín was, like Tina Modotti, a sex cult figure of the bohemian 1920s. See Elena Poniatowska, *Tinísima* (México: Era, 1992); Adriana Malvido, *Nahuiolín. La mujer del sol* (México: Diana, 1993).
4. Included in *La esquina es mí corazón.*
5. Judith Butler, *Bodies That Matter: On the Discursive Limits of "Sex"* (London: Routledge, 1993) p. 21. In her earlier *Gender Trouble: Feminism and the Subversion of Identity* (New York: Routledge, 1990), she tended to insist on the parodic.
6. Teresa de Lauretis, "The Seductions of Lesbianism," in *The Practice of Love: Lesbian Sexuality and Perverse Desire* (Bloomington: Indiana University Press, 1994), p. 191.

7. Gloria Anzaldúa, *Borderlands/Fronteras: The New Mestiza* (San Francisco: Aunt Lute Books, 1987) pp. 84-85.

8. Gloria Anzaldúa, "Ya se me quitó la verguenza y la cobardía," Conversation with Claire Joysmith, *Debate feminista* 8 (September 1993): 16.

9. See for example de Lauretis, *The Practice of Love,* especially the discussion of Moraga's play, "Giving up the Ghost," pp. 205-15.

10. Joan Rivière, "Womanliness as a Masquerade," in Burgin, Donald and Kaplan, eds., *Formations of Fantasy* (London: Methuen, 1986).

11. Marjorie Garber, *Vested Interests: Cross-dressing and Cultural Anxiety* (London: Penguin Books, 1992).

12. Donna Haraway, "Gender for a Marxist Dictionary," in *Simians, Cyborgs and Women: The Reinvention of Nature* (London: Routledge, 1991), p. 136.

13. Butler, *Gender Trouble,* p. 17.

14. Butler, *Bodies that Matter,* p. 13.

15. Ibid., p. 21.

16. Ibid., p. 137.

17. George Yudice, from *We Are Not The World,* forthcoming from Duke University Press.

18. Roger Lancaster, *Life is Hard: Machismo, Danger and the Intimacy of Power in Nicaragua* (Berkeley: University of California Press, 1992), p. 256.

19. See for example David William Foster, *Gay and Lesbian Themes in Latin American Writing* (Austin: University of Texas Press, 1991).

20. Lancaster, *Life is Hard,* p. 269.

21. José Donoso, *El lugar sin límites (1966)* (Barcelona: Seix Barral, 1987).

22. Klaus Theweleit, *Male Fantasies* (vol. 1): *Women, Floods Bodies History* (Minnesota: University of Minnesota, 1987).

23. Paz Errazuriz and Claudia Donoso, *La manzana de Adán (Adam's Apple)* (Santiago: Zona, 1990), p. 121.

24. Quoted in Theweleit, *Male Fantasies* (vol. 1), p. 387.

25. Nelly Richard, *La insubordinación de los signos: Cambio político, transformaciones culturales y poéticas de la crisis* (Santiago: Editorial Cuarto Propio, 1994).

26. Julia Kristeva, *The Powers of Horror: An Essay on Abjection* (New York: Columbia University Press, 1982), p. 4.

27. Michael Taussig, "America as Woman: The Magic of Western Gear," in *Mimesis and Alterity: A Particular History of the Senses* (London and New York: Routledge, 1993), pp. 176-92. Note: I wrote this chapter before the publication of the November 1994 issue of *Revista de crítica cultural,* which was devoted to the Dávila affair.

28. Nelly Richard, *Masculino/Femenino: Prácticas de la diferencia y cultural de-mocrática* (Santiago: Franscisco Zegers Editor, 1989), p. 68. The translation is mine.

29. Diamela Eltit, *El padre mío* (Santiago: Francisco Zegers Editor, 1989).

30. Julio Ortega, "Diamela Eltit y el imaginario de la virtualidad," included in Juan Carlos Lértora, ed., *Una poética de literatura menor: La narrativa de Diamela Eltit* (Santiago: Editorial Cuarto Propio, 1993), p. 79, translation by Deborah Shaw.

GENDER POLITICS: LUISA VALENZUELA'S *COLA DE LAGARTIJA*

CLAUDINE POTVIN

Over at least the last decade, postmodernism has challenged the main master narratives—such as truth, reason, knowledge, science, authority, originality, progress, unity—that have dominated Western culture since the Enlightenment period. Within the same deconstructionist frame, various contemporary feminist discourses continue to question essentialist notions about such identities as gender, race, class, ethnicity, nationality. As they try to redefine the positioning of women in Western society and to situate themselves in function of the postmodern theory, critical feminist approaches focus on cultural and theoretical practices in their relation to gender. Gender issues and gender intersections with class, race, work, are at the center of many women's studies programs and departments today. The whole of postmodern thought and aesthetics cannot be totally understood outside gender considerations.

Obviously, the concept of gender goes far beyond the simple sexual differentiation and cannot be reduced to the anatomical categories of male and female. To be a man or a woman at any given historical time is the result of a cultural construct. The way a certain world sees, portrays, forms, educates, and conditions women, or men for that matter, is directly linked to the interests of a social class or a particular religious, economic, or military context (among other elements). It is a cliché to remind ourselves that we use women during periods of revolution and war and return them to their homes after victory or defeat by using totally opposite arguments (women can work as well as men; women's place is in the home). Gender dichotomy does not correspond to a so-called natural division that has been established since time immemorial and cannot be reversed; on the contrary, challenging gender dichotomy leads to the need to reexamine the notion of gender per se, since it is impossible to speak of a generic "woman." As Jane Flax writes, "no such person exists except within a specific set of (already gendered) relations—to 'man' and to many concrete and different women."[1] In order to displace the classical episteme, gender theory has to take into account all these aspects susceptible to indicate of whom we are speaking and from which perspective we are doing so.

In Latin America, the notion of gender is generally looked at through the lens of political reality. Women's freedom usually comes after the country's liberation. Although it may seem logical to think this way considering the oppressive governments and the conditions of poverty in which the population lives, this philosophy remains based on reactionary views of women's role and function within the family's traditional structures and social order. Gender politics is essentially a male politics, as history and literature have constantly shown. Gender issues are strongly inscribed into fiction, particularly in women's writings, which tend to subvert the literary established modes of representation of archetypes and feminine mythology (motherhood, care, education, virginity, passiveness, submission, etc). In order to write, Latin American women need to find their own voice, record it into their own landscape, elaborate a new text woven from archaeological threads of Her/story.

Without entering into the debate over the existence of a masculine or feminine literature, it is useful to mention how the history of women writers reveals that when they decide to write, despite the repression and against all odds, women writers manifest an intent to appropriate a language reserved for centuries to "the other." Interestingly enough, when asked in an interview if she was conscious of a clear distinction between a feminine and a masculine voice in her works, the Argentinian author Luisa Valenzuela answered: "What I am looking for is perhaps a kind of feminine discourse in which I have full command of the words of the phallocentric discourse. There are terrible markings put on a woman's language. They have given us a heavily charged

210

vocabulary. I would like to have command of that language and give it a feminine charge."[2] Neither active in the public world nor able to speak (about) it, women have been condemned in many ways to a marginal existence, since they did not belong to the center and did not participate in the instances of power or decision-making. Traditional textbooks have presented women as having played a minor role throughout history. Their pseudo absence of participation in the making of history corresponds, however, more to "one" vision, a biased reading of reality, than to a recount of "objective" facts.

If women have been silenced time after time, confined to an interior and private space, their stories, their point of view, were often judged insignificant, irrelevant, merely sentimental or not sufficiently universal. This is partly why Valenzuela insists on using all the existing language but above all on transforming the "masculine" (and I must add, "sexist") charge that language contains in a patriarchal culture. Valenzuela's comment refers to the power of language; words have their own energy and the political, cultural, social, or ideological meaning, and the power of a word varies according to the position of genders in society and in function of its use or its value. In the novel discussed here, *Cola de Lagartija (The Lizard's Tail),* Valenzuela not only speaks and writes, giving herself the status of narrative character, but inverts the gender categories and stereotypes, playing with words, reducing to silence and insignificance (lack of pertinence and meaning) the figure of the dictator, the ultimate power, manhood itself, and becoming herself the voice that chooses to speak or remain silent only when she wishes.[3]

Looking at *Cola de Lagartija,* in which Valenzuela questions patriarchal and dictatorial society's values and the concept of power which has traditionally excluded women's discourse and gender categories, we can see that three voices dominate the text: the military dictatorship, the Gran Brujo's prophecies, and the writer's narration itself. Ultimately though, the woman writer tends to erase the other texts, allowing the (re)production and the circulation of signs.

According to Mikhail Bakhtine, whose work on texts is critical to the analysis of language and identity, every *énoncé* (enunciation) is the product of a complex social situation in which it first appeared. Following this concept, Tzvetan Todorov added that no individual exists outside of society and that any human being becomes historically real and culturally productive only as part of the social entity, within and through its social class. Thus, we are not only born physically but socially. Individuals are born landowner or farmer, "bourgeois" or proletarian, Russian or French.[4] Needless to say that human beings are equally born gendered, that is man or woman, not only in sexual and biological terms, but ideologically inscribed within the social construct and the fabric of a value system linked to the relations between genders and their representation. By excluding the concept of gender, Bakhtine limits his own notions of alterity, dialogism and multiplicity.[5] In "Female Grotesque: Carnival and Theory," Mary Russo affirms that "Bakhtine, like many other social theorists of the nineteenth and twentieth centuries, fails to acknowledge or incorporate the social relations of gender in his semiotic model of the body politic, and thus his notion of the Female Grotesque remains, in all directions, repressed and underdeveloped."[6] As a matter of fact, in any dialogue between languages, classes, cultures, races, ethnic groups, nationalisms, generations, and so on, impurity has to be spoken or seen equally in terms of sexual difference. Furthermore, women who write need a new language, hybrid in its essence, subversive, transgressive, which Valenzuela's novel exemplifies in many ways. Women writers conscious of this necessity tend to invent a double tongue, capable of imagining a map without limits, where the feminine body allows the circulation of her own law, her self, her pleasure, her desire.[7]

For Bakhtine, however, as with Luce Irigaray, no words are to be considered neutral.[8] Dialogism, in this context, implies that women's discourse is always double because it contains simultaneously the sign of its own desire and that of the other (man, father, chief, etc.) Dialogism belongs in that sense to the self and the other's voices. Bakhtine writes that dialogism sees in every word a commentary directed to the word itself and considers that for a word to be fully significant, this polyphone or intertextual space is necessary.[9]

Women's postmodern writings in Latin America illustrate this type of multiple language made of a plurality of discursive signifiers: coexistence, interaction, simultaneity, plurivocalism, mixture of literary genres, deconstruction of authoritative discourse, decentralization of narrativity, and so on.[10] Parody and irony characterize their works, in which numerous formal and semantic distortions invert the concepts of truth, law, and order. Their novels appear often as infinite conversations spoken by feminine characters relegated to the margins of society. The characters affirm nonetheless their identity as they develop within the narrative schemes according to their own perception of their stories and His/story: from the masculine territory, public and apparently universal or generic to the feminine sphere, domestic and private.

The dialogue of narrative genres in Valenzuela's novel and the constant exchange between the "I" of the author/narrator/character and the reader create a multiplicity of voices and narrations, a coexistence of plural aesthetics as well as sociopolicital contexts: popular/erudite culture, right/left ideologies, past/present history, individual/community, body/intellect, mouth/ear, sacred/profane, writing/reading. As the author establishes a permanent dialogue between reality and fiction, facts and illusions, she re-reads and re-writes Argentina's history in her novel, reversing the official social discourse of the politicians who maintain a whole population under an absolute repression through fear, torture, superstition, and ignorance. Through a sarcastic and acerbic critique of the Argentinian military regime, *The Lizard's Tail* subverts and questions the whole Western patriarchal civilization and its limited concept of gender. The author proposes to re-think the process of governing and not only shows how women's words or silences may change the course of history but focuses on the relativity itself of the concept "gender" associated to the exercise of power, since the dictator is neither male nor female but androgynous.

Originally, the novel's title was "El Brujo Hormiga Roja, Señor de Tacurú, Amo de Tambores, Ministro de Bienestar, Serruchero Mayor, Alto Sacerdote del Dedo, Patrón de los Desamparados, Dueño de la Voz y su hermana Estrella [The Sorcerer Red Ant, Señor of Tacuru, Master of the Drums, Minister of Welfare, Head Sawer, High Priest of the Finger, Patron of the Forsaken, Owner of the Voice and his sister Estrella]." This litany of titles indicates clearly the political importance of el Brujo, the Sorcerer, and above all, his intrinsic divine quality as well as the enormity of his power. He controls and owns the right to speak, the capacity to say or help, the ability to open or close all doors, the knowledge of magic; he is the hand that cuts, the finger that shows the road, the index that punishes and condemns, the one that erects himself over the crowd, the phallus that governs, the logos that possesses the truth, and the authority. While the novel was renamed by the editor for obvious reasons, the new title, *The Lizard's Tail,* highlights some of the major concerns of the book.

Although his name is never mentioned, the novel tells the story of López Rega, a self-proclaimed witchdoctor, President Isabel Perón's minister of social welfare from 1974 to 1975. Although a minister of state, López Rega governed and maintained his dictatorship through his underground existence and his hallucinating and cruel art of witchcraft. At the very beginning of the novel, an "advertencia" (a warning), informs the reader that "Nuestra arma es la letra" ("our best weapon is the letter") after announcing the intention of the author/narrator to let the Brujo speak. As we know from the prophecy that follows the warning, a river of blood will flow through the country and devastate it before peace can occur. Now, blood, torture, violence, murder, disdain, slavery, every military technique of persuasion, are the only methods known to the Brujo in order to dominate the world and acquire absolute power.

In that context, the new title seems particularly relevant. Sharon Magnarelli, in "The Lizard's Tail: Discourse Denatured," points out: "First, the

213

Spanish title is a translation of a guaraní term which refers to a type of whip that inflicts great pain and is used to punish. Itself an instrument of torture, the whip is an effective trope which evokes the torture and terror of the era described in the novel and the attendant abuse of power."[11] As a sceptre, the whip becomes a symbol of religious authority. The sexual connotations are equally abundant: the lizard's tail is used to undress the girls, the servants, creating at the same time pain and erotic pleasure. Furthermore, the tail is obviously a phallic symbol, and "it is believed that the lizard itself can be both male and female and that, in the Sorcerer's style, it can reproduce by means of hermaphroditism."[12] Finally, the English translation allows the double reading of tail and tale, which corresponds to the Spanish text where somebody tells the never ending story of tyrannies, massacres, and *colas*, long and painful waiting lines of anonymous faces. This implies a series of multiple versions that vary according to the narrator and her/his "vision" of facts.

The novel contains three parts, precisely numbered "One," "Two," "Three," in function of the predominance or appearance of different narrators. The first part, called "El Uno," is written mainly in the first person and portrays the Sorcerer as a megalomaniac in the act of composing his autobiography. Being essentially centered on his own self, all the names and functions he successively assumes reduce him to a unique, perfect, complete, superior, self-sufficient person; saint, God, el Señor, all his attributes confirm that he represents the Verb, "the Moebius strip, Klein's bottle, Pascal's sphere, Red Ant's antenna. I move about in an ever so flat space, says he, because there are no obstacles whatever for me, neither mountain nor gully; I am in all places and in none. I am what I am not and also am, I can even be kind, splendid, and magnanimous."[13] According to him, he is writing his journal, a great novel, the Novel, the Bible. A Christian fantasy of "auto/redemption" articulates his conception and representation of his own life; he does not need women, of course, and will eliminate the notion of gender itself. Creator of his own persona, he will also engender himself and become the only son, the "I" of all mirrors and possessions. We must remember that his lair, the pyramid, is covered with mirrors that reflect solely his image and that during the celebration or the carnival that he improvises, all participants must wear a mask that reproduces his figure. Masks or mirrors, far from hiding, reveal a particular truth, one side of reality.

In the second part, Valenzuela intends to assume responsibility for the fiction by intervening directly within the narration, by doubling herself as author/character involved in the storytelling. Originally, for this new Valenzuela authenticated by the author's signature at the end of the narration, writing

214

the story means making, modifying, changing the events, the role of protagonists, past and present, the reading of national history; but as she gets more involved in her fiction and in the problem of representing the true reality, she realizes to what extent to name (El Brujo possesses about fifty different names) supposes a process of creation, a desire to en/gender, to give existence and voice that becomes as dangerous as the masses' or women's silence.[14]

The author/narrator is then learning to play the double game of revealing/hiding the truth. This is why she chooses to first write a biography, in which she intends to recount the life of the Sorcerer; however, in the best of cases, biographies constitute a distortion of facts or at least one interpretation among many possible. Later on she decides to withdraw, to abandon the pen, in the name of the futility of literature when innocent people are being tortured, and also because "By erasing myself from the map, I intend to erase you [Borrándome del mapa pretendo borrarte a vos]."[15] This way, the ball is in the camp of El Brujo, who is also narrating the same story of his life. An autobiography is supposedly always closer to the truth than a biography, since it is written by the main actor concerned. But this man's illusions of grandeur and sense of delirium put a serious veil or mask over his eccentric characterizations. So, the apparent movement of the author appearing suddenly as an outsider is nothing but a feint, a ruse, since the other Valenzuela is taking over.

The subtitle of the novel's second part, "D*OS," indicates through the asterisk between the two first letters a parenthesis, an interval, the presence of the other, a linguistic, semantic, and literary intervention and a separation between OS and the rest of us, the world, the others, the freedom: intervention of an author who decides all of a sudden to insert herself into that first version, far too unilingual, far too monologic, far too uniquely male oriented. Women's fictions insist on the plurality of avenues or answers and henceforth on the multiple readings as modes of resistance. "D*OS" supposes two discourses, a second voice, another reading of His/story. Comparing and commenting Valenzuela's *Lizard's Tail* and Allende's *House of the Spirits,* Magnarelli writes, "In both cases the female narrators may occasionally feel impotent, marginal, and/or out of control in relation to the male narrators; yet the narrative frames underscore the subtle, but very conscious power of the female characters as both readers and writers," capable of using their own discourse as a very effective weapon.[16]

It is in the second part that we learn about the newspaper owned by El Brujo called La Voz (The Voice), opposed to any possible democratic voice or to any chance of integrating a different voice, that of women or others. Expert in the art of dissimulation, the owner gives the daily paper a new orientation, occult sciences, and obliges the journalists to report exclusively his vision of things. The notion of free press or freedom of expression disappears totally, replaced by a total submission to the rulers. However, Valenzuela notes that if this particular newspaper does not report facts or real news, it has the advantage of teaching the reader to read between the lines. So *siempre* (always) must be read as *a veces* (sometimes), *a veces* (sometimes) as *nunca* (never), and so on. Finally, worried with the invasion of El Brujo whose life is becoming greater and greater as the biography progresses, Luisa Valenzuela, alias Rulitos, abandons her project to write the Sorcerer's biography. In reality, she erases the possibility of the Brujo's survival. To write is to give life; consequently, as she remarks, "Without my biography, it will be as if you had never had a life. So long, Sorcerer, happy death (Sin mi biografía es como si no tuvieras vida. Chau, brujo, felice morte)."[17]

The political connotation of part two is obvious: why dedicate all these words to a military regime that annihilates every person who talks, reads, and writes. If the words constitute weapons in the Sorcerer's arsenal, the absence of language or the refusal of a certain discourse (the biography, for instance) represents also a powerful gun for the rebellious woman writer. Valenzuela uses a number of genres, literary or not, most of them qualified as minor or inferior by the Academy: from police report to newspaper article to publicity ads, from epic poems to dramaturgy, from dialogues to interrogations, from burlesque representations to (auto)biographies, and even the formula of political and religious speech. The first type of discourse often presented under the form of a sermon, the Gospel according to El Brujo. By doing so, she subverts the official discourse and the erudite literature and affirms the power of her fiction and of women's words. Ultimately, she revises the double meaning of gender and genre, in terms of ideology and literary institution, rewriting the place of women within fiction and history, creating frontier utopias centered on the otherness. *The Lizard's Tail* is clearly an allegory of Peronism, but it is also a verbal commitment of a woman writer looking at a certain (male) universe. In this work of frontier, that is off-limits. To use Emily Hicks's comment on the author, Valenzuela selects "several codes, including the Lacanian, the political, the semiotic, and the feminist, and she reveals how the ruptures and gaps in each are filled in by the others."[18]

Emily Hicks considers that "Border writers give the reader the opportunity to practice multidimensional perception and nonsynchronous memory."[19] By multidimensional perception, she refers to the ability to see not just from one side of a border, but from the other side as well, that is with two sets of referential codes in mind. The relationship of nonidentity will replace the notion of functional unity and desirable assimilation of ethnic groups. Without reading too much into the novel, the third part appears extremely revealing within that context. The concept of gender itself is here totally subverted in the main character's physical evolution.[20] Gender is a frontier that human beings cross constantly. Here, the exchanges, the slips or overlaps between sexes, the multiple forms of transvestism, the shifts from one erotic desire to another, the absence at other moments of definite female or male forms, the masks, the covering, the dressing up, the metamorphosis deny all possibility of centering the discourse. According to Valenzuela, "every human being is transsexual and the idea of a perfect, true sex is false. We all have both sexes; just as we have many masks, so we are both sexes only because there is no further choice."[21]

From the very beginning, we have learned that El Brujo has three testicles. He is then more macho than anybody else since he has more balls than any other man. His masculinity is slightly diminished however; as a matter of fact, his third testicle is feminine as it personifies his sister Estrella, whom he cherishes. El Brujo's greatest dream is to have a son from her, a son who will be the ultimate extension of himself, an ego bigger than any imaginable future, an egocentric and uniform version of one I/eye, one image, a fascist vision of an absolute domination and control of the entire world. In order to get this result, the operation is arranged through artificial insemination. As the Garza, his slave, empties the sperm from his phallus to transfer it in small tubes, reproductions of phalluses, El Brujo ironically looses his virile attributes and acquires ambiguous, grotesque characteristics of an impotent creature. As he proclaims himself:

> Thus, my virility remains on deposit in these test tubes that are like glass phalluses and I can go along letting myself be penetrated by the female principle. My whole person, my total person will come to be Estrella so I give myself back my seed, reintegrate myself by giving origin to I, who will not be just a doubling but a totallity, in him we shall be the three-in-one: I. I will pass from one to the other of my manifestations to reach I.[22]

El Brujo's metamorphoses into a bride and a mother on one side, the confection of a white, pure, "a pure white theater curtain for the grand finale; the birth," a curtain/tent made of "the finest cloth, lacework, embroidery, trim, things made of the purest white, purified in the sun," and may be from "an altar cloth, a wedding gown" from the Dead Woman.[23] On the other side, we have the great mutant, the consecrated virgin: "Now neither man nor woman, nothing but transition, s/he can't be classified and new genders and new pronouns have to be invented. Not neuter ones, because there is nothing neuter about the Sorcer *[le Bruj]*. Mutant pronouns are needed."[24] At this point, the reference to the

GENDER POLITICS IN LATIN AMERICA

name of the Sorcerer is transformed and he becomes only a "Sorcer" since he has been losing letters, attributes, and above all power.

In this third part of the novel, called "¿Tres?," the interrogation signs contained in the subtitle raises considerable doubts about the principle of the Holy Trinity recreated previously by El Brujo. During that operation, sexes and sexuality were abolished in the name of other types of perversions and obscenities.[25] It is clear that we cannot interpret El Brujo's movement as an intent to a pluridimensional and dynamic recreation of his or her self. On the contrary, his main objective is to reduce all mirrors to the unique, to the principle of logocentrism, oneness, to an "I" whose only limits reside in the image of unity. In that sense, his mutations are static and do not belong to an intention of crossing the frontier in both or any direction. His limited and closed explorations of sexes and gender categories are not the ones that will lead to the writer's rejection (the writer within the book) of the male's power and knowledge. The writer herself will be the one to confront and break through her writing the spatial barriers of repression.

The desire to go beyond, to explore new territories, to refuse the closeness or the prison of sexes, languages, and cultures, is doubly inscribed in the parody of the self-reflexive intellectual's interventions and in the act of deconstruction of the political operation. Both processes allow Valenzuela to elaborate in her fiction a subject woman which Jardine refers to as "the putting into discourse" of woman. "The object produced by this process is neither a person nor a thing, writes the critic, but a horizon, that toward which the process is tending: a gynema. This gynema is a reading effect, a-woman-in-effect that is never stable and has no identity."[26] So the title of this section ("¿Tres?") suggests the idea of the trinity (the father, El Brujo, the son). Without doubt, the question mark supposes the author's irony, as it remits to the reduction of the Sorcerer, the imaginary condensation of all male powers in one I/eye and the absurd and ridiculous transformation of the original monumental figure into a weak creature without identity. A figure ultimately converted into a little thread of blood instead of the expected river of fire promised in the warning given at the beginning of the story. We read in the text: "Transvestite, transsexual, sodomite, catamite Sorcerer, witchdoctor, magician of mere hormonal transformations, necromancer of confused gonads, warlock, no one even dares write about you any more, who points at you now? Who looks at you, who follows you with one eye and handles you a little and sometimes tells about you, orally, because your story no longer even deserves to be written?"[27] It is really as if the character Valenzuela, the one who was trying to write El Brujo's biography, takes over again, but this time with no intention of narrating "the other."

We are envisioning here the building of a self, the putting of a self together, a self always becoming as well as being. It is a matter of "sexing the self" to use Elspeth Probyn's expression.[28] In *The Lizard's Tail*, Valenzuela opposes a process of deconstruction, obviously postmodern, of myths, legends, lies, truth, birth, death, that is origin and end, to the more problematic process of national reconstruction which may imply the destruction of the individual. The novel finishes with an apparent accomplishment of the prophecy, a return to the very beginning of the narration: the Sorcer (linguistically diminished) transforms himself into the promised river of blood. But this turns out to be nothing more than a minuscule "trickle of sanguine liquid." In the last paragraph of the novel, Valenzuela says that history tends to repeat itself. Tyrannies, presidents, generals keep succeeding one another.

The paradigm of anthropophagy completes this picture: the need to devour the other, to incorporate him into "us." Although the concept may often be dynamic and signify renewal, linked to El Brujo's character, it has a connotation of destruction. The constant allusions to cannibalism are interspersed with references to vomiting. Human beings gobble each other and are victims of their own indigestions. In the same manner, the military regime throws up its "garbage" or "excess baggage," making large sectors of the population disappear. This is the law of El Proceso; it is also the dictator's "letter" and the Father's law which disposes generously of women's bodies.

In conclusion, by exposing the body, allowing the fluidity of language, fragmenting the self into multiple others, transforming narratology, refusing the control and unity of meaning, Valenzuela opens the gates of representation and signification. This is how words and metaphors become powerful "látigos" or whips under her pen. Valenzuela's strategies of writing and reading represent forms of cultural resistance.[29]

This textual and ideological resistance (narrative form and content) expressed through the re-writing of gender dichotomy takes its full significance within the sociopolitical Argentinian context. The novel clearly attacks the abuses of power proper to any authoritarian regime and offers a denunciation of all forms of repression. Rebellion is suggested through a feminine intervention (the author as character), which counteracts the protagonist's intention to impose himself as the only text. Valenzuela's replacing or displacing the sexes establishes a necessary relation between gender and politics. Women acquire a voice in the novel that allows them to re-read and re-write the national history between the lines of multiple blank sheets that have disappeared over the years inside the numerous holes left by the regime's (lack of) memory. Valenzuela speaks for the minorities and for all oppressed human beings. Since she does it from a feminist perspective and by reversing the usual gender categories defined by absolute power, she shows the dangerous connection between the "art" of governing and the institution of patriarchy.

NOTES

1. Jane Flax, "Postmodernism and Gender Relations in Feminist Theory," in Linda J. Nicholson, ed., *Feminism/Postmodernism* (London: Routledge, 1990), p. 56.
2. Fernando Burgos and M. J. Fenwick, "In and Around Memphis with Luisa Valenzuela: a Conversation," *River City* IX, no. 1 (1989): 69.
3. Luisa Valenzuela, *The Lizard's Tail* (New York: Farrar Straus Giroux, 1983).
4. See Tzvetan Todorov, *Mikhaïl Bakhtine. Le principe dialogique* (Paris: Seuil, 1983), p. 51.
5. The notion of dialogism refers here to the simultaneous presence of the "I" and the "other" in the discourse, which implies the fragmentation of the subject, consequently the fact that the "I" interpels necessarily the "alter" (ego, destinatary, difference). Since a number of discursive instances permeate all texts and all words, by extension, the dialogue established between words and discourses is infinite; in that sense, the plurality of voices, the multiplicity of languages, and the confrontation of ideologies deny the principle of identity, or uniformity, or monologism, and the possibility of an absolute or fixed meaning within the literary text. The official authoritarian discourse of patriarchy tends precisely to ignore the differences (women's voices, ethnic groups, immigrant's perspectives, minorities, working classes, etc.) and offer a limited or one-faceted vision of reality.
6. Mary Russo, "Female Grotesque: Carnival and Theory," in Teresa de Lauretis, ed., *Feminist Studies, Critical Studies* (Bloomington: Indiana University Press, 1986), p. 219. Russo refers to how the theorizing of the signifying systems of the social body tends to evacuate the gender category. If theory is to consider the production of signs, it must include all the signs as semiotic subjects.
7. Hélène Cixous uses Lacan's concept of *jouissance* to refer to the circulation of the feminine desire within her words and her world, made possible by her own agency. See for example Hélène Cixous, "Sorties," in Hélène Cixous and Catherine Clément, *The Newly Born Woman* (Minneapolis: University of Minnesota Press, 1986).
8. According to Irigaray, "speaking is never neutral." Since the creative subject has always been masculine, whatever is spoken by this subject is necessarily informed or biased by it and continues to construct history, culture, ideology, and discourses in function of an "original" position. See Luce Irigaray, *Parler n'est jamais neutre* (Paris: Minuit, 1985).
9. Mikhail Bakhtine, *La poétique de Dostoïevski* (Paris: Seuil, 1970), p. 13.
10. See for example the works of Valenzuela, Peri Rossi, Mercader, Somers, Traba, Poniatowska, Lispector, Heker, Ferré, and Albalucía.
11. Sharon Magnarelli, "The Lizard's Tail: Discourse Denatured," *Review of Contemporary Fiction* 6, no. 3 (Fall 1986): 100.
12. Ibid.: 101.

13. *The Lizard's Tail,* p. 185.
14. Francine Masiello, having studied the dialectic of silence and denunciation in a dictatorial context through the example of the Mothers of the Plaza de Mayo in Argentina, wrote that: "in the conflict between the one who speaks and the one who is reduced to silence, since men have lost the possibility to speak, women appear as a solution because they offer a powerful voice against the military regime" (my translation). See Francine Masiello, "Cuerpo/presencia: mujer y estado social en la narrativa argentina durante el proceso militar," *Nuevo Texto Crítico* 2, no. 4 (1989): 156.
15. *The Lizard's Tail,* p. 227.
16. Sharon Magnarelli, "Framing Power in Luisa Valenzuela's *Cola de Lagartija* and Isabel Allende's *Casa de los espíritus,"* in Lucía Guerra Cunningham, ed., *Latin American Women Writers in Search of Themselves* (Pittsburg: Latin American Literary Review Press, 1990), p. 57.
17. *The Lizard's Tail,* p. 227.
18. D. Emily Hicks, *Border Writing: The Multidimensional Text* (Minneapolis and Oxford: University of Minnesota Press, 1991), p. 82. In Valenzuela's novel, the Lacanian code refers to Freudian psychoanalysis and, in particular, to the Oedipal configuration of the subject within the symbolic order.
19. Ibid., pp. xxiii, 12.
20. The Garza or the Egret, the castrated assistant/slave of El Brujo, is equally revealing in this respect and could be discussed from the same perspective.
21. See Evelyn Picon Garfield, *Women's Voices from Latin America. Interviews with Six Contemporary Authors* (Detroit: Wayne State University Press, 1985), p. 157.
22. *The Lizard's Tail,* pp. 234-35.
23. Ibid., p. 247.
24. Ibid., p. 246.
25. Susan Rubin Suleiman refers to the possibility of dreaming "beyond not only the number one—the number that determines unity, of body or of self—but also beyond the number two, which determines difference, antagonism, and exchange conceived of us as merely the coming together of opposites." See Susan Rubin Suleiman, *Subversive Intent. Gender, Politics, and the Avant-Garde* (Cambridge and London: Harvard University Press, 1990), p. 136.
26. Alice A. Jardine, *Gynesis. Configurations of Woman and Modernity* (Ithaca and London: Cornell University Press, 1985), p. 25.
27. *The Lizard's Tail,* p. 256.
28. Elspeth Probyn, *Sexing the Self: Gendered Positions in Cultural Studies* (London: Routledge, 1993), p. 172.
29. For more on the concept of cultural resistance, see Teresa de Lauretis, *Alice Doesn't: Feminism Semiotics Cinema* (Bloomington: Indiana University Press, 1982), p. 7.

CONCLUSION: POST BINARY BLISS: TOWARDS A NEW MATERIALIST SYNTHESIS?

NANNEKE REDCLIFT

Gender theory has always been diverse, fractured by differences in basic premises. The liberal, socialist, and radical feminisms of the 1970s and 1980s were not just conflicting alignments within the women's movement. They were distinctly different kinds of explanation for sexual inequality, and therefore of producing theory. If there was ever a moment in which one could talk of gender theory in a general sense, it was perhaps only in reaction to conventional, ungendered, or gender-blind theory, premised on the absence of a female subject. Shared ground was forged through critical opposition to dominant models, a questioning of the terms on which knowledge is produced.

At a deeper level, even this commonality may have been more apparent than real. The assumptions lying behind the profusion of research on gender have sometimes been explicit but have often been tacit. For example, as Fiona

Wilson pointed out in her review of research on gender and agrarian change in Latin America, different views of what the family was and, more importantly, what it should be lay behind a number of studies carried out in the 1980s.[1] Whether the family was seen as a source of support or a locus of oppression made a difference to the framing of research and the evaluation of data. The premise held in common was a recognition of the need to "gender" political economy, and to link any examination of economic transition with an account of family and household systems. A more complex set of values and principles about what kinds of change are desirable was left only partly articulated.

Research on gender has been carried out primarily within three different conceptual frameworks, deriving from different intellectual traditions. These include theories of exchange and appropriation, arising out of contemporary patterns of social organization; theories of symbolic power and value grounded in enduring systems of thought, located in the nature of culture itself; and materialist theories which regard inequalities as the result of historical trans-formations of the relationship between production and reproduction. While not mutually exclusive at an empirical level, these approaches represented major differences in orientation when it came to offering explanations for gender difference.

New intellectual movements characteristically begin by redefining a space and transforming conceptual language; this is then followed by a proliferation of rich detail, in which the questions that drive the enterprise are seen as self-evidently necessary. It is only later that terms are re-examined, and new knowledge is applied to fundamental assumptions. At the same time, theory is shaped by real-world practice and commitments. Critical perspectives them-selves have social effects, both purposive and unforeseen. There is regrouping, incorporation, as well as backlash and countermovement. An institutionaliza-tion of ideas takes place, however uneven, so that what was once radical becomes conventional.

Thus, there are now feminisms rather than feminism. There is no longer an intrinsic connection between feminism and gender studies. The politics of research on "woman" or on gender raises new issues about the goals of academic inquiry. Discussions of "difference" have revealed the limits of common interest, and in the hands of feminist philosophers have led to "standpoint" theories of knowledge, which may refer as much to differences among women as between women and men.[2] As Franco and Rowe have argued in this volume, contemporary sexual politics and the reclaiming of stigmatized sexualities have destabilized the connections between bodies and identities, between margins and centers. The older geography of theory-making (the North thinks, the South does), even though recalcitrant and unresolved, can no longer pass without question. The hidden assumptions of generalizing models (usually Western) have been confronted by the specifics of local worlds (everywhere else).

As the contributors to this book show, ways of thinking about masculinities and femininities, about sexuality and sexual difference, are being reassessed. They strain against the confines of old models, taking issue with concepts which have become outgrown. This sense of turbulence is captured by the "cross-currents" of the title of the original conference, where many of these chapters first took the form of papers.[3] Cross-currents implies both disorientation, flux, and uncertainty, but also a meeting point and mingling of different streams and approaches.

Latin American research has been marked by particularly strong disciplinary traditions. Each has also developed its own stance in relation to currents of thought, and its own versions of the tension between local and "northern" knowledge. Theory has also taken on a different emphasis in different regional settings. However, when we turn to examine the production of gender through the lens of recent research, the lines of demarcation begin to blur. It seems that it is only by crossing the boundaries that any sense of adequacy in describing the complexities of changing experience can be attained. "Power" and collective action (the defining concepts of politics), "representation/imagination" (the critical tools of literary analysis), "family/household/production" (the particular preserve of sociology), and "symbolic meaning" (a central concern of anthropology), must be brought together in any attempt to understand the nature and performance of gendered identity. History, too, and more particularly memory and "memory work," the recognition of the past in the present, and the present in representations of the past, has taken on a new significance in revealing the multilayered relationship between political and economic power and sexual differentiation.[4] As several of this volume's contributors, notably Dore, Nazzari, and Ramos, demonstrate, history-memory has helped us to see more clearly the interactions between long-term structural changes and the *mentalites* of individual identity and moral worth around which masculinities and femininities are created. It is not only the advent of "intellectual" postmodernism with its notions of plurality and difference, but also the nature of contemporary politics and social movements that have led to this questioning of previous assumptions. Merely "gendering" the intellectual inquiry is no longer enough.

This chapter explores some of the ways in which earlier frameworks have been developed and transformed, leading to a more fundamental questioning

224

of positions. To acknowledge the diversity of Latin American economies, societies, and gendered identities and the totalizing stereotypes of Hispanicist discourses is also to become aware of the fragmentation of knowledge, in which generalizations are quickly unmasked and contested.[5] Do exhortations to context-specific understanding lead toward new models which might encompass both similarity and difference or to the rejection of models? Is there a theory "beyond the binaries"?[6] Or have we reached the end of theory, as well as the end of history, in the questioning of authoritative positions from which to speak?

PAST PARADIGMS, PRESENT PARADOXES

In Latin America feminist work grew out of and was a rewriting of the sociology of the "dependentista" theorists, creating a particular kind of Latin American materialism, strongly conscious of the shaping power of wider economic forces and political relations.[7] In 1979 Marysa Navarro could write, "Most Latin American scholars currently engaged in research on women see themselves either as resolving interesting theoretical or methodological questions, or as exploring social inequalities ultimately explained by the prevailing sociopolitical system."[8]

Concern with divisions of labor, production and reproduction, and the effects of historical change produced notable regional studies, which were particularly strong on the interplay between gender constructions, divisions of labor and resource use, and the penetration of capitalist relations.9 The examination of the relationship between family/household and production systems was built on a number of premises. First, a desire to show the mutability of gender constructs, changing in relation to new forms of productive relations. Second, a need to evaluate the gendered effects of capitalism as negative or positive for women, and to question Western progressive models of change. Third, an underlying assumption that changes in women's relationship to production would enhance their social value and power. The issue of causality was also uppermost, since the two domains of production and reproduction tended to be kept conceptually separate. How did household and family composition condition women's ability to enter the labor market? How did changing economic conditions affect the structure of the household, gender ideology, and the nature of power and authority within it?

Because of this orientation, the discussion of "difference" that developed in the 1980s was strongly politicized. Without wishing to underplay the variety of positions in this debate, I will focus particularly on (1) the examination of the different relationship of women and men to the production of symbolic

225

meaning and the generation of sexual difference;[10] and (2) the recognition of the mutual constitution of gender, class, and race.

The model on which the mutual constitution of gender, class, and race was based tended to view the production of gender and the production of goods as separate systems or circuits, intersecting at the point of household reproduction.[11] The division of labor, internationally, nationally, and domestically, formed a kind of core principle around which power and ideology were woven. Recent studies have brought increasing subtlety to this conceptualization through greater detail. The "before and after" approach which examined the impact of economic change on gender relations has given way to a more complex understanding of the ways in which a gendered economy is infused with ideologies of sexual differentiation, of spaces, skills, tasks, and values.[12] Local economies, reacting in diverse ways to the crisis of the 1980s, have demonstrated a mosaic of responses and new forms of labor force participation by women, not easily captured by the simplification of terms like "marginalization" or "incorporation."[13] Comparative studies of urban economies show, for example, that similar processes may lead to different outcomes. Increased income earning capacity has in some local labor markets led to a possibly greater say in household decision-making, for specific income groups. At the same time, in other contexts, the reverse trends are evident.

It remains hard to see what kind of change this may represent in the longer term.[14] In Guadalajara, Mercedes González de la Rocha found that women's enduring responsibility for children's well being continues to dominate their struggle to devote incomes and efforts to food and nutrition. Their management of subsistence remains a key aspect of their moral worth. Despite the fact that these incomes are a vital part of livelihood, they are virtually invisible, subsumed into collective provisioning. The economic stresses of the "lost decade" of the 1980s and the entrenchment of neoliberalism have probably exacerbated this invisibility, producing a "privatization" of the crisis, in which hardship is absorbed by an intensification of work and domestic management. Women are obliged to accept male violence as the price paid for some minimal support and to strike an implicit bargain with the ideological value given to the father's role as provider. The need to increase household income and women's greater contribution has therefore taken place "in a context where no alternative ideological models exist" and has not led to their creation.[15]

Perhaps, therefore, Audre Lorde's statement "the master's tools cannot demolish the master's house" begins to take on wider relevance.[16] Lorde drew on Nietzsche's phrase to question whether racism can be challenged within the terms of a discourse that is dominantly white. Similarly, if the economic system is constructed *through* gender (as much effort has been expended to demonstrate), it may not be the vehicle through which gender inequalities can be challenged. Thus, we can describe the ways in which poverty is gendered; we can describe the way in which economic structures draw on gender ideology to segment the labor force; we can describe how the retreat of the state is premised on the reproductive obligations which women fulfill, but this does not amount to a "theory" of gender, nor does it give an account of the likelihood of change. The productive system, being gendered, cannot in any straightforward way provide the means to transform gender relations. As Fiona Wilson points out, the "conflation ... between the image of the household as a protected domestic space and the physical concealment characteristic of many deregulated economic activities in Latin America ... centers on the cultural construction of womanhood and on the sanctity accorded familiar relations."[17]

Class, gender, and race, therefore, are not merely connected, they do not simply intersect. Chapters by Dore and Nazzari show the complex way in which they *are/stand for* each other. The reproduction of upper-class endogamy in both seventeenth-century São Paulo and rural Nicaragua depended on a sexual system requiring both the chastity of élite wives and the "dishonoring" of women beneath them. It cannot make sense to talk of "subordination" in any general sense in this context, and it becomes rather tautological to try to understand the changing nature of Paulista or Nicaraguan gender relations primarily through economic structures or transformation. The economic dimension is a key part of the picture. But we need to know about the reproduction of moral and symbolic boundaries through concepts of sexual and racial purity to understand the changing definitions of property and class.[18]

A similar shift is noticeable in Latin American work on women as political subjects. Women did not "lose their specificity" in the process of mobilization in the 1980s.[19] Whether through revolutionary participation, through human rights protests, or in the struggle for collective consumption, they tended to become politicized in ways which often confirmed existing meanings of womanhood. In fact, it has often been by drawing on images confirming their difference (stereotypical, essentialist, and apparently conservative) that exclusion was translated into action. What kind of power does this represent? Not an entry into the power of the system as constituted. Rather, it represents a subversion of the assumptions on which power is based, and of the practices of "misrecognition" which dissimulate and conceal its real nature and purposes.[20] Characteristic of these movements is not a taking of power in the conventional sense, but a nonetheless significant process of political redefinition and delegitimization of the "embodying" violence of the state, which works by denying the values of power or of politics itself.[21]

It is therefore possible to identify three aspects of earlier approaches that have more or less disintegrated in the light of the research that they themselves generated. First, the rigid separation of binary oppositions (public and private, sex and gender), has come to be seen as both overuniversalized and as often representing the inappropriate imposition of Western categories. As Cubitt and Greenslade point out in this volume, these categories are better seen as representations, justifying the assumptions of liberal democracy and often contradicted by practice in which the associations of particular spaces are contravened (i.e., workshops in the domestic domain, struggles for political power via family structures). As images, rather than theories, they are often powerful nonetheless.

Second, unitary models and conceptions of power (such as the idea of a transhistorical patriarchy, or of women as an analytic category) have been superseded by a greater emphasis on the power to control the terms of dominant discourse. Greater attention is given to conflict, contradiction, and negotiation and a recognition that power is not so much a property (of groups or persons) but an activity, accessible in different spheres at different times and not always reducible to "having" or "not having."

Third, what I will term "simple" materialism in the form of straightforward associations between productive systems and gender identities has been qualified by a better understanding about the way work is experienced and livelihoods are related to values, expectations, obligations, and other aspects of social identity.[22] The relation between production and reproduction may be different for different groups, and is often a key area of political control.

Finally, the "abstracted empiricism," in which the definition of research on "others"—whether women or genders—tends to reflect dominant philosophical traditions and political positions (freedom, autonomy, empowerment, identity), and to create a homogenized object of analysis (Mexican women, Latin American gender), has raised critical questions about the relationship between theorizers and theorized, about the geographical division of theory and practice, and about the grounding of theory itself in a specifically Western gender epistemology.[23] As Collier and Yanagisako suggest, "Instead of asking how the categories of 'male' and 'female' are endowed with culturally specific characteristics, thus taking the difference between them for granted, we need to ask how particular societies define difference."[24] Rather than the application of *a priori* universal categories, the diverse social meanings of male and female and the specific ways in which masculinity and femininity are constituted in particular cultures becomes more compelling than attempts to explain the relative position of the sexes schematically. This has been complemented by a critical examination of the terms of Western discourse, suggesting that the concepts used to explain sexual inequalities are themselves part of our own folk model. The task in each context, therefore, is not to ask how "natural differences" acquire cultural meanings, but to examine which attributes and characteristics provide markers and boundaries configuring the relations between individuals and social groups. The categories and domains of analysis have themselves come under attack, and ambiguity, heterogeneity, and contradiction have made inroads on earlier unities and dichotomies.

REEXAMINING POWERS: HISTORY AND CONSCIOUSNESS

What circumstances lead to changes in gender identities and consciousness? What is the dialectic between this and other forms of inequality? What representational strategies are implicated in the transformation of gendered meanings? Like some other issues in feminist theory (the domestic labor debate, nature and culture, etc.) the attempt to develop the notion of multiplicity, and to give some shape to the mutual constitution of gender, class, and race has tended to run itself into a tedious impasse, full of exhortations to consider the interrelationship of each but lacking in real substance. The chapters in this volume push the discussion forward constructively in a number of ways.

One implication suggested by these chapters is that the idea of a matrix of identifications and interests may be a more appropriate way to think of the concrete histories and everyday practices through which opportunities and constraints are negotiated. Alison Scott's account of the experience of working-class families in Lima in the 1970s provides a case in point. Scott describes the dynamic nature of an economy in flux, showing considerable diversification, with the potential for growth in some sectors, and the chance of mobility for a significant proportion of the population. Dualistic models of urban economies based on a straightforward division between formal and informal sectors, or a simplistic separation between class and gender as a basis of identity or consciousness, would not be adequate to analyze this dynamic. Although Peru remained a highly unequal society, in which the gap between rich and poor was undoubtedly widening, increasing relative inequality was not incompatible with an absolute improvement in living standards for the poor. This was reflected in a family ideology of mutual support, solidarity, and self-improvement, and what she describes as a "latent radicalism" expressed in a consciousness of the interests of *trabajadores* (workers) against the rich, who were seen to derive their incomes from hereditary wealth in land or property. This broad identification transcended other labor-market divisions, but did not give rise to political action because of widespread alienation from the political system itself, a product of the long history of repression and sectarianism.[25]

Furthermore, the extreme gender segregation of the labor market, while evident, was unlikely to generate an independent basis for identity or women's mobilization, since their experience and actions were shaped by the common class interest of the family. A high proportion of married women withdrew from the labor market with the birth of children and became dependent on the male wage, so that their own best hope of mobility lay through marriage to an upwardly mobile man (reinforcing particular sexual scripts and images). The important popular and neighborhood mobilizations actively involving women in defense of housing and community issues should be seen primarily as class-related phenomena rather than gender-related ones. The very constitution of class groups emerges in part out of the negotiation between women's tradeable skills in the labor market and decisions about childrearing and reproductive replacements for mothers' time. Women's work thus has implications not only for their empowerment but for the class structure as a whole. Ideologies, resources, and cultural aspirations work themselves out in practice in the context of the particular constraints for groups at different places in the class hierarchy.

We can build multiplicity into the notion of systematic forms of power, as Deniz Kandiyoti has argued, by seeing patriarchy not as a monolith, but as a discourse that is played out, negotiated, and possibly subverted in various ways.[26] The interrelationship between gender and class creates shared interests between men and women in some contexts and divergence of interests in others. The structure of opportunities for securing a livelihood and the nature of family and kinship ideology in Lima in the 1970s allows Scott to show why the first is often the case.

Looking retrospectively and comparatively at the *longe duree* of persistence and transformation in gender relations that is being unearthed in the many contexts of Latin American history adds another dimension to this multiplicity. In colonial New Mexico, for example, family status, ethnic supremacy, and control of production, as expressed though the idiom of honor and ideals of social conduct, meant that action based on personal desire and sexuality, particularly that of women, threatened the reproduction of the élite through kinship relations.[27] "Love" was seen as a "subversive sentiment," and one which was hardly present in discourse until the end of the eighteenth century, because it undermined the concerns of hierarchy and status. Arranged marriage,

230

sexual segregation, and the high valuation of female virginity emphasized collective contract and curtailed individual feeling.

Although control was incomplete and transgressions showed that the interests of parents and children did not necessarily coincide, the development of a language of personal emotion and the imagery of the heart as a symbol for passion began to emerge at the beginning of the nineteenth century. This coincided with the growth of a market, the development of a middle class of merchants, the growing mobility of autonomous workers, and changing public political relations. Sources of authority were increasingly internalized through the idea of the conscience, and the rise of a concept of romantic love was linked to the shift from consideration of family honor to individual motivation in relationships between men and women. In some ways, wives became more economically dependent on their husbands, casting doubt on any simple association between honor systems and women's subordination. As in the case of São Paulo described by Nazzari in this volume, this had contradictory effects, both in terms of social hierarchies and in terms of personal autonomy. The seclusion and valuation of women's virtue continued to play an important role for a shrinking élite, marking a status boundary with "other" women, for whom the loosening of familial bonds confirmed their subordinate social position. In this sense, the divisions "within" the category "women" are not an aberration, a betrayal of gender solidarity, or a failure of theory. They are an intrinsic and integral strand in the web of gender ideologies.

All of these changes reveal the interconnections between struggles for control of rights and resources and the metaphors and symbolic associations surrounding masculinities, femininities, and sexualities. As JoAnn Martin notes, the analysis of gender ideologies has often described a system of male domination and "then ... illustrate(d) the fit between the symbolic construction of gender and the subordinate position of women."[28] The dangers of this are that the power of gendered images in their own right (of mothering, nurturing, suffering, etc.), both as compelling symbols of nation or group and as personal constructs for individuals which may be both embraced and resisted, can easily be lost in an oversimplified opposition.[29] They are ambiguous in that while they may serve to constrain or even to victimize they may also provide "root metaphors" for other aspects of social experience.[30]

The way in which the public body politic utilizes and recreates ideas of the sexed body for its dominant metaphors has been usefully expressed in Irene Silverblatt's use of the term "semantic structure." Her case is that of conquest, but the point is relevant to contemporary gender significations too. The value of this concept is that it allows us to encompass the political/economic and the representational/moral aspects of cultural orders. It also allows us to integrate the different injunctions/values and images surrounding women of different classes or ethnicities, as well as covering both "reproduced and transforming definitions of masculinity and femininity."[31] Silverblatt's panorama of first Inca and then Spanish appropriations of Andean societies attempts to unravel the way in which a people can be penetrated conceptually and existentially by their colonizers. Divisions of labor, rights, obligations, tribute, the historical "events" of conquest are underpinned and enabled through the more subtle (and hitherto more hidden) ways in which cosmology and cultural systems of meaning can be rewritten to serve a new logic. In this view, gender systems are "metaphors as well as conduits for the expression of power." Views of procreation, fertility, the relation between human and natural world can be framed by the dominant in the terms of their own ontologies, creating political hierarchies and also providing a new language for relations between people.

According to Silverblatt, the Inca conquest transformed the symbols of Andean gender parallelism to accord with the new political economy in two notable ways. First, the conquerors grafted their own deities onto local ones and harvested the procreative body of the subject communities by monopolizing the icons of their fertility. Second, by "gathering" élite girls, they brought about a major structural transformation in the reproductive organization and imagery of local kin groups, creating both accommodation and resistance.[32] Whatever comments one might make about whether Silverblatt analyzes history or creates mythology, her argument suggests rapprochement between the material basis of productive control and the "social imaginary" of concept and language as the producers of meaning.

CONCLUSION: TOWARDS A NEW MATERIALISM?

The post-binary world is still an uncertain one, if indeed it is where we are. It is fashionable to describe Cartesianism as in crisis and Enlightenment views of linearity, progress, and metanarrative as an arrogant modernism. Yet even as we attempt to deconstruct, we reinvent, and it would be naïve to think that merely through self-critique we step outside the structures of knowledge. In laying siege to Western metaphysics we retain an undeniable power of representation. The value of this partial paradigm shift is perhaps not least a further indication of how deeply "naturalized" our gender assumptions are, so that public and private, sex and gender, or the organizing framework of a specific gender history can be imposed without self-consciousness on the meaning systems of others, not only in practice, through conquest and through the globalization of images (in which they become rooted and reincorporated as inseparable from local constructs), but as supposedly neutral and disinterested theory.

But there is a further point. It is not just that dichotomies are appropriate for us and inappropriate for others; as Iris Zavala argues, we can see them now as part of a wider and newly interesting process, as "sustaining fictions ... narratives which participate in the constitution of the self."[33] Even the body itself, that apparently transhistorical guarantor of unity, is the subject of the imagination and the gaze; it has no prediscursive, precultural existence, and cannot be read outside the forms in which cultures are able to visualize it.[34] Yet the body has usually been seen as "given," a passive recipient of the shaping activities of culture and, ironically, taken for granted and therefore excluded from theories of sexual difference.[35] "By positing matter and meaning as exclusive terms," write V. Broch-Due et al., "both erase the unsettling effects produced by the intersection between the mental and the material."[36] In this intersection, dualities need not so much be abandoned as available for reexamination as one mode of giving sex to the body and inscribing it in social space.

Such a reexamination might open the way to a wider theory of subject formation, drawing in the multiplicities and ambivalences of gendered identities. Zavala comments that we might remember "Marx's insight that language is practical consciousness as it exists for other men."[37] Perhaps what emerges most strongly from recent work, in Latin America and elsewhere, is a new view of the semantics of the political and personal body that may form a pointer to new theoretical pathways. The recognition of this is hardly "blissful," though perhaps it is salutary.

NOTES

1. Fiona Wilson, "Women and Agricultural Change in Latin America: Some Concepts Guiding Research," *World Development* 13, no. 9 (1985): 1017-1035.
2. Chandra Mohanty, "Under Western Eyes: Feminist Scholarship and Colonial Discourse," *Feminist Review* 30 (1988): 60-88; Marnia Lazreg, "The Perils of Writing as a Woman on Women in Algeria," *Feminist Studies* 14 (1988): 81-107; Donna Haraway, "Situated Knowledges: The Science Question in Feminism and the Privilege of Partial Perspective," *Feminist Studies* 14, no. 3 (1988): 575-599; Sandra Harding, "The Instability of the Analytic Categories of Feminist Theory," *Signs* 11, no. 4 (1986): 645-664; E. Grosz, *Sexual Subversions: Three French Feminists* (Sydney and London: Allen and Unwin, 1989).
3. In July 1994 the "Latin American Cross-Currents in Gender Theory" conference at Portsmouth University brought together scholars and activists from different disciplines from Latin America, North America, and Europe to discuss a wide range of gender related issues in Latin American contexts.

4. Frigga Haug, *Female Sexualization: A Collective Work of Memory* (London: Verso, 1987).

5. Sarah Radcliffe and Sallie Westwood, eds., *Viva: Women and Popular Protest in Latin America* (London: Routledge, 1993), p. 3.

6. Thanks to Pieter Geschiere for this phrase.

7. For an analysis and critique of dependency theory, see John Weeks and Elizabeth Dore, "International Exchange and the Causes of Backwardness," *Latin American Perspectives* VI, no. 2 (Spring 1979).

8. Marysa Navarro, "Research on Latin American Women," *Signs* 5, no. 1 (1979): 120.

9. Verena Stolcke, *Coffee Planters, Workers and Wives: Class Conflict and Gender Relations on São Paulo Plantations, 1850-1980* (Basingstoke: Macmillan, in association with St. Anthony's College, Oxford, 1988); Kate Young, "Modes of Appropriation and the Sexual Division of Labor," in Anna Kuhn and Anne Marie Wolpe, *Feminism and Materialism: Women and Modes of Production* (London, Boston: Routledge and Kegan Paul, 1978); Carmen Diana Deere and M. León de Leal, "Peasant Production, Proletarianization and the Sexual Division of Labor in the Andes," in Lourdes Benería, ed., *Women and Development: the Sexual Division of Labor in Rural Societies* (New York: Praeger, 1982); Carmen Diana Deere, *Households and Class Relations: Peasants and Landlords in Northern Peru* (New York: Praeger, 1990).

10. C. Hugh Jones, *From the Milk River: Spatial and Temporal Processes in North West Amazonia* (Cambridge: Cambridge University Press, 1979); L. Nadelson, "Pigs, Women and the Men's House in Amazonia," in Sherry Ortner and Harriet Whitehead, eds., *Sexual Meanings* (New York: Cambridge University, 1981); Olivia Harris, "The Power of Signs: Gender, Culture and the Wild in the Bolivian Andes," in C. McCormack and Marilyn Strathern, eds., *Nature, Culture and Gender* (Cambridge: Cambridge University Press, 1980).

11. See: Lourdes Benería and Martha Roldán, *The Crossroads of Class and Gender: Industrial Housework, Subcontracting and Household Dynamics in Mexico City* (Chicago: University of Chicago Press, 1988); Alison Scott, *Divisions and Solidarities* (London: Routledge, 1994).

12. T. Ehlers, *Silent Looms: Women and Production in a Guatemalan Town* (Boulder: Westview Press, 1990).

13. Scott, *Divisions and Solidarities.*

14. Sylvia Chant, "Women, Work and Household Survival Strategies in Mexico, 1982-1992: Past Trends, Current Tendencies and Future Research," *Bulletin of Latin American Research* 13, no. 2 (1994): 3-33.

15. Mercedes González de la Rocha, *The Resources of Poverty: Women and Survival in a Mexican City* (Cambridge, MA and Oxford: Basil Blackwell, 1994), p. 290.

16. Audre Lorde, *Sister/Outsider* (Trumansburg, NY: Crossing Press, 1984), p. 110.

17. Fiona Wilson, "Workshops as Domestic Domains: Reflections on Small Scale Industry in Mexico," *World Development* 21, no. 1 (1993): 67.

18. As Ruth Behar comments, "In work on women in Latin America, the part/whole problem surfaces in another form. There the incompleteness of women as social

actors is shown in the overwhelming emphasis placed on the political and economic aspects of women's experience." See "Rage and Redemption: Reading the Life Story of a Mexican Marketing Woman," *Feminist Studies* 16, no. 2 (1990): 229.

19. Maxine Molyneux, "Mobilisation without Emancipation: Women's Interests, the State and Revolution in Nicaragua," *Feminist Studies* 11, no. 2 (1985): 227-254.

20. Pierre Bourdieu, *Outline of a Theory of Practice* (Cambridge: Cambridge University Press, 1977).

21. JoAnn Martin, "Motherhood and Power: the Production of a Women's Culture of Politics in a Mexican Community," *American Ethnologist* 17, no. 3 (1990): 470-490; Radcliffe and Westwood, eds., *Viva,* pp. 14-15.

22. Wilson, "Workshops as Domestic Domains."

23. Aihwa Ong, "Colonialism and Modernity: Feminist Representations of Women in Non-Western Societies," *Inscriptions* 3/4 (1988): 79-93; Lazreg, "The Perils of Writing as a Woman"; Mohanty, "Under Western Eyes."

24. Sylvia Yanagisako and Jane Collier, *Gender and Kinship: Essays Toward a Unified Analysis* (Stanford: Stanford University Press, 1987), p. 35.

25. Scott, *Divisions and Solidarities.*

26. Deniz Kandiyoti, "Bargaining with Patriarchy," *Gender and Society* 2, no. 3 (1987): 274-290.

27. Ramón A. Gutiérrez, "From Honor to Love: Transformation in the Meaning of Sexuality in Colonial New Mexico," in Raymond T. Smith, ed., *Kinship Ideology and Practice in Latin America* (Chapel Hill: University of North Carolina Press, 1984) and "Honor, Ideology, Marriage Negotiation, and Class-Gender Domination in New Mexico, 1690-1846," *Latin American Perspectives* 12, no. 1 (Winter 1985).

28. Martin, "Motherhood and Power": 486.

29. Lynne Phillips, "The Power of Representations: Agrarian Politics and Rural Women's Interpretation of the Household in Coastal Ecuador," *Dialectical Anthropology* 15 (1990): 271-283.

30. John M. Ingham, *Mary, Michael and Lucifer: Folk Catholicism in Central Mexico* (Austin: University of Texas Press, 1986), p. 185.

31. Irene Silverblatt, *Moon, Sun and Witches: Gender Ideologies and Class in Inca and Colonial Peru* (Princeton: Princeton University Press, 1987).

32. For example, "Ayllu procreation and ayllu well-being, which used to be in the hands of the goddess whose support was localized were now tied to the welfare of the empire's upper-class. Pachamama had become the benefactress of the empire through her bonds with the lords of Cuzco," See Silverblatt, *Moon, Sun and Witches,* p. 49.

33. Iris Zavala, "The Social Imaginary: the Cultural Sign of Hispanic Modernism," *Critical Studies* 1, no. 1 (1989), p. 30.

34. T. Laqueur, *Making Sex: Body and Gender from the Greeks to Freud* (Cambridge, MA: Harvard University Press, 1990); V. Plumwood, "Do We Need a Sex/gender Distinction?" *Radical Philosophy* 51 (Spring, 1989); M. Gatens, *Feminism and*

Philosophy (London/Bloomington: Polity Press and Indiana University Press, 1990).

35. Judith Butler, *Gender Trouble: Feminism and the Subversion of Identity* (New York: Routledge, 1990).

36. V. Broch-Due, I. Rudie, and T. Bleie, *Carved Flesh, Cast Selves: Gendered Symbols and Social Practices* (Providence and Oxford: Berg Publishers, 1993), p. 57.

37. Zavala, "The Social Imaginary": 26.

CONTRIBUTORS

RICARDO CICERCHIA is Professor of Latin American History at the University of Buenos Aires and is co-director of the Family History Project at the Latin American History Programme (PROHAL, Instituto de Historia Argentina y Americana "Dr. E Ravignani"). He is also National Researcher at the Argentine National Council of Research (CONICET) and director of the National Curriculum of Social Sciences at the Ministry of Culture and Education.

TESSA CUBITT is Principal Lecturer of Sociology at the University of Portsmouth. She is author of *Latin American Society* (Longman, 1994).

ELIZABETH DORE is Senior Lecturer in Latin American History at the University of Portsmouth. She has published widely on class and gender in Peru and Nicaragua, including *The Peruvian Mining Industry: Growth, Stagnation and Crisis* (Westview, 1988) and *Nicaragua: A Myth of Modernity: Property, Gender and Patronage in Rural Granada, 1840-1979* (forthcoming).

ANNA FERNANDEZ PONCELA is Titular Professor at the Universidad Autónoma Metropolitana in Mexico City. She has published *Participación Política: Las Mujeres en México al Final del Milenio* (El Colegio de México, 1995).

JEAN FRANCO is Professor Emeritus of Latin American Literature at Columbia University. Her many published works on gender and cultural theory include *The Modern Culture of Latin America* (Pall Mall, 1967) and *Plotting Women: Gender and Representation in Mexico* (Verso, 1989).

237

HELEN GREENSLADE is researching her doctoral thesis, "Gender and the Public Sphere in Cuba: Political Representation and Participation 1900-1995," at the University of Portsmouth, where she is a Research Assistant for the Gender and Development in Latin America Research Team.

ELIZABETH JELIN is Professor of Sociology at the University of Buenos Aires and National Researcher at CONICET, and has produced numerous studies on the family and social movements, citizenship, and gender. She is the editor of *Family, Household and Gender Relations in Latin America* (Kegan Paul International, 1991) and *Women and Social Change in Latin America* (Zed, 1991).

SHARON McCLENAGHAN is completing her doctoral thesis, "Power, Ideology and Identity: A Comparative Study of Salaried and Non-Salaried Women in the Dominican Republic," at the University of Portsmouth.

ANN MATEAR is a Lecturer in the Politics and Modern History of Latin America at the University of Portsmouth.

MURIEL NAZZARI is Associate Professor of History at Indiana University, Bloomington. She is author of *The Disappearance of the Dowry Women: Families and Social Change in São Paulo* (Stanford University Press, 1991).

CLAUDINE POTVIN is Chair of the Women's Studies Program and is Professor of Quebec and Latin American Literature in the Department of Modern Languages and Comparative Studies at the University of Alberta, Canada. She has written on medieval Castillian poetry and published a collection of short stories, *Détails* (L'instant meme, 1993). Her work on women's writing and feminist literary theory has appeared in various journals.

CARMEN RAMOS ESCANDON is Associate Professor of Latin American History at Occidental College, Los Angeles. Her books include *Género y Historia* (Universidad Autónoma Metropolitana, 1992); *El Género en Perspectiva* (UAM, 1992); and *La Industria Textil y el Movimiento Obrero en México* (UAM, 1987).

NANNEKE REDCLIFT is Senior Lecturer in Anthropology at University College, London. She has edited, with Thea Sinclair, *Working Women: International Perspectives on Labour and Gender Ideology* (Routledge, 1991); with Janet Sayer and Mary Evans, *Engels Revisited: New Feminist Essays* (Tavistock, 1989); and with Enzio Mignione, *Beyond Employment: Household, Gender ans Subsistence* (Blackwell, 1985).

WILLIAM ROWE is Professor of Latin American Cultural Studies at King's College, London. He is co-author, with Vivienne Schelling, of *Memory and Modernity: Popular Culture in Latin America* (Verso, 1991).

DEBORAH SHAW is Senior Lecturer in Latin American Literature at the University of Portsmouth. She is author of "Gender and Class relations in Elena Poniatowska's *De Noche Vienes"* in *Bulletin of Hispanic Studies,* January 1995, and "The Mexican Woman Writer: A Critical Invention" in *Beyond Solitude: Dialogues Between Europe and Latin America* (Birmingham University Press, 1995).

238

INDEX

DATE DUE

OCT 2 8 2006

MAR 0 6 2007

MAR 0 5 2008

JUN 0 9 2009